Chasing Black Butterflies

"Just when the Caterpillar thought her life was over, she looked up, noticed her wings and began to fly."
- Black Butterfly

A Memoir

Angela Maradiaga

Library of Congress Cataloging-in-Publication Data available upon request.

ISBN: 978-0-578-82543-4

Cover Design: 13th & Joan Publishing House
For more info, please visit *ChasingBlackButterflies.com*

*D*EDICATED

to all my **Black Butterflies**.
You can either be two things in this world,
a victim or a survivor.
I chose to fly ...

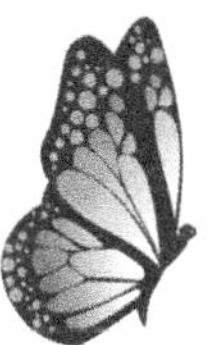

TABLE of CONTENTS

TABLE of CONTENTS

Intro
Black Ovum

GROWING UP I FELT SO DIFFERENT from everyone else. I was the black sheep, the one that was always fucking up, the one that had no daddy, the one everyone hated before even getting to know, and the one no one could control. I tried so hard to be good, but trouble would always find me no matter what I did. Like a dark shadow, it followed me everywhere, waiting for me to become vulnerable enough to pull me back down its black hole. I desperately struggled to break free from it, sometimes even losing a piece of myself in the process. I was so tired of fighting, tired of running away and pretending to be someone I wasn't.

It felt like I was stuck in quicksand, and the harder I tried to get out, the deeper and deeper I would go. Feeling exhausted, I was ready to give up and let it consume me, but then I felt a ray of hope when I saw a man who had been stuck in the same quicksand as I pull himself out. And not only did he manage to free himself, but he also helped to free others. It was at that moment I found the strength to pull myself out once again, but this time I had a whole different perspective on life.

The day I saw the Antwone Fisher story was when I started to see the silver lining in my life. If I could use what I had gone through to help others, it would give my life purpose and make everything somehow worth it. From that moment on, I decided to turn all of my mistakes into learning lessons and my struggles into inspirations. I was even starting to think maybe I had been chosen to go through all of this because God knew I would be strong enough to survive it. I'm a firm believer that the bad things that happen to us in life, put us on the path to experience the best things. You can't enjoy the rays of the sun if you've never experienced the thunders of the storm.

"She was a rare flower that proved you can blossom amidst darkness when your soul shines brighter than the sun." – Black Butterfly

Chapter I
Hatching Chaos

IT'S CRAZY HOW YOU CAN LOOK BACK on your life and remember the exact moment your childhood was altered to the point where it changed the course of your entire life. I was around four years old when that happened to me. As kids, we live in such a bubble, not knowing the danger that surrounds us every day, and all it takes is one little crack to shatter our world forever.

Before I get to that moment, I feel like I should give some type of warning to those of you who don't know me. When I speak, I am very blunt and have no filter, and I wrote my book the same way. It contains real-life shit like graphic violence, a lot of strong-ass language, adult situations like fucking, and a whole bunch of other shit you might not want to hear if you all sensitive and shit. Readers' discretion is strongly advised and is intended for mature audiences only.

So anyways, I was born somewhere in Hollywood on February 1, 1981. My mother was only sixteen and living in a group home for girls when she got pregnant with me. Still, to this day, I don't know why she ended up there. My mom doesn't like to talk about her past and once you've met my grandmother, you'll know why. She's the sweetest bitch you'll ever meet. She has a way of saying the coldest things in the politest way. Like if she thought you were getting too fat, she would say something like, "You should be eating lady portions," or "No one is going to want you if you get any bigger." But the way she would say it would make you have so many insecurities about yourself you never knew you had. She kind of reminded me of Kathy Bates in "Misery," minus the killing.

Although I wouldn't be surprised if we found a dead body in her basement, just kidding. She doesn't have a basement. But for real, my grandmother was a nice and sweet old lady, but at the same time could be controlling and evil if you ever pissed her off. So I could understand why my mom shuts down all the time and is so secretive, but what I couldn't understand was how my amazing grandfather could allow her to end up in a group home. All I know is that's where she met my godmom, who I called my G-mom.

They were like the Black Thelma and Louise, always getting into trouble together. My G-mom used to tell me so many stories like the time they thought it would be funny to instead of handing out candy to kids on Halloween, they would spray them with whip cream. Unfortunately, one of the parents didn't think it was too funny and ended up kicking in one of their windows, but they didn't care, and it didn't stop them from spraying more kids.

My mom was the last girl to arrive in the group home, so she had to share the whole top floor with my G-mom since no one else wanted to. They were all scared of her, and since her grandmother owned the group home, she always felt this entitlement and acted like she ran shit. But as soon as my mom moved in, they instantly hit it off and became two peas in a pod. My mom was very sweet and soft-spoken but had a sneaky vindictive side if you ever crossed her, just like my grandmother. My G-mom was the opposite. She was loud, blunt, and in your face, but always kept it real.

Since my mom was so soft-spoken, girls always thought they could run over her, but my mom could fight, and one of the girls in the group home found that out the hard way.

She was constantly antagonizing my mother. For a while, she tried to ignore her and tune her out until one day she had finally had enough and quietly got up, walked over to the girl, and beat her ass senseless without even saying a word. Then she went back to reading her book like nothing ever happened. Even my G-mom was caught off guard. She always thought she would have to jump in if they ever fought since the girl was much bigger than my mom, but that was far from the case. After that, no one else in the house fucked with her again.

She and my G-mom became so close they even decided to get pregnant together and try to deliver each other's babies. My G-mom ended up getting pregnant first, and my mom bought all kinds of books on how to deliver the baby from home. However, that all went out the window the moment she felt her first contraction.

"Fuck this shit! Take my Black ass to the hospital now!!" my G-mom shouted.

After she gave birth to a healthy baby boy, my mom desperately wanted to have a baby of her own, so she started going on the hunt for potential mates. While volunteering at Kaiser as a candy striper, she met my father, who was a janitor. He was much older than her and barely spoke English but was a very handsome and charming man who somehow convinced her to go out on a date with him even though he had to bring his cousin along to translate everything. He had always dated Spanish girls, but there was something about my mom's dark chocolate skin that enticed him. It must have been a really great date because it translated into me being conceived, and nine months later, I was born. My father was only around for the first year of my life. After a trip back to his hometown in Honduras, my mother never saw him again.

A year after my father disappeared, my mom met my brother's dad, who was this tall White German man, and two years after that, Ryan was born. His dad didn't stick around either, so my mom ended up moving us into a small apartment. For a while it was just the three of us.

One afternoon, I was in the living room, helping my mom change Ryan's diaper. We laughed as she opened it up and pee squirted out, almost hitting us in the face. After we cleaned him up, I asked if I could go outside and play. She said yes but to make sure I stayed right out front. I agreed and walked outside, where I saw the two White boys from next door standing with their pit bull named Chance. Since we had no pets, I loved going over there, so I asked if I could play with him. They both said yeah, so I ran over, but before I made it to Chance, I noticed something pink hanging out of his stomach, which stopped me in my tracks. My eyes got really big, thinking his belly button had just popped out or something. With concern, I asked, "What's wrong with Chance's belly button? Why is it hanging out like that?"

The boys looked at Chance and started laughing then they whispered to one another. I felt like they were making fun of me, so I began to get angry, and this time I asked again with a little bit of attitude and one hand on my hip. "Stop laughing and tell me what's wrong with Chance," I said, more demanding.

"Are you sure you want to know?" one of the boys asked as he looked back at his brother and began to smile.

"Yes," I said.

"Well, if we tell you, you can't tell anyone. This has to be our little secret," the other brother said.

"Okay!" I shouted as I rolled my eyes. Anxious to hear what it was.

"You have to pinkie swear because if you say anything, they will take Chance away and kill him, and you don't want him to die, do you?"

"No, I don't want him to die. Why would they kill him?" I said with a sad frown on my face as I looked down at him, still panting heavily with his pink thing hanging out.

"Okay, then give me your pinkie and say *I pinkie promise I won't tell anyone about our secret.*"

I grabbed his pinkie with mine and promised not to say anything. He then took me by the hand and started to pull me in their home, but I pulled back and said, "Where are we going? My mom told me I have to stay out front."

"We have to show you inside!" he said.

"I can't. I'll get in trouble," I sighed.

"Okay, fine then, but you won't know what's wrong with Chance." I turned and looked back to see if I could see my mom through the front window, but I couldn't. He grabbed my hand again and said, "Come on, let's go. It won't take long. Your mom won't even know you're gone."

I followed them to the back and was expecting to see their dad along the way, but they told me he went to the store to grab a pack of cigarettes, so we had to be quick. When we got to their bedroom, they laid me down on one of the beds. One of them stood over me and unzipped his pants. He pulled out something that resembled Chance's pink thing then told me to touch it. He grabbed my hand and wrapped it around his thing, and I started to feel it grow harder and harder than he said, "This is what Chance has." I began to remember this was also what my brother had when we changed his diaper, and I started to pull my hand away.

Just then, I felt another hand gliding up my dress, going in between my thighs and pulling my underwear to the side. I started to sit up and pull away, but the boy standing over me pushed me back and held me down while the other stuck his finger inside me. I began to scream, so he covered my mouth.

After what seemed like forever, their father burst through the bedroom door and yelled, "WHAT THE HELL IS GOING ON? GET OFF HER!"

"Dad, we were just playing around!" both brothers tried to explain. Their dad rushed over and yanked me off the bed by both of my arms and said, "You need to go home right now, and don't you dare say anything, or I will tell your mom what you did, and you will be in big trouble. You hear me?" I shook my head yes as tears flowed down my face.

He took the rag that was hanging out of his back pocket and wiped my tears away. Then he took me by my hand and shoved me out the front door. Before I could even make it down the stairs, I heard him yelling and screaming at them. I was so scared I ran inside my home and went straight to my bed, where I crawled underneath the covers. A few moments later, my mom came in and asked me what was wrong. I paused as everything that had just happened flashed through my head. I wanted to tell her, so I took a deep breath and swallowed hard, but the words would not come out. I didn't even know how to say what just happened. Instead, I told my mom I wasn't feeling well and wanted to take a nap. She felt my forehead and pulled the covers over me.

After my nap, I lay there, unsure if what had happened was real or just a bad dream. *Yeah, it was just a bad dream*, I tried to convince myself. I got up and walked into the living room where my mom was getting ready to change my brother's diaper again. She asked me to help by handing her the diaper bag off the chair. I grabbed it and put it down next to her as she took his diaper off. As I looked down at my brother, who I had once looked at with so much innocence and love, I started to feel this anger, disgust, and shame. Tears started to fill my eyes, so I ran to the bathroom and muted my cries with the towel hanging from the wall. It was then I knew this wasn't just a bad dream.

I don't remember seeing them again after that, but I know we ended up moving back to the group home shortly after, which I was so glad about. I loved living there and always felt protected, especially around my G-mom, who would kill anyone who ever laid a finger on me or my brother. For a while, things were great again and felt back to normal. My mom was a huge picture person and constantly took pictures of us. Since we were back at the group home, she wanted to take us to Sears to get some more pictures taken of me and my brother.

She put me in this pretty pink dress with two pigtails and told me not to mess up my hair or get my dress dirty, so instead of playing outside, I went upstairs to play with my godbrother, which somehow led to us chasing each other around the room and having a pillow fight. A few moments later, I heard my mom calling for me, so I ran downstairs. As

I met her outside, I could see the anger fill her face when she saw that my hair was completely messed up. She knew she wouldn't have time to fix it before the bus came.

"Didn't I tell you not to mess up your hair? Now we're going to miss the bus!" she said, hitting me with her purse on the side of my stomach. I braced myself for another hit but felt nothing. When I opened my eyes, I saw her standing there as if she had just seen a ghost. My mom was a beautiful dark-skinned woman, but all the color had been drained from her face. Then I started to feel something wet dripping down my leg. When I looked down, I noticed my pink dress begin to turn red, then I began to scream when I realized it was blood.

My G-mom heard my cries and rushed outside. "Oh my God, what the fuck happened?" she shouted at my mom, who was still standing there frozen in shock.

"I don't know! I don't know! I hit her with my purse and forgot my knife was in there, and it must have gone through."

My G-mom grabbed me and rushed me in the house, placing me in the kitchen sink to rinse off the blood, where I blacked out. The next thing I remember was waking up in the hospital with nurses standing over me with a big-ass needle. I had never seen a needle that big before, and once I saw that I started flipping out. It took four nurses and my grandfather to hold me down. My grandfather was short, dark and handsome, and the sweetest man I have ever known. Before he moved to Texas a few years later, he would always stop by to check on us, so when my mom called to tell him what happened, he was the first one to meet us at the hospital.

I ended up just getting a few stitches since only the tip of the knife had gone through. We didn't live in the best neighborhood, so she would always carry a butcher knife in her purse for protection. Even though we might not have lived in a fancy neighborhood, my brother and I were still super spoiled growing up and had everything we ever wanted. Christmas always looked like the pages out of a

Sears catalog. But after this happened, my spoiled-ness went up to a whole other level. I knew my mom felt so bad, and I milked every moment of it. Anytime she would tell me no to something like no eating dessert before dinner, I would quickly remind her how she almost stabbed me to death, and she would end up letting me get my way. Occasionally my G-mom would catch me doing this and tell my ass no, but when she wasn't around, I would start milking it again. That was until my mom met him.

HIS NAME WAS CURTIS. HE WAS A TALL, skinny Black guy from Compton who looked just like MC Hammer, but he didn't take any shit from anyone. He came to the group home to visit his sister for the first time, who had been staying there for a couple of months, but when he noticed my mom, he started coming over more frequently. Eventually, she fell for him, but my G-mom couldn't understand why. He was such the opposite of my and Ryan's dads. My G-mom always felt like he was too much of a thug for her and couldn't see what she saw in him.

As soon as they had my youngest brother Christopher, they got married. My mom wanted a better life for us, so she decided moved us down to the Inland Empire (I.E.), to some apartments in San Bernardino. At the time, San Bernardino was still hood but an upgrade from Los Angeles. As soon as we moved in, he made it clear that he was the man of the house and wasn't tolerating any of our spoiled ways.

My first whoopin' was when I was around six. My mom asked me to help her bring in the groceries, but I wanted to finish watching "He-Man," so I flipped her off behind her back, not knowing my stepdad could see me. He snatched me up so quick, pulled down my panties, and beat the shit out of me with his bare hands. My G-mom would sometimes pop us if we were acting up, but it was nothing like this. This was the first time I had my ass beat. He hit me so hard I could barely breathe, and it felt like I was going to die.

At first, I hated that we moved, but I quickly made friends and started to like it. The first girl I met was named Laneshia. As soon as she saw me playing outside, she walked up to me and introduced herself. She said she and her family had been living there for years, so she knew right away that I was new, and that I could play with her anytime I wanted. Laneshia was a tall cocoa, brown-skinned girl who was a little bit older than me, but I liked that because it was like having an older sister. I knew if anyone ever messed with me, she would have my back. I started going to her house almost every day. My mom wanted to meet her parents, so she and my stepdad met Laneshia's parents, and they all became friends just as quickly as Laneshia and I had. Her parents were still together and would sometimes take turns watching us. Laneshia also had an older sister and brother, and sometimes Laneshia's older sister would watch us too when all the parents went out together. We were around each other so much that they became like a second family to us.

That summer, I had my first kiss. All the neighborhood kids were outside playing hide and go get it. I thought it was just a newer version of hide and go seek but learned it meant something else when this boy Brandon told me that I had to kiss him since he found me. Before I could even say anything, he leaned in and kissed me with his snotty-ass nose. All I remember was thinking how disgusting that was, and that I would make sure I didn't get found again.

My brother Ryan was also outside playing with us. As we all took off to go hide again, I decided to hide underneath a car. As I started to crawl underneath, I heard a bloody scream coming from Ryan, so I jumped up and saw him hanging from a fence with blood pouring down his arm. He had tried to hop over but slipped, and the wire fence went through his hand. I tried to pull him up, but he screamed even more, so I ran inside to get my mom.

He was so clumsy and always getting hurt. Like the time he fell down a flight of stairs while carrying a big piece of watermelon when he was two. That time he didn't cry, but another time he was climbing on some logs at our grand-auntie's house and fell off and cut the side of his face right next to his eye. Just a quarter of an inch more, he would have cut his eye and possibly gone blind, the doctor told us. I was super protective over Ryan, but that all changed when Chris was born. Once he was born, I was instantly bonded with him and would walk around like he was my baby. Ryan would get so jealous he would start fights just to get attention, which made us grow further apart.

After the summer ended, I started first grade, and our neighbor's daughter named December would walk with us to school every day. I couldn't stand her because she was always so sensitive and fragile. Anytime someone would say anything to her the wrong way or crack a joke, she would cry, and I hated that. So I would pick on her even more to try and toughen her up.

At school, there was this boy Jovan who was my first crush. He was the cutest boy in school, and I wanted him to be my boyfriend, but he was always so mean to me. He would take things out of my hand, hide my belongings, and this one time, as we were in a single file line headed to the cafeteria, he kicked me, causing me to fall, and everyone laughed. I had finally had enough. I turned around and pushed him back, knocking him down to the ground and asked why he kept picking on me. By this time, everyone had turned the corner, and when he realized no one could hear him, he said, "Because you're my girl." Then the teacher yelled for us to catch up, and I smiled as we both ran inside. After that, he was nicer to me and would even bring me stolen gifts from home.

One day when I was playing on the monkey bars, this boy Richard, who also liked me, came over to me and gave me one of his cookies. I smiled and said thank you but noticed Jovan in the background with this mad look on his face. The next day Jovan brought a butter knife to school and pulled it out on Richard and told him to stay away from me because I was his girl. After that, I never saw Jovan again and heard he got expelled from school. I was so mad he got kicked out and blamed it all on Richard, who I didn't talk to for the rest of the year.

My mom and stepdad always argued, but the first big fight I remember was when I was playing in my room, and I heard my mom scream out for me. I ran into their bedroom, where I saw Curtis on top her with his hands around neck. She yelled for me to call the police, so I ran to the living room and grabbed the phone, but he came out right behind me and snatched it out of my hands before I could even dial 911. Then he grabbed me by my arms and dragged me into my room, where he threw me on the floor and told me to stay my ass there.

About ten minutes later, I heard the police knocking. I cracked open my bedroom door and listened to them tell my mom they had received a call from one of the neighbors complaining about a domestic dispute. My mom reassured them everything was okay and that it was just a little argument, but she was fine. The cops started looking in the house, and when one of them made eye contact with me, I quickly closed the door. I then heard my stepdad confirm what my mom said, and they eventually left.

After that, things were good between them for a while. My mom was even in such a good mood that she let us help her make brownies. But there was something always in the back of my mind that I couldn't shake about calling 911. I was curious about what would happen if I called them. So one day when Curtis was at work and my mom was putting Chris to bed, I snuck into the living room and called the police, then hung up each time they answered.

Then I ran back and hopped on the couch to continue watching TV. Next thing I knew, the police were knocking on the door again. "Hi, ma'am, we got a couple of calls that were traced back to this location." My mom looked so puzzled and told them she didn't call them. Then he asked if there was a baby in the household because they could hear a baby crying in the background. She said yes, but he was sleeping, so it couldn't be the right house. Both looked at me, and I shook my head and said I didn't call them. I was so scared I would get caught but also thought it was so funny and was trying so hard not to laugh out loud. He kept asking her repeatedly, but once she explained it was just her and her three kids in the house, and none of us called them, they had no choice but to leave.

The next day my mom was on the phone laughing with one of her friends about how the police came to the wrong house. Since I could tell she thought it was funny, I confessed it was me. "Mom, guess what? That was me that called 911," I said as I began to laugh, thinking she would be laughing right back. But her laughter quickly turned to anger, and she told her friend she would have to call her back. After she got off the phone, she yelled at me for calling them and told me to go to my room and wait for Curtis to get home. When she said that, I knew I was in deep trouble and cried until he got home to beat my ass again. That was the last time I played on the phone like that.

I don't know what it was, but I always like doing things I had no business doing. Like the time we all went to Blockbusters, and my mom and stepdad went inside to return some movies. They had left the keys in the car, so I decided to hop in the front seat of my mom's black Camaro and pretend I was driving all my friends around. As I was turning the steering wheel back and forth, I noticed the car start to roll backward down the sloped parking space we were in.

Luckily, I remembered my mom always pulling the emergency break up, so I quickly grabbed it and yanked it. We came to a hard stop in the middle of the street. Before I had a chance to hop back in my seat and pretend the car had moved by itself, they saw me, and I got another whoopin' as soon as we got home. Looking back on it, their asses should have been the ones in trouble, not me, for leaving three kids in the car with keys in it.

But anyway, the next summer, we moved again to this small trailer park in Mentone after the apartment next door to us caught on fire, killing December's mom, who had fallen asleep while smoking a cigarette. I felt so bad about how I'd treated her. I swore to myself I would never be mean or pick on anyone else again.

When we moved into the mobile home, I thought my mom had hit the lotto. We had always lived in tiny apartments, but now we lived in this big house with a huge backyard, park and a community pool. It only had two bedrooms, but my mom promised they would turn part of the dining room into a bedroom for me so that I could finally have my own room. A few months later, they put up the walls and built my bedroom as promised. It was the first time I didn't have to share a room with my two brothers.

My mom got a government job and worked a lot, so my stepdad mostly watched us. I think he started to resent my mom for being the breadwinner, because he got even meaner when he lost his job at Popeyes, which I missed because we used to get free chicken and biscuits all the time. He was always harder on Ryan and me than with Chris, but I got it the worst since I had a smart-ass mouth.

Plus, around this time, Ryan's dad, who always reminded me of Ned Flanders from the Simpsons, had come back into the picture because my mom had filed for child support. Now that he was ordered to pay money, he felt obligated to pick Ryan up every other weekend. I was extremely jealous of my brothers since they had dads and I didn't. It seemed like everyone but me had a dad. I was so desperate for one that I even asked Ryan to ask his dad if he could pick me up on the weekends too, but course he said no. So I would just sit in my room and daydream that one day my dad would find me like Ryan's dad had found him.

I hated living in the house with Curtis. When he first started giving us whoopin's, we would fight back or run and hide from him. He got so frustrated with us running he started tying us to the bed and hitting us with everything from extension cords to belts, shoes, and even blocks of wood. One time I got beat so bad with a block of wood I had bruises all over my back, and my wrist was so swollen I couldn't even make a fist. When I tried to tell my mom, he told her I was acting up and said I was doing things I didn't even do to justify why he did it.

Then I got a whoopin' the next day for snitching, so I stopped trying to tell her things. Curtis even had me and Ryan turning against each other. We were so afraid of being spanked that we would blame each other for things we did to avoid getting hit, which made us hate each other even more.

There was only one time I could remember where I was having fun with Curtis, but it was short-lived. I was around ten years old, when he took us swimming, which I loved to do but would always stay on the shallow end since I didn't know how to swim. When he noticed this and said he would teach me, and for the first time, I felt like I had a real dad. He taught me how to hold my breath under water without plugging my nose and held me up as I practiced kicking around the pool. Then he asked me if I wanted him to teach me the way his father taught him. I smiled and said yeah as we walked over to the deep end. We got to the edge and he showed me how to bend my knees and told me to put my hands together a point them forward.

Before I knew it, he'd pushed me in. I remember everything going into slow motion as I inhaled a gulp of water and struggled to swim to the top, but the harder I tried, the more I started to sink farther to the bottom. I began to lose all my energy in my legs and arms, and the water began to get darker and darker. Just then, I felt this strong force lift me out of the water. After I coughed up a lung and caught my breath, I looked up and saw my stepdad standing over me laughing. I was so angry that began to cry and told him that I hated him and wished he was dead.

People around us began to stare, so he sternly whispered to me, "You know what, I was trying to show your little ass how to swim, but since you wanna act up and be a brat about it, we're all going home." He yanked me by my arm and pushed me to go get my brothers so we could leave, then he yelled at me the whole way to the house. When we got there, he told me to go to my room until my mom got off work.

The next day he snapped at me for every little thing, like a toy being left out in the living room, which my youngest brother had done. I got tired of being yelled at all the time, I started to talk back more and more. He got so mad when I told him I hope my mom divorces him, that he got up off the couch and grabbed me by my arm to take me into their bedroom so he could grab his belt and give me another whoopin'.

Just before we made it into their bedroom, I was able to snatch my arm away from him and told him if he hit me one more time, I would tell my mom he touched me in my private area. I don't know what in the world made me say something like that when he had never done anything like that to me, but it was all I could think of at the time to prevent him from whoopin' me again. I knew I would never really tell my mom that, but I wanted to say something that would scare him, and it did. He was so hurt that those words came out of my mouth. He looked like he almost wanted to cry. "Why would you say something like that?" he asked. I shrugged my shoulders with this smug smile and said, "I didn't know." He didn't even say anything as he went into his room and closed the door.

I felt bad that I'd said that, but it also felt liberating that I'd finally found something to stop him from hitting me, which it did. After that, I don't remember him spanking me ever again, even when I got into trouble on a school field trip to the Calico Ghost Town Regional Park. Our class was walking through the stores, and I was double dared to steal a rabbit's foot, so I did, and one of the boys overheard us bragging about it on the bus and told one of the teachers. She came over and asked me to show her the receipt for it, which I couldn't do, so she told me she was going to call my parents when we got back to the school.

As soon as we got back, she called my stepdad, who told her to put me on the phone. I was so scared he was going to yell at me about getting a whoopin', but to my surprise, he calmly said that he was disappointed in me and not just because I'd stolen something but because I did it off a dare.

"If you're going to do something, do it because you want to do it and not because someone else told you to. Did you even want the rabbit's foot?" he asked.

"No," I replied.

"Then why would you risk getting in trouble for something you didn't even want? You need to start having a mind of your own and make your own decisions. If they wanted the rabbit's foot so bad, they should have taken it themselves. Not have you do their dirty work." Then he told me I was grounded for a week, but for the first time, I paid attention to what he was saying, and that message has always stuck with me even to this day.

Even though my whoopin's had stopped, the fights between him and my mother started to get more frequent and intense. Usually, when they argued they would just have makeup sex, and everything would be good again. I know this because after a heated argument, I peeked under their bedroom door when I heard loud moaning to make sure he wasn't hurting her. I could see him on top of her, kissing her with his ass in the air and her legs spread open. I ran to tell Ryan, and when he looked, he started laughing so loud they heard us and yelled for us to go back to our room.

After that, I knew every time they went into the room and closed the door, that's what they were doing, especially after Ryan and I came across one of their VHS porno videos that they accidently left in the VCR. When it first came on, I knew it was wrong for us to watch, so I told Ryan to leave, but he didn't want to go. He was just as curious as I was and said he would tell if he didn't get to watch too. We both stood there, laughing about what we were seeing. Then we quickly turned it off when we heard them come out of the room. I couldn't stop thinking about it, so later that night, when everyone went to bed, I watched it over and over again. I was so drawn to it and felt these weird sensations all over my body.

When the fights between my mom and Curtis got physical, she would always cry out for me, and I would run out to see him either on top of her, choking her or behind her with his arm around her neck. Sometimes he would stop when I ran in, but this last time he didn't, and her scream was much different from the ones before. She had a fear in her voice I had never heard before, almost as if she thought she was about to die.

When I ran out of the room, I saw them on the floor with his back against the wall and my mom in between his legs with the phone cord wrapped around her neck. He yelled for me to go back to my room, but this time I was frozen. I had never seen fear like this in my mom's eyes before, and I desperately wanted to do something. I thought about grabbing a knife, but I knew he would see me coming since they were facing the kitchen. I couldn't even call the police because he had the phone wrapped around her neck. I felt so helpless and had no idea what to do.

"I'm not going to tell you again. Get your fuckin' ass back in the room," he yelled as if he was the devil himself.

Seeing my mom that scared made me even more scared. "What the fuck did I just say! Get your ass in the room NOW!" he yelled.

This time I snapped out of my trance and ran into my brothers' room, where I woke Ryan up, crying that he was going to kill Mom. We both rushed over and listened underneath the door to see if we could hear anything. A few moments later, I heard my stepdad scream, then a few seconds after that, the door slammed, and a car sped off. Then it was dead silence. We were too scared to find out what was on the other side of that door. So many thoughts ran through my head, and my biggest fear was seeing my mom dead.

Every time I would reach for the door, something told me not to, so I lay in the bed with Ryan waiting for our mom to come in and tell us everything was okay, but she never did. There was a loud knock at the front door. Moments later there was a bright shining light in our faces, asking if we were okay. When I saw that it was the police, I ran out of the room, where I saw a blood trail leading from the kitchen to the living room.

"Where's my mom?" I shouted.

"Go back to your room. We need to talk to your dad," one of the officers said. That's when I saw Curtis sitting on a chair with a shirt wrapped around his thigh and blood pouring down his leg. I looked around but I couldn't find my mom anywhere. I went back to my brothers' room and put my ear on the door. Chris had slept through the whole thing and Ryan was waiting on the bed for me to tell him what was going on.

I could hear the officer ask him how he got stabbed in the leg and where my mother was. He told them he had accidentally cut himself, and she went out to get bandages. Once I heard that, a big sigh of relief came over me, knowing my mom was okay, so I crawled back into bed and fell asleep until I woke up the next morning to find my mom cooking breakfast in the kitchen like nothing ever happened. Hours went by, and I noticed Curtis never came out of the room, so I went to look and noticed he wasn't here. I then went into the living room where my mom was and asked where he was. She said she didn't know but that he was never coming back. And he never did. That was the last time I ever saw him again, but he frequently called the house until she finally changed the phone number.

MY G-MOM PLAYED A MAJOR PART IN MY life growing up, but she never liked Curtis, and their friendship suffered because of it. I was around ten years old the last time I saw her before she ended up moving to Vegas and losing contact with us. It was on the 4th of July. My G-mom, godbrother, and a couple of his cousins came over to watch the fireworks. Whenever my mom had friends over, all the kids would camp out on the living room floor. Even though I had my room by this time, I still slept out there with the rest of them.

While everyone was passed out and snoring, I lay on the floor watching TV until I finally started to doze off. Just as I started to close my eyes, I felt a hand start rubbing me down there.

I turned to my godbrother, who was just one year older than me, pushed his hand away, and asked, "What are you doing?"

He said, "Shhh, I'm just rubbing on you." He started to do it again, and this time, a chill went down my body that I had never felt before. It felt good, and I didn't want him to stop, but I was so scared we would get in trouble, so I pushed his hand away again.

"Stop before we get in trouble," I whispered.

"Then let's go to your room," he whispered back as he got up and pulled me up. We crept slowly into my bedroom, and I lay on the bed where he crawled on top of me and started to dry hump me. I didn't know what was going on, but all I knew was that it was feeling weird but good at the same time.

Just then I heard a soft voice whisper, "What are you guys doing here?"

It was his sixteen-year-old cousin. She had been sleeping on the couch and saw us sneak into my room. We both jumped up frantically and looked down, scared to say anything. She asked us again, and we both said we weren't doing anything at the same time.

She then said, "Okay, well, if you don't tell me what you were doing, I'm going to go tell on you, and you'll both miss out on the fireworks tomorrow."

"Okay, okay, I was just laying on top of her," he whispered.

"Show me," she said with a smirk on her face.

"Show you?" we both said.

"Yeah, show me, or I'm telling right now."

I sighed as I lay back down, and he crawled on top of me again and continued where he'd left off. I was so humiliated my face turned red with embarrassment. After a few seconds, I pushed him off and ran back into the living room, where I lay back down until I finally fell asleep.

The next day we were all getting ready to go outside to play. My G-mom was sitting in the living room watching TV, drinking a cold beer while my mom went to the grocery store. My godbrother's cousin told me my mom had asked her to help me get dressed.

I headed toward my bathroom, but she stopped me and said, "No, go to your mom's bathroom since it's big enough for the both of us."

The both of us? I thought. I walked in my mom's bathroom, where there was already a bubble bath halfway filled up. She told me to take off my clothes, but I hesitated.

"Don't be shy. We're both girls and have the same thing, look," she said. I was too afraid to look up, so I kept looking down as she took her clothes off, then mine. I covered my private parts with my hands and stepped out of my clothes, rushing into the tub where I started to play with the bubbles. When I looked up, I was shocked to see her naked body slowly getting into the tub. She had hair down there, unlike me and her breasts were much bigger than mine. I looked down, embarrassed at my bird chest, covering them up with as much bubbles as I could.

She sat down across from me and I couldn't take my eyes off her breasts. I started to imagine me having a chest like hers. She giggled and asked what I was looking at. I bashfully looked down and said nothing.

"Whatcha scared of? You never seen titties before?" she asked.

"No," I replied with my head still down.

She then grabbed my hand and pulled me closer, placing my finger against her nipple, which started to get hard. I had started to feel the same feeling when my godbrother was touching me, but this was a girl, so I got scared and pulled my hand away. She grabbed my hand again and said, "It's okay, you can touch them. One day you are going to have some just like these."

"She was taught her curiosity would kill her. A cage would tame her wild thoughts, but instead, it was a slow death."
– Black Butterfly

Chapter II
Burning Larva

NOW THAT MY STEPDAD WAS OUT OF the house, it felt like a scene out of the movie "The Wiz" when Dorothy killed Evillene. My brothers and I woke up every morning singing, "Can't you feel a brand-new day, can't you feel a brand-new day?" I was expecting things to go back to the way they had been before he came into our lives, but they never did. Something had changed in my mom. She had never been the type to show much affection. Never gave us a hug or kiss or even told us she loved us, but she always had a way of showing her love through gifts and taking us places to make memories. However, when he left, it's like this coldness came over her, and she would get mad over the littlest things. She never spanked us, but sometimes her words would cut deeper than a knife.

I was around twelve when we moved out of our mobile home into a three-bedroom apartment that my mom let me pick out. I wanted to be in the same complex as my best friend Kristin, who I had been best friends with since the 4th grade. Luckily, they were affordable enough that my mom agreed, and I was even happier to find out that we had moved directly across the street from her. That was one of the happiest times I remember as a child. Every day felt like Christmas.

Kristin and I always had so much fun together. She was the prettiest and most popular girl in school, and we became friends over a game of tetherball. She had sandy blond hair with ocean blue eyes with the cutest freckles. Everyone used to say she looked like a younger Christie Brinkley. All the girls wanted to be just like her, including me.

When we first moved to Mentone, I was one of the only Black girls in my school and always felt different from everyone else, but I was very athletic and funny, so I never got picked on. Especially since one of the most popular girls was one of my best friends. She never made me feel different and would always compliment me on how beautiful my brown skin was even when I didn't think so.

The only ones that would make me feel bad about being Black were some of the adults. One of them was my friend DJ's mom. He would sometimes walk me home from school since he lived around the corner from me, but one day, his sister saw us and told his mom. The next day, he told me he wasn't allowed to walk with me after school anymore because I was Black. He wanted us to still be friends but only at school because he didn't want to get in trouble. That was the first time I felt my color was a problem, and I couldn't understand why it was.

Another time I went over to one of my Spanish friends' house after school, and when her mom came home, she told me I had to leave. When I walked out the door, I overheard her telling my friend not to bring any niggers to her house. I immediately ran home crying and told my mom what happened. My mom was a very sweet lady but did not play when it came to her kids. She could quickly turn into a lioness when it came to protecting her cubs. She threw on some sweats, tennis shoes, pulled her hair back into a ponytail, and told me to take her back to my friends' house. My mom started banging on the door and yelling for her mom to come out, but she never did, and her daughter never talked to me again after that.

That was the first time I saw the hood come out of my mom. The second time was when some of my friends and I were outside playing ding dong ditch, and this White guy got so mad and started yelling at me to take my nigger ass back to Africa where I belonged even though the kid that rang the doorbell was White. I was so embarrassed I ran home again to tell my mom. I knew she was going to light his ass up, which she did. She had the whole neighborhood outside watching as she cursed him out and told him if he ever talked to me like that again, she would beat his ass. He apologized and that was the last time he said anything to me, even after we rang his doorbell a few more times after that.

Although my mom defended me, and I knew what they were saying was wrong, I started to hate being Black and constantly wished I was White. It wasn't just because of what the adults said. It was also because all the boys liked the White girls. Even the few Black boys that went to our school only wanted the White girls.

I'll never forget when I finally worked up enough courage to ask the only Black boy in class to dance to a slow Keith Sweat song at our school dance, but he told me no and to ask Kristin if she wanted to dance with him instead. I played it off like I was cool, but that was the first time I had my little heart broken. I went to the corner and shed a couple tears, wishing he would get hit by a school bus the next day and die. As you can see, the apple didn't fall far from the tree.

Besides the boys always wanting to be with White girls, I was mostly jealous of their hair. I hated my curls and wanted my hair as straight as possible. So straight that I even tried to straighten it with an iron just like one of my Mexican friends did, but it didn't work out too well and I ended up frying my ends off. I was so envious. White girls never had to worry about sweating it out or the rain or getting it wet when they went swimming, although sometimes Kristin's hair did turn green afterward, but I didn't care. At that time, I would rather have had green hair than my nappy hair.

Being twelve years old was such a confusing time for me. I started to feel all these different emotions and sexual desires that I couldn't explain or talk to anyone about. I used to stay up late on the weekends after everyone went to bed to watch all the weird shit people did on the HBO show, "Real Sex." Even the way I played with my Barbie dolls started to change. They were no longer interested in cooking, cleaning, and wearing different cute outfits to school. Now they were interested in wearing sexier clothes to get Ken's attention so they could make out and hump in the back of his red Corvette.

That summer when Kristin came back from a family trip, she was way different than she had been the last time I'd seen her. She was stealing cigarette butts from her mom's ashtray and smoking them outside in the orange groves behind our complex. She got me to try it a few times, but I always ended up coughing up a lung, so I hated it. She was also sneaking out wine coolers, which I loved because they tasted just like Kool-Aid.

One day I went over her house to hang out, and we went to her room to talk. She pulled out a wine cooler she had hidden in her closet. As we were drinking, she started telling me how her parents had been arguing a lot lately, and she thought they might be getting a divorce soon.

I could see her eyes start to fill up with tears, so I tried to change the subject by telling her about what my godbrother had done to me over the 4th of July weekend, which worked because her eyes quickly turned from sadness to curiosity.

"What do you mean he rubbed on you down there and humped you?" I told her again what he did and how his cousin made us show her.

"How did she make you show her? Show me what he did," she asked with a big smile on her face.

I was so confused she would even say that. I thought she was joking. "What do you mean, show you? How?" I asked.

"Come on, if you can show her, you can show your best friend. Plus, I have seen a lot of weird things in my dad's porn box, so I won't be freaked out. Just get on top of me and do what he did to you on me." I sat there next to her on her bed so scared like I was being set up, and as soon as I tried, she was going to yell "Just kidding" and tell the whole school about it.

"Nooo, I can't do that," I said. As I was about to get up, she grabbed my hand and started rubbing it on herself down there. "See, I'm not freaking out," she said. Then she lay back, closed her eyes, and whispered for me to get on top and not to stop rubbing her. So I did. I got on top and kept rubbing on her. Then she told me to kiss her. I had never kissed anyone before, besides the time Brandon had kissed me during hide and go get it, so I wasn't sure how to do it. I just gave her a small peck like I used to always do on the back of my hand when I would practice at home.

Just as I was about kiss her again, there was a knock on the door, and we both jumped up like the police were about to bust in. Her mom knocked again and asked, "Do you guys want pizza for dinner?" as she opened the door. We both stood there like we had just gotten caught stealing something. "So do you guys want pizza or not?"

"Su-su-sure," Kristin stuttered.

"Umm, no, thanks. I have to get home," I said and ran back home to my room, where I just lay on my bed thinking about what happened. Even though I was a little turned on, it felt wrong, so I started daydreaming that it was this older boy named Carlos who lived up the street that I had a crush on.

After that happened, things were a little awkward at first, but we just pretended like it never even happened. A few months later, she ended up moving to her grandma's when her dad came out as gay, and her parents decided to get a divorce just like she said they would. She had only moved a few miles up the street, but we both cried at the fact we were no longer going to be neighbors. Kristin, her mom, and her brother all moved in with her grandma, and her dad got his own place.

When we'd first moved there, I thought things would be so great since Curtis was gone, and I got to move next door to my best friend. But now everything seemed to be falling apart, and my world felt like it was coming to an end. Ryan and I started fighting a lot more, especially after he broke my cheerleading trophy on purpose, and I threw his "Whoomp There It Is" CD off the balcony.

We always did spiteful things to each other like when he peed in my hair gel, and I used his toothbrush to scrub the toilet. I also sprayed him in the face with Raid once. Even my mom and I started not to get along, and it was like the clash of the Titans every time we saw each other. I don't know why, but everything she said and did always made me so mad.

Things started to go downhill when she went into my room and found love letters from a boy at school, describing all of the sexual stuff he wanted to do to me. I had just gotten home from school, and she was sitting on the couch with the shoebox of letters I had hidden underneath my bed. The first thing out of her mouth was, "What the hell are these?" I tried to play dumb like I had no idea what she was talking about, but she wasn't going for that and hounded me until I confessed.

I was so pissed that she'd had the nerve to go into my bedroom that she paid the rent on and go through my things that she'd bought and read my private letters that she had no right to read. I felt like my privacy had just been violated, so I told her I hated her as I stormed into my room, where she followed right behind and told me I was grounded for two weeks. *Life was so unfair, why would I be grounded for something a boy wrote me?*

That was the first time I thought about running away, but we lived on the second floor and there was no way out except through the front door, which she watched over like a guard dog. Over the next couple of weeks, I just stared out the window at all the other kids playing and having fun outside and daydreamed a lot about Carlos. He was around sixteen and looked like "Benny the Jet" Rodriguez from the movie "The Sandlot." I would imagine myself sneaking out the window, using my bedsheets to climb down, and he would toss me his for me to climb up through his window, and we would make out until the sun came up. However, in real life, he never even looked my way.

My mom had started going out a lot more. She didn't know but I could tell by the evidence left behind on her neck that she was going out on dates. She only brought a man to the house once on the weekend my brother Ryan had gotten picked up from his dad, who, by the way, I was still extremely jealous of since my dad had yet to be found. Even my youngest brother's dad Curtis would call the house from time to time to check on him after he finally found our new number.

Every time I would ask my mom about my father, she would say she didn't know where he was, which started to make me resent her. But anyway, back to my mom's date. She invited this guy over and told my youngest brother and me to stay in our rooms for the night, but I kept finding reasons to come out and ask for something.

I don't know what made me so desperate for his attention, but my mom wasn't having it. She got up so fast, grabbed me by my ear, and pulled me back to my room, where she yelled for me to stay until tomorrow. That was the first and last time she ever brought a guy over.

After that, my mom had an attitude with me every time I did or said anything she didn't like. One day she asked me to do the dishes, but I didn't feel like doing them because I wanted to finish watching "Martin," so I told her I would do it later. She got mad and started yelling for me to do them NOW!

"Why don't you ever do the dishes?" I said under my breath as I got up and walked toward the kitchen, rolling my eyes.

"Because this is my house, and I pay all the bills around here, and if you don't like it, then you can get out."

Get out? You know what, maybe I should, I thought. This would be the perfect opportunity I needed to finally run away, plus it would give me an excuse to go to Kristin's house on a school night. So I threw the plate in the sink and started to head toward my room to grab my things, but she blocked me and told me everything in the house belonged to her, and I wasn't taking any shit with me. I shrugged my shoulders and said fine with a smirk on my face as I walked out.

I ran and walked the five miles to Kristin's house. Once I got there, I played victim by telling her mom that my mom had kicked me out for not doing the dishes, and I needed a place to stay. They felt sorry for me as the fake tears flowed down my face. Her mom hugged me and showed me to the dinner table where they had all been eating pizza, my favorite. Behind my sad face was a big-ass smile. I got to leave my evil mom's house, spend the night at my best friend's house, and eat my favorite food.

Everything was going as planned. I was so happy and thought I'd be staying there forever until the next morning when the police knocked on the door looking to take me back home. I had to leave, but I'd gotten my very first taste of freedom. It was like a cub tasting blood for the first time. I wanted more. This became a constant ritual between us. I would either run away or she would kick me out every time we argued, and then later, she would send for the cops to bring me back home.

ONCE KRISTIN AND I WENT TO MOORE Middle School, we started to drift apart. It was an all-year-round school, and we had different tracks, so we rarely got to see each other anymore and started hanging around different people. I tried hanging out with these Black girls in my class, but they would always make comments about me like "Oh, you think you cute, huh?" or "He only likes you because you light skin." So I stopped trying to tag along with them.

One of the first girls that was nice to me was this chick named Olivia. She had a quarter Black in her but was mostly Spanish and was hanging around all the Mexicans. I thought since I was mixed with Spanish, I would fit right in, but that was far from the case, since I looked more Black than she did. At first, they were cool with me because of Olivia. We would ditch school, and I would always be their watchdog when they would make out with their boyfriends in abandoned houses or jump girls into their gangs in the bathrooms. I wanted to get jumped in so bad.

I even started to switch my look up from wearing cute colorful shirts with leggings to wearing dickies, overalls, and tube tops with brown lip liner and dark lipstick. My mom didn't allow me to wear make-up yet, so I had to always sneak and use hers when she left for work. Some of the girls didn't accept me because I was too dark, but Olivia would always stick up for me.

I was finally starting to feel like I was fitting in in junior high—that was, until the boys started noticing me more and more, including one of the hottest chicos in school. Like Olivia, every girl had a crush on him, but he never showed much interest in the girls at our school. All his girls were older and in high school. One day I left class to go to the bathroom, and when I turned the corner, he was walking straight toward me. I thought he was just going to walk right past, but he stooped and grabbed the hoop on my Dickies and pulled me close to him.

"Whatz up, chica, I'm really feeling this new look on you," he said, backing me against the lockers. He leaned in like he was going in for a kiss, but I quickly turned my head.

"You know my homegirl Olivia really likes you," I said, trying to pull away.

"Well, I'm not feeling your homegirl, I'm feeling you," he said as he put both hands over my shoulders to preventing me from moving away. I was so ecstatic that he liked me and wanted to make out with him right there on the lockers, but I knew I couldn't do that to my girl.

He went in for another kiss, but I ducked and went underneath his arms and said, "Nah, my homegirl will be so mad if she found out."

"So you do everything your homegirl tells you?" he said, walking backwards toward his class.

"Bye, Casper," I said, smiling as I headed back in my class.

Lunchtime came, and I went out looking for Olivia like I always did during lunch. As I was walking through the grass, I noticed a large crowd starting to form around me, then I felt a hard push from behind. I turned around and saw Olivia's cousin Lil Scrappy. I smiled and thought she was playing around at first, but this time she pushed me again, knocking the books out of my hands.

"So I heard you were trying to get with Casper behind Olivia's back," she said, pushing me for the third time.

"No, I wasn't. What are you talking about?" I said, throwing my hands up in confusion.

"Yes, you did. Maria saw you and Casper making out by the locker."

I then saw Casper step out of the crowd. I thought he would come to my rescue and say that it wasn't true, but he just stood there smiling as if he was trying to get a better view of the fight.

"That's a lie. I wasn't trying to get with him at all. You can even ask him. He was the one trying to get at me, but I said no because of Olivia," I said, backing away from her.

The crowd started chanting for us to fight. Olivia just stood right behind her with her arms folded like she didn't even know me anymore.

Casper then yelled out, "Bitch, you lying! You got at me, and I turned your ass down. I don't want no Black bitch."

The crowd started laughing, and before I could even turn my head back toward her, she grabbed my hair and pulled me down to the floor. Somehow, I got on top of her and started punching her as hard as I could until one of the teachers yanked me off and took us both to the principal's office.

I tried to explain how I hadn't started the fight, but that didn't stop him from giving me three days of suspension and giving her a week. My mom was so mad. She didn't even want to hear my side and grounded me for two weeks and threatened to kick me out if I got into any more trouble.

When I got back to school, all of my friends including Oliva had turned on me. They started purposely bumping into me, throwing stuff at me during class or knocking my books out of my hands in the halls. I just tried to ignore it, hoping it would all blow over.

"Why do you keep letting them do that to you?" said this light-skinned girl with long curly hair sitting next to me in class. She had the prettiest curls I had ever seen, like the Noxzema Girl. I started to wish I had my curly hair again, but I had permed it out.

"Because I'm trying not to get suspended again. My mom said if I do, she's kicking me out, and I don't have anywhere else to go," I whispered.

"Oh well, they are going to keep doing that to you if you don't do anything back. I'm Tatiana, by the way," she whispered back.

"Yeah, I know. We have all our classes together," I said. We kept talking until the teacher told us to stop, and just like that, we became instant friends.

It wasn't long before my bad girl ways started rubbing off on her, and we were getting into trouble together. We were always late for class and constantly laughed and joked around so much that one of our teachers finally had enough and ended up separating us. We no longer had all the same classes together. But that didn't stop us from hanging out during lunch and after school.

Moore Middle School was diverse yet segregated at the same time. For the most part, all the Blacks, Asians, Mexicans, and Whites were in their own little sections during lunch. This was nothing like it was in elementary school, where everyone played together. During lunch, Tatiana and I would sit near the Black area by the basketball courts. I was getting ready to take a bite into my chimichanga when I saw Maria, aka Dipples, who was the fat ringleader of the Spanish girls, walking toward me with her crew following right behind, including Lil Scrappy.

"What's up perra? I heard you were talking shit about me," she said, towering over me.

"What are you talking about? I haven't said shit about you," I said, rolling my eyes and feeling so irritated that I couldn't take a bite out of my chimichanga.

"Well, I saw you mad dogging me in class, so I know you were talking shit," she said.

"If I were talking shit, I would say it to your face," I said, standing up and throwing my chimichanga down on the floor so she would know I was serious.

"Oh, look who has some cojones now," she said, laughing. I knew I couldn't let all the Black kids see me getting punked, especially when I was trying to fit in with them. As she got closer, I pushed her back so hard even I was surprised at how far back she flew. Just as she gained her footing and rushed toward me, a loud whistle blew, and one of the teachers came over to break it up. She told us to go back to class before we all got detention.

"This ain't over, puta," she said, bumping into me with her shoulder as she walked by.

I was so proud that I had finally stuck up for myself. I felt this confidence come over me and even had a smirk as I walked in class and saw Maria's fat ass squeezed in between the desk and chair, mad dogging me. After school, I got on the school bus headed home, but my confidence quickly turned into shit when I saw Maria and a bunch of her girls waiting for me in the Circle K parking lot next to my home.

When I got off the bus, I pretended like I didn't see them as I tried to hurry past, but they quickly surrounded me, pushing me back and forth into each other. Maria then punched me, and the rest jumped in. I knew the more I fought back, the longer it would be, so I just covered my head and took the punches and kicks until a store clerk rushed out to break it up. They all scattered like roaches back into a red Honda Civic and took off.

The clerked helped me up and into the store, where she handed me some napkins to wipe the blood from my lip. She then told me I could have a free Slurpee, which, I'm not going to lie, did kind of make me feel better. I used to always have to scrap up loose change out the couch to get one. I was just glad the fight hadn't happened at school where everyone could see. And thank God this was before social media and camera phones.

After the fight, Maria and her clique bullied me for a couple more weeks, but eventually, they turned their target on a new girl. Tatiana had become my best friend by this time, and we constantly hung out after school with her sister who was one year older than us, and her sister's two best friends. They were all very pretty, light-skinned with natural shoulder length or longer hair. They also had a lot of jealous females hating on them in school and gave me advice on how to deal it.

Her sister's crew was always getting into trouble. They were ditching school, sneaking out to go to parties and were even having sex already, which made me curious about it. Tatiana was a goodie two-shoes and wanted to wait to have sex. She was the good angel on my shoulder who always tried to talk me out of all the bad shit I wanted to do, but once we started hanging out with her sister even more, I knew which ear I was going to listen to.

I was so naïve, for the longest time I thought I had lost my virginity when I was four and that White boy had stuck his finger inside me, until the day I took a sex education class. The teacher started to explain the birds and the bees. I raised my hand and asked if fingers counted. The whole class started laughing as I slumped down in my chair, embarrassed about what I had just asked. The teacher said no and then she started explaining about inappropriate touching. Afterwards she told us if there was anything we wanted to talk about or if we wanted to ask a question to write it down on paper and put it in this safety box.

She then said if we didn't put our name on it, we would remain anonymous, and the questions would be answered at the end of each class. So I grabbed a piece of paper and wrote, "When I was four years old, two boys from next door touched me down there. Was it my fault since I went into the house with them when my mom told me to stay out front?" I had always known what they did was wrong, but I also thought it was my fault. I guess I just needed confirmation it wasn't and that I was still a virgin. At the end of class, the teacher read and answered a few of the questions from the box. Then she got to one that she didn't read out loud. Instead, she looked right at me, and I immediately looked away. After the class was over, she asked me to stay behind. *Oh no, she knows it's me*, I thought.

"Angie, did you write this?" she asked.

"No!" I tried to deny it.

"Listen, if you wrote this, I need to know. You are not going to be in any trouble. I just need to know so we can talk about it. I know you asked the question about the fingers before, and this looks like your handwriting. So did you write this?" I took a long pause and put my head down and nodded. "It's okay, to answer your question, noooo, you didn't do anything wrong. You were only four years old, and those boys should have known better. What they did was very wrong, and I really think we should talk to your mother about it."

"Noooo, no, no, no. Please, Mrs. Wilson. Please don't tell my mom. She's going to be so mad," I cried out.

"She's not going to be mad. I promise. I will talk to her," she reassured me.

I was so scared to go home that day. When I got home, my mom sat me on the couch and asked why I'd lied to the teacher about something like this.

"I'm not lying," I said.

"Then why wouldn't you say anything about it before?" she asked.

I didn't have an answer for that, and I couldn't explain why I'd never said anything until now. Things started to feel uncomfortable, so I then asked if I could go outside and play. Feeling just as uncomfortable as I was, she told me I could go. When I opened the front door, she said, "You know, if there's anything you ever need to talk to me about, you can always tell me." My mom never expressed much emotion, so I was shocked to hear that coming from her and felt some sort of relief as I walked outside.

Now that I knew I was still a virgin, I wanted to lose it. Tatiana and I were the only ones still virgins, and I didn't want to be the last one. I didn't want to lose it to anyone other than with this boy named Ricky. Pretty Ricky was what they called him—no, seriously! When I first saw him, I was thirteen and had to take my brother to his karate class during the summer. We would catch the bus and then walk past Ricky's apartment to get to the Redlands Community Center. He was sixteen and the sexiest boy I had ever seen. He had cocoa brown skin, with deep black waves in his hair and a set of full, juicy lips every girl wanted to kiss. He looked like a young Warren G and was always outside talking to a different girl every time I walked by.

Some days he would smile at me, and I would daydream on the bus about him pushing those girls aside, sweeping me up in his arms, and kissing me passionately. I was in such a deep daydream that I even missed our stop and ended up on the wrong side of town and without any more money. Luckily, the bus driver felt sorry for me and my little brother and put us on the right bus to get home.

Summer was damn near over, and he still hadn't said one word to me. My brother only had a couple more weeks of karate class before it was over, and I wouldn't have a reason to walk past his house anymore. So the next day I wore my cutest sundress my mom had just bought for school and put some of her makeup on. I got off the bus and was anxious to see him, but this time he wasn't outside, and my heart sank. I took my brother to his class, and as we were headed back to the bus stop, I heard a voice out the window say, "Cute dress." I turned, and it was him smiling out the window, drinking a Coke. I swear I could see hearts surrounding his head.

"Thanks," I said as I walked up to his bedroom window. "Why aren't you outside?" I asked.

"Oh, I'm on punishment and have to stay inside. I been seeing you walk by all summer but never seen you in a dress before. What you lookin' all cute for?" He smiled as if he knew I was only wearing it for him.

"Uh, my brother is getting ready to graduate in his karate class, and they had a celebration." I smiled.

"No, we didn't. I don't graduate until—"

Before my brother could finish, I covered his mouth and pushed him out of the window's view. "Ugh, okay, so the truth is I thought the celebration was today, but it's in a couple of weeks, so I got all dressed up for nothing." My face was beet red from embarrassment.

He gave me that *sure okay* nod with a smirk on his face as if he knew I was making it all up. "Well, you look cute. You should wear dresses more often." My heart skipped like five beats as I blushed and smiled. "So how old are you?" he asked.

"Umm, fifteen," I said as I looked back down at my brother like he better not say a damn thing.

"Fifteen, huh? Why haven't I ever seen you at school then?"

"Ooooooh, I just moved here," I said.

"Yeah, from where?" he asked with a side-eye squint.

"Umm, Rialto." I spoke with a slight hesitation.

"Ooooh, I got family out there. What school did you go to?"

FUCK! I had no idea what schools were out there. "Huh?" I said.

"You not really fifteen, are you?" he asked and looked at my little brother, who started giggling. I rolled my eyes at him as I looked back at Ricky and mumbled under my breath, "No, I'm thirteen."

"Haha, I already knew you were thirteen. I asked your girl Sandra about you after I had seen y'all talking." Sandra lived in the same apartment complex as him.

I was so embarrassed. I just wanted to sink into the grass and disappear. I just knew a sixteen-year-old would never be interested in a thirteen-year-old. I didn't even want to talk anymore, so I grabbed my brother's hand and started to walk away.

"Hey, wait," he said as he handed me a white piece of paper through the window. "I think it's cute you tried to lie about your age, but you don't have to do all that with me. Here's my number, call me."

I screamed so loud in my head but played it off cool as I took his number and said, "Okay, I'll call you when I get home." I was on cloud nine the whole bus ride home and daydreamed about us falling in love, getting married, and having babies.

Over the next couple of weeks, we were always on the phone and spent time together during my brother's karate classes. But when school started, we didn't get to see each other as much, so one day he asked me to ditch school and come over. We talked, played video games, and then started making out on the couch. He stood up, grabbed my hand, and pulled me into his bedroom. I lay on the bed as he turned on the radio, and "Before I Let You Go" by Blackstreet started playing as he began to take off his shirt. He hopped on the bed, and we began to make out again. He started kissing my neck, leaving trails of him behind. Then he began to slide my panties off, but I stopped him.

"Wait, I haven't done this before," I nervously said. Even though I wanted to lose my virginity to him, I was nervous about actually going through with it.

"What do you mean you never done this before? You're a virgin?" He looked confused.

"Yeah, of course I'm a virgin," I said.

"It's okay, I'll go slow." He began to kiss me softly on my lips then on my barely existing breasts. My pussy began to throb as he pulled my panties off. He kicked his pants off the bed and slid his drawers to his ankles.

He started to rub his dick against my pussy and push his way inside, but it was too tight, and I kept pulling away, so he licked one of his fingers and stuck it inside me. I slightly pulled back as he started going in and out, rubbing all of my pussy juices around my pussy lips until I was soaking wet. I was more turned on than I ever had been in my life. I bit my lip as he pulled back up and pressed himself inside me. This time the tip went in, and I clenched.

"Oouch," I said as I tried to pull back.

"Just relax," he said as he kissed me again softly on my lips, and the next thing I knew he was entirely inside me, stroking it harder and harder. At first, it was hurting so bad, but I didn't want him to stop, so I just lay there and took it. It was over as quickly as it had started, and I stared up at the ceiling in disbelief that I had finally done it. I felt like I had just become a woman.

He got up, looked down in confusion, and said, "Wait, there's no blood. Thought you said you were a virgin?"

My heart sank to the bottom of my stomach. I thought after we had sex, we would have this unbreakable bond knowing that I gave myself to him, but he didn't even believe I was a virgin, and I was just as confused as he was. What made it even worse was while I was getting dressed, he said, "Girls always be lying about losing their virginities." I had always heard stories about your cherry popping and blood coming out, but he was right. There was no blood. Maybe my teacher was wrong; perhaps I did lose my virginity when that boy stuck his finger in me. Or maybe I did lose my virginity and blocked it out. I mean, what else could it be? I had no explanation, so I didn't say much as I put my clothes on and headed back home.

When I got home, I went to the bathroom to wash up and noticed a little bit of blood on my underwear and on the washcloth. I knew it. I knew I was a virgin. I hurried to call and tell him, but he still didn't believe me and brushed it off. I couldn't believe the way he was starting to treat me. I felt like shit, like it was my fault for not bleeding right after. The weekend came, and he wasn't answering or returning any of my calls.

That Monday, rumors of me spread like wildfire, and soon everyone at school knew I was having sex, and just like that, my reputation was ruined. I became the school slut. Now all the guys wanted to fuck me, and all the girls hated me even more. I was so depressed I wanted to drop out of school and never go back, but having Tatiana, her sister, and her friends made things a lot more tolerable, mostly since they had gone through the same thing but had a *don't give a fuck* attitude about it. Not to mention one of them had also fucked Ricky too, so it made me feel better knowing I wasn't the only one.

It's crazy how men can fuck a million girls and become the man, but a girl can give her prize possession away to one and become a ho. It was then I learned never to give my heart away to a boy again and to stop giving a fuck about what others thought. I started being the player and playing boys left and right, ripping hearts out like I was Kano from Mortal Kombat.

BY THIS TIME, I WAS RUNNING AWAY AND drinking a lot more. Alizé was my drink of choice, but I always had to depend on a guy to buy it, which usually came at a price. So when I saw this grocery store closing down, I thought it would be a perfect time to steal one for myself. I was with my girl Sandra, and I decided to sneak out with a bottle of Alizé in my pants. During this time, I was dressing like TLC. I was more like Left Eye and Sandra was like Chili with her skinny body, dark complexion and long weave down her back. We wore colored T-shirts and baggy pants, so I thought it would be easy to hide the bottle of Alizé. As we were walking out the door, the store manager ran over and grabbed us both by the arms, and as soon as he did, a police car just happened to drive by, so he flagged them down as some of the employees held us back from running away.

The cop came in and put both of us in the back seat of the car. As the cop was in the store taking down the statement, I saw one of my homegirls from class walk past, and she threw her hands up to ask what happened. We weren't handcuffed, so I pointed for her to open the door. She quickly ran over, opened it, and took off like she was Felicia in Friday. I yelled to Sandra for us to hurry up and run, but she chickened out and kept saying we would get caught and in even more trouble.

I should have just taken off and left her, but before I could even get another word in, the cop threw me against the car, handcuffed me, and placed me in the back seat again. He put Sandra in a choke hold as he tried to get her hands behind her back, but she started to put up a fight. When I saw him choking her, I begin kicking at the car window and screamed to let her go. He wrestled around with her for a few moments but finally got the cuffs on her and threw her in the back seat next to me.

When we got to the station, they kept trying to interrogate us to tell them who let us out of the car. But no matter how many times they asked, I stuck to my story that it was a stranger that was just walking by. When my mom came up to the station to get me, I could see the steam coming from the top of her head as soon as she walked in. When she got close, she smacked the shit out of me right in front of all the cops. I was expecting them to arrest her for assault or something, but they all just laughed, and she grounded the shit out of me. I couldn't do anything for weeks.

Since I was grounded and couldn't go to this house party, I snuck out when my mom had gone to sleep and met this boy named Mike. Tatiana, her sister, and her friends were all there, and they ended up talking to his boys too. They belonged to this little crew called NEP "Never Eating Pussy," and I was determined to make him eat mine. I love challenges and making boys do things they said they would never do. It made me feel more like I was the one in control, and they couldn't play me. I was in 8th grade, and he was in 11th and went to a different school, so I lied about my age and said I was a little older than I was.

After the party, we exchanged numbers and I would sneak on the phone and talk to him for hours. I told him my brother Ryan was getting picked up by his dad this weekend, and my mom had to be at work at by 5 am that Saturday, so he should come over late Friday night and stay the night, and I would sneak him in my window. I had snuck a guy in like this once before, and it worked, so I was confident we wouldn't get caught.

That weekend he caught a ride to my house, and I snuck him in when my mom had gone to bed. I didn't have a lock on my door, so I would push my dresser in front of my door to prevent anyone from just coming in. He came in, and he went right to making out. He reached straight for my panties since I was only wearing a T-shirt, but I pulled his hand away and said no, not yet. We made out for another thirty minutes, then he tried again, and this time I told him I needed to get more in the mood, and he needed to go down on me. "HELL, NO," he yelled.

I covered his mouth and said, "My mom is in the next room asleep, remember."

"Hell no, I'm not doing that. My boys would clown me," he whispered.

"Okay, but I'm not having sex until you do," I said as I flipped him on his back and got on top. I started kissing his neck, his chest, then back up to his lips. I softly moaned as I rubbed the tip of his dick against my warm pussy until he finally said, "Damn, okay, fine, but if I do, you better not tell anyone." He flipped me back over.

"Okay, but if you don't make me cum then we still not having sex. It's not fair guys always cum, and I don't," I said as I threw my hands behind my head and smiled as he went down on me. Every time he tried to come up to have sex, I stopped him and said, "Nope, you still haven't made me cum yet."

After about a half hour of this, he was so pissed he gave up and said he was going to bed. It was too late for him to catch the bus or a ride back, so he was stuck there until the next morning, and we both fell asleep naked. I woke up to the sunlight shining on my face and the doorknob jiggling. "Angie, open the door. I need my comb," my mom said as she tried to open the door.

"Oh, shit," he said as he jumped up.

"Hide in the closet! … Okay, Mom, I'm coming," I said as I wrapped the sheet around my naked body and pushed the dresser to the door's side.

"What are you doing here? And why you are blocking the door with the dresser?" my mom asked, looking at me suspiciously. "Nothing, I just didn't want Chris coming in my room, so I blocked the door," I said as I handed her the comb that was sitting on my dresser.

She took it and pushed the door open more and started looking around. "Did you sneak out last night?"

"Nooo!" I said.

"Then what's that black bag back doing over there on the floor next to the window?" she asked as she got closer to it, realizing it was a boy's bag. We both looked down at the bag, then I don't know why but I looked toward the closet, and then she looked toward the closet. Everything started moving in slow motion as she walked over and opened it to see him standing there like a deer caught in headlights with his hands covering his dick.

My mom ran into her room and came out with a small handgun and waved it at him to get the fuck out of her house. He grabbed his clothes and backpack and ran out of the house naked just like in the movies. "I have to go to work, but I will deal with your ass when I get home. Don't leave this fuckin' house," she said pushing me out of her way as she walked by. I had never seen her with a gun, let alone pull it out on someone, so I knew I was going to be in so much trouble when she got home, and I didn't want to stick around to find out. I packed up everything I could fit in my backpack and ran to the streets.

Chapter III
Tormented Caterpillar

AFTER BEING KICKED OUT AND running away so many times, I ran out of places I could go. My friends' parents got tired of the cops always showing up at their house looking for me, so I wasn't allowed to stay there anymore, including Tatiana's. I had no idea where I was going to go, but I knew I wasn't going to stay home and feel my mother's wrath when she got off work. It was starting to get dark, and I was running out of time.

I was walking the streets of Redlands, when I realized I was passing my girl Tina's house. She was a small skinny Vietnamese girl with braces and one of the sweetest girls I ever knew. She would give you the shirt off her back if you needed it. We hung a lot at school, but I had only been to her house once since her parents were so strict. I saw her bedroom light on and slightly tapped on her window. She was shocked to see me, but after I told her what happened, she didn't hesitate to sneak me in and tell me I could sleep in her closet for the night. She said I had to be super quiet because her parents would be pissed if they found out.

She made a cozy spot in her closet for me so I could lay down. I was so exhausted from walking around all day and just wanted to sleep. She asked if I was hungry, and I was, so she went into the kitchen to fix me something to eat. When she came back with the food, her mom must have noticed something strange or heard us because she came barging in the room screaming at me to leave. When I tried to go out of the bedroom door, she told me to go back out the way I came in, so I climbed back out the window and could hear her screaming at Tina all the way down the street. I felt so bad I had gotten her in trouble.

I had no choice but to go back home, but instead of knocking on the door, I climbed up on the roof, where I would occasionally go to watch the stars, and slept there until I could figure what to do the next day. That morning I heard my mom leave for work, so I climbed down and knocked on the door. Ryan came to the window and yelled that Mom had said not to let me in.

"Just open the fuckin door, Ryan," I shouted back. My little brother Chris tried to unlock the door, but Ryan pushed him out of the way. I pretended like I was walking away but came around back until I was able to find Chris and told him to open the back door, which he did, and I was able to get in. Once I was in, I pushed Ryan and called him a stupid bitch for not opening the door, and we began fighting. I was older and bigger than him, so I always won, and he ran in his room, crying that he was going to tell Mom. I washed up, ate breakfast, and went to school, hoping one of my friends would let me stay with them after telling them what happened.

When I got to school, Tina had a black eye and told me that she and her mom had gotten into a really bad fight after I left. I felt so bad she went through all of that for just trying to help me out. She said her parents were so strict she hated living there and wanted to run away with me, but I had nowhere for us to go.

After school, I couldn't find anywhere to stay, so I ended up going back home and taking my punishment. My mom had cooled off by this time, so it wasn't as bad as I thought it would be, and I just ended up getting grounded for a month.

Usually when she grounded me, I would still sneak and use the phone or have friends over if Ryan was at his dad's house. Since she was a single mother of three and worked all the time, it was easy to get away with things. However, when Ryan was home, he always felt the need to always tell on me, which only heightened my hatred for him.

I was in the living room watching TV while my mom was in her room, taking a shower to get ready for bed. Ryan came out and snatched the remote out of my hand and said he wanted to watch TV, plus I wasn't supposed to be out here since I was grounded. I stood up and tried to snatch it back, but he elbowed me, so I pushed him hard, and he flew across the room. He stood up and charged at me like Jean Claude Van Damme, kicking me in the chest and knocking the wind out of me.

I was caught off guard and surprised at how much strength he was starting to have, so I grabbed the broom stick and beat him until he crawled into a ball on the floor. Then I kicked him in his nose and stomped on his head. He was screaming so loud, but all I saw was red. Then my mom came running out to break it up. His nose was so swollen it looked like it was broken, and she said if it was, she was kicking me out again. I told her he had started it and kicked me first, so she sent us both to our rooms. She had to wake up at five in the morning to go to work and didn't feel like dealing with it.

As I was sitting in my room, I started to feel bad for what I'd done. Even though I couldn't stand Ryan, I didn't want to see him that hurt either. A couple of hours later, I got up and went to the bathroom across the hall, and all I heard was a loud yell, and then I felt a hard thump on the back of my neck. When I turned around, I saw Ryan, all dressed in black, coming at me again with a crowbar, but I ducked the second time, and he hit the bathroom door, leaving a big hole. He charged again, but I managed to get in the bathroom and lock the door. Blood was pouring down my back.

My mom woke up, and I heard her screaming at him about the hole in the door, so I came out crying and said, "Look at what he did to my neck."

She turned and smacked him and told him to go to his room, and that he was grounded too. That was the first time I had seen her get that mad at him for anything and take my side on something.

For the rest of the school year, I didn't get into too much more trouble, but Tina, who had always been such a good girl, started hanging out with the wrong crowd. She met this girl at church who was running with this Asian gang called Tiny Rascals. Once she started hanging out with them, she started running away and ditching school. It was becoming routine for her not to show up at school for weeks at a time. So I wasn't too surprised when I didn't see her on the first day at Clement Middle School, which was for 9th graders only.

I was really excited about starting this new school. It felt like it would give me a fresh start. My mom had rented a three-bedroom single family house that was walking distance from the new school. Now Tatiana and I lived up the street from each other and could hang out a lot more. My mom and I had even started getting along again. She bought me all these brand-new outfits and got my hair done, so I was looking extra cute on the first day of school.

The first person I noticed was this brown-skinned, green-eyed, athletic built boy named Cornell. I usually didn't date guys at my school because I didn't want everyone in my business, but I was about to make an exception for him. A lot of girls wanted him too, so it wasn't going to be easy. Luckily, we had science and PE together, so it gave me a chance to talk to him, but I played it off like I wasn't interested in him and just wanted to be friends.

During lunch, one of Tina's mutual friends came up to me and asked if I'd heard what happened to her.

"What do you mean, what happened to her?" I asked.

"She's dead!" she replied.

"No, she's not, I just saw her right before summer," I said.

"No, for real she's dead. I spoke to her stepdad, and I saw it in the newspaper. She went to a house party with her boyfriend, and his friends raped her, and when she threatened to call the cops, they told her they were going to take her home, but they shot and killed her and left her body in the ditch."

Even after her tearful account of what happened, I still didn't believe her until I saw it for myself in the papers and broke down and cried. It was the first time I'd ever lost a friend, and I wished I could have done something to save her.

Besides hearing about Tina, everything at school was going great. I even heard from a mutual friend of Cornell's that he thought I looked good. I just needed an opportunity to get him alone. He was always surrounded by his boys or a bunch of girls. I was late for school and had gotten called into the principal's office. As he was lecturing to me, we got interrupted, and he had to step out. When he was gone, I noticed a bunch of hall passes on his desk, so I took a few. He came back and scolded me some more and said I would get detention if it happened again. I said it wouldn't and headed back to class. I made a stop in the bathroom and thought of the perfect idea to get Cornell alone. I wrote up a fake note on the hall pass, stating that he was wanted in the principal's office.

I was so nervous I would get caught when I walked into his math class and gave the note to his teacher. "Cornell, you have to go to principal's office," she said, as the class oooo'd at him. He grabbed all his belongings, and we both walked back toward the main office.

When we got far enough from his class and near in an empty hallway, I yelled, "Just kidding! You're not really wanted in the principal's office. I just wrote up a fake note to get you out of class." I laughed.

"What, are you serious? Damn, I thought I was in trouble or something. I heard you were a bad girl. I guess you really are." He laughed. I told him how Ricky had broken my heart, and I wasn't this bad girl everyone thought I was. "I'm not gonna lie, I noticed you on the first day of school, but everyone kept telling me all these things about you," he said.

"Well, are you the type to always listen to what everyone else tells you or do you make your own decisions?" I said, giving him an old quote from my stepdad with a flirtatious smile.

"Come on now. I run this school. You should already know the answer to that," he said.

"Okay, then. Find out about me for yourself and not based on what everyone else said." I smiled and leaned in like I was going to give him a kiss but just walked around him.

"Aight, I will. Here's my number. Call me after school. I'm going to go back to class before we get caught." He smiled as he handed me a piece of paper, and we both went back to class.

After school, I called him, and we talked on the phone until the sun came up. We had so much in common and talked every day after school. Not long after, he asked me in a letter if I would be his girlfriend, and we were officially the new it couple. I'd dated a few boys before but never had a real boyfriend like this, and the fact that he was still a virgin made me like him even more. Even though he was my first real boyfriend and I really liked him, I still wasn't going to give my heart to him completely just so it could be crushed again. So I constantly cheated on him and hooked up with other guys, especially since he wasn't ready for sex yet. One of those guys was this boy named Jason who was older and from another school that I met at Tatiana's church.

After a couple of months of dating, Cornell and I were walking over to Tatiana's apartment after school. Tatiana was still at school working on a project and was going to meet us there later, but her sister was home to let us in. Cornell and I were holding hands when I saw Jason drive by. My heart dropped, and I quickly let go of his hand. I told Cornell

I'd race him to Tatiana's house. When we got there, I told Cornell to meet me in Tatiana's room, and then I told her sister to tell Jason that I wasn't there. When I got into the room, I nervously waited for the knock on the door. Cornell began to grow suspicious, but I told him I would explain in a minute. I was waiting for Jason to leave and to come up with a good lie to tell Cornell.

I had my ear to the door and could hear them talking then it got quiet. I felt the door open hitting me in the head. I stepped back, and it was Jason. "Hey, what's up, babe?" he said, kissing me on the cheek and giving me a hug. Then he turned and saw Cornell sitting on the bed. I stepped back and sat on the edge next to him. Jason then sat on the other side of me, and they both looked at each other in confusion.

Then Cornell put his arms around me, and Jason asked, "So what up? You with this dude?"

I was so at a loss for words and so pissed off that Tatiana's sister had let Jason in the house. "Yes, we're together," I finally answered.

"So what about us?" he asked.

"What's he talking about?" Cornell jumped in.

They both stood up and stared at me, waiting for me to answer. Before I had a chance, Jason said, "You know what, fuck it! You can have her." And he slammed the door as he stormed out.

Cornell grabbed his bag and said, "I can't believe you played me like that. We're done." And he followed right behind Jason.

"Thanks a lot," I yelled to Tatiana's sister, who was standing in the hallway there with a smirk on her face, enjoying all the drama.

"He said he saw you come in with Cornell, so what was I supposed to do?" she replied.

I rolled my eyes and walked home, thinking about how I was going to get both of them back.

Later that night, I called Cornell and pleaded that I was sorry and told him Jason was someone I was seeing before we had even gotten together. And I didn't know how to break it off because I didn't want to hurt him. I figured since we didn't go to the same school that it would eventually fade away since we barely saw each other. I was expecting Cornell to say fuck you and hang up, but he actually believed me and decided to work things out.

I tried to call Jason, but he wasn't answering my calls. I wanted them both but didn't care as long as I got Cornell back. The next day at school, a few of Cornell's groupies started talking shit about me, calling me a ho for cheating on him. He had told a couple of his boys what happened before we made up, and now all of his friends were pissed at me. Even though we made up, he was acting different and kept his distance from me when his friends were around.

I got so mad I went into the bathroom to cool off, and a group of females followed in after me. This tall one who looked like a female version of Snoop Dogg started calling me all kinds of bitches and hoes.

"Why the fuck do you even care what I do?" I said.

"Because that's the homie and he deserve better than you. I told his ass you were nothing but a ho," she said, getting all in my face.

"Well, if you want him so bad, then take him," I said, trying to walk past her, but she pushed me back, and I slipped and fell. As I stood up, she grabbed me by my hair and started banging my head into the mirror. I quickly started swinging back and somehow got her in a headlock. A couple of teachers rushed in and broke it up. Just like the last fight, I tried to explain how she started it, but it didn't stop them from suspending me again. My mom was so mad we got into a heated argument.

"You're such a bitch. You never take my side on anything!" I shouted at her.

"If you weren't out here hoeing around, these girls wouldn't be trying to fight you all the time," she said.

"Like you can talk. You're the one with three kids by three different daddies. So what does that make you?" I smirked.

That must have hit a soft spot because she slapped the shit out of me and said, "Your dad left because he didn't want you, and you know what? I wish I never had you either." Then she told me to get the fuck out of her house. That was the first time she said anything like that about my father, and that cut deep. My eyes filled with tears as I ran out of the house and over to Tatiana's.

Her mom felt bad for me and let me stay the night but told me it could only be for one night because she didn't want the police to come to her house again. I made a bunch of calls and called this girl I'd met at the Black history parade in San Bernardino. She was hella cool, but she lived too far for us to hang out, but we would still talk on the phone. She told me she would call around and call me back. About fifteen minutes later, she told me her Uncle Ronald said I could stay with him. I was so happy I didn't have to go back to my mom's. I honestly didn't even care who he was.

He picked me up outside Tatiana's house in a dark El Camino. He was in his thirties and looked just like Flavor Flav. I was a little nervous at first, but he told me on the way to his house that his mother lived with him because she had health problems, and he was helping to take care of her, and that he could use the help. I started to feel more comfortable about the situation until he gave me a weird smile as he looked me up and down and said, "It's going to be nice to have such a beautiful girl around the house." I gave a half-ass smile back and stared out the window until we arrived at his ranch style house.

When we walked in, he introduced me as his niece's friend from school who needed a place to stay. His mom looked at me but didn't say anything. She looked like she was out of it. I said hi, and he showed me to his bedroom. "This is my room and where you will be sleeping. You can put your stuff down over there in the corner, and I'll make you some space in the closet later. I'm about to make some dinner. You hungry?" he asked.

I shook my head yes and smiled as he left the room. I'd thought I would have my own room or sleep on the couch. I didn't know I would be sleeping in the same bed as him, but I was afraid of offending him, so I didn't say anything.

The next day he showed me around the house and all the medications to make sure his mom took and headed out to work. I wanted to make myself useful, so I cleaned up around the house and had dinner ready by the time he got back.

"Wow, you catch on quick," he said, walking in from work and placing his keys on the small table by the front door. We ate dinner like a family, and the next day I repeated the same thing. It soon became a daily routine, and everything seemed cool. I knew I was missing a lot of school, and eventually I would have to go back, but I wasn't quite ready yet, especially after he bought me this beautiful pink diamond ring, which eventually turned my finger green, with some flowers to thank me for doing such a great job around the house. He leaned in for a kiss, but I quickly turned my head, and he settled for a kiss on the cheek. I was so grateful for everything he was doing for me but felt disgusted at the thought of him touching me. After that, I started to notice him becoming more and more touchy-feely with me.

When I first got there, he didn't touch me at all when we slept together, and now he was rubbing on me when he thought I was asleep. I was starting to feel so uncomfortable, but I didn't want to mess up my living situation, so I keep quiet. That Friday, he went out drinking with his friends after work, and when he came back, he reeked of alcohol. He stumbled into the bed where I was half asleep. He tried rubbing on me, and this time I pushed his hand off, but he became more aggressive and pulled down my shorts and panties. I sat up, pulling them back up, and asked what he was doing.

"What you think I'm doing? Did you think you were just going to live here for free? I pay all the bills, buy your food and buy you nice things. This is the least you could do," he said, pulling my legs down until I was flat on my back.

"But I'm not staying here for free. I thought by me helping out around the house that would be in exchange for me to stay here," I said, holding on to my shorts to prevent him from pulling them down any farther.

"Do you know how much that ring was that I bought you? Don't you like it? Don't I treat you nice? I'm sure none of those other boys you dated ever did anything like that for you before. I can take care of you like you deserve. This is why you need to be with a man." He started kissing up my legs all the way to my inner thigh. He had a long tongue that somehow made it to my pussy without my legs being all the way open. I tried to resist, but it was feeling so good. He kept getting deeper and deeper until his tongue was completely inside me and he was sucking on my clit.

It's too late now to stop it. He's already tasted it, I thought. I released my grip on my shorts and let him continue to pull them off. He spread open my legs and dug his tongue so deep inside me felt like a dick. I had never felt it like this before. Usually, when boys went down on me, they would just lick around but not go deep inside like this. I moaned in ecstasy as he continued to suck on my clit until my legs trembled, and my stomach muscles began to spasm. I didn't know what was happening. All I knew was this was the best feeling I had ever felt. It felt so good I didn't even care anymore that he was touching me or that he was now inside me.

The next morning, I woke up to him on top of me going at it again, but I knew I couldn't keep doing this. Later that day, I convinced him I needed to go back to school. I told him I had missed way too many days and didn't want to fail my classes. He was hesitant at first and told me he would think about it, but eventually agreed to take me. That Monday, he dropped me off at the front and said he'd be here right after school to pick me up. I had only been gone a few weeks, but everyone looked like they had seen a ghost when I walked through the halls to my class.

As soon as I sat down, my teacher called me up to the front and asked me where I had been. I told her I had got kicked out and had been staying with a friend. Next thing I knew, I was being called to the principal's office, where a police officer was also there waiting for me.

"So who is this friend you have been staying with?" the officer asked.

"Just an uncle of one of my friends. Why?"

"Because you have missed three weeks of school, and we need to know where you have been. What's the name of this uncle?"

I didn't want to get him in trouble, but they were very persistent and wouldn't let me leave until I told them. I told them his name, and the officer left for about fifteen minutes. When he came back he said, "This man has a long criminal record, and you shouldn't be living with him. You should be at home with your family. I'm sure your mother misses you."

I rolled my eyes when he said that. "Have you two been intimate with each other?" he asked.

"Look, he took me in after my mom kicked me out, because I had nowhere else to go. I don't want to get him into any trouble. He was there for me when no one else was."

"You're not going to get anyone in any trouble. We just want to talk to him and take you back home," the officer reassured me.

"What about all my belongings? They're at his house," I asked.

"We'll make sure to get all of your belongings for you, but you need to be truthful and tell us everything that happened while you were there. Have you two been intimate with each other?"

I paused for a minute, looked down, and said, "Yes."

The officer and the principal both looked at each other, and then he asked if he was picking me up from school and what kind of car he had. I was so ready to be done with this whole thing I told them everything. Finally, he told me I could go back to class.

All of my friends were excited to see me, including Cornell, but I only told Tatiana what happened. After school was over, I walked over to where Ron said he would pick me up and saw him surrounded by police. Then I saw them putting him into handcuffs and in the back of one of the cop cars. My heart dropped, and I felt so bad. I didn't want to have sex with him, but he had taken good care of me, so I felt incredibly guilty that I had gotten him into trouble for trying to help me out. Looking back on it now, he deserved to go to jail for fucking a fifteen-year-old, but at the time I didn't see it that way.

The same officer who'd spoken with me in the principal's office was the same one that took me home and told my mom about everything that had happened. She didn't say much to me after he left, but I could tell she was disgusted with everything she had heard and even more with seeing him in court a few weeks later. I had to testify about everything that had happened in front of her and a courtroom full of people. He was later sentenced to three years.

While in jail, he called me collect over and over again, so I finally answered it. He was crying on the phone about how I'd ruined his life. I tried to explain to him how I didn't mean to, and how they forced me to do it, but he didn't believe me. I was feeling so guilty I hung up on him. I couldn't take hearing his cries anymore. After that I never saw or spoke to him again.

The judge had told my mom in court that I should see a therapist, which I had started shortly after the sentencing. At the time, I thought therapy was a dumbass idea, so I didn't open up to her at all. When the cops lied to me about getting all of my things back from Ron's house, I know I couldn't trust anyone who got a paycheck to help people, including therapist. I knew they didn't give a shit about me and was doing it because it was their job. I had lost so much at Ron's house. My baby albums, savings bonds my grandmother had giving me and all of my clothes and personal belongings. I had so much anger bottled up inside of me. I knew it was just a matter of time before one day I would explode.

Cornell had felt so bad about the fight which got me suspended and kicked out of the house that when I came back to school, he was being extra sweet to me—walking me to class, holding my books, and sometimes buying my lunches. For a while, things were great between us. We even had sex for the first time in my room when Ryan was at his dad's and my mom was at work. It was the first time he had ever had sex, but he didn't fuck like a virgin. He wanted to keep going over and over again. We were drenched with sweat by the time I threw in the towel.

Cornell had a best friend who I nicknamed Smokie because he looked just like Chris Tucker on Friday, plus he smoked hella weed, and he was funny as fuck, just like Smokie. He always had us dying laughing. Once I felt like I was going to throw up from laughing so hard. That day during lunch we were having such a good time we didn't feel like going back to class, and we all decided to ditch school and go back to my place. It was me, Tatiana, Smokie, and Cornell. When we got there, Cornell and I went into my mom's room to have sex on her waterbed while Smokie and Tatiana watched TV.

While looking through my mom's drawer for some sexy lingerie to put on, I stumbled across the gun she had pulled out on Mike. I pulled it out and showed Cornell. We played with it for a couple of minutes, then we put it back and began having sex on her bed. After we finished, Cornell asked if he could scare Smokie with the gun. I thought it would be funny, so I said okay, and he grabbed the gun and walked in the living and yelled out, "Put your hands up, you mark-ass trick!" as he pointed the gun at Smokie. Smokie's eyes got so big, he looked like he had just shitted himself. We all started laughing hysterically. After Smokie caught his breath, he jumped up and wanted to see it. He played around with it for a little, but I was starting to have a bad feeling, so I grabbed it and told them I was going to put it back in my mama's drawer before she killed me.

We started watching "Saved by the Bell," when Smokie remembered a trick he wanted to show us. He told me to get him a lighter and some perfume, which he sprayed on his jeans' leg and set it on fire. The second time he did it, the fire didn't get put out as fast as the first one, and he jumped up in a panic but was able to put it out quickly, and we all busted out laughing over it. It was starting to get late, so we decided to head back to class. Smokie asked if he could use the bathroom, and when he came out, we all walked back to school just in time to hear the bell ring.

That evening I was coming out of the kitchen from washing the dishes, when I noticed my mom charging right at me. I stopped in my tracks, dropped the hand towel as she grabbed me by my hair.

"Where the fuck is my gun?" she yelled.

"What, what are you talking about? I don't know where your gun is at." I was so confused.

She dragged me over to where a vase was sitting on the dining room table and hit me over the head with it. "I'm not going to ask you again, where the fuck is my gun?" she yelled grabbing me by my shirt to prevent me from running away.

Luckily the vase didn't break, but it still hurt like hell, and I started screaming as I grabbed my head, checking for blood, "I don't know where your gun is at." She went to hit me again with the vase, but I put my hands up and cried, "OKAY, okay, wait! My friends and I ditched school today, and I showed them your gun. Maybe one of them took it." She put the vase back down on the table and dragged me over to the phone and told me to call my friends right now and find out where it was.

The first person I called was Tatiana, but she had no idea about it, so I called Cornell. He had no idea either but said he would call Smokie and find out if he'd taken it. About ten minutes later, he called and told me Smokie had it. I begged and pleaded for him to get it back, and he assured me he would. An hour later, there was a knock at the door, and it was Cornell's uncle, who'd gotten the gun and brought it back. Once he gave the gun to my mom and saw how attractive she was, he tried to hit on her, but she quickly slammed the door right in his face.

I was so relieved when she got it back and thought she would be too, but as soon as she put the gun away, she came up to me and said, "I can't fuckin' stand your ass. I wish I never had you. I wish when I stabbed you, you would have just died."

"Well at least you had a choice because if I did, I would have never made you, my mother. And I know my father didn't leave because of me, he left because he didn't want to be with your ass," I shouted back. Before I could get another word out, she smacked me harder than she ever had before, and I seriously contemplated grabbing the kitchen knife and stabbing her in the throat with it. The blood in my veins began to boil. I'd never felt angry like this before, and it scared me.

She noticed me staring at the knife, and yelled, "Get the fuck out of my face and go to your room. I can't even stand to look at you right now."

I went to my room and thought of a million ways to kill her. Stabbing her would be too messy, and she was strong as fuck, so I knew she would probably gain control over the knife. And by now, I was sure she had hidden the gun somewhere where I couldn't find it. So I knew I couldn't shoot her. *That's it. I'm going to set this whole fuckin' place on fire.* I poked my head out the door and whispered to my little brother, "Chris, come here. I need you to do me a huge favor. I need you to stay in your room and jump out the window when I knock on it. I'm about to burn the house down." He was so scared and confused but knew by the tone in my voice and the fight he'd just overheard between my mom and me that I was serious. I went into his room, cracked his window, and popped out the screen. Ryan was in the living watching TV, and I wasn't telling him shit. Chris was the only one in my life that I truly loved.

When my mom went to bed and the coast was clear, I snuck into the garage and found the jug of gasoline she used for the lawnmower. Just before I began to pour it around the house, she came into the garage and grabbed me by the arm. Then she snatched the jug out my hand. "What the fuck are you doing? You're really about to burn this house down with me and your brothers inside?" she asked.

"No, I was going to save Chris," I said, wiping the tears from my face. The look on her face was like her heart had just broken into a million pieces. She grabbed me by my hair again and dragged me into the house. She picked up the phone and called Laneshia's mom, Ms. Bates, "Please come get this girl before I kill her."

MS. BATES AND HER HUSBAND WERE best friends with my mom and Curtis, but not too long after Curtis moved out, Ms. Bates caught her husband cheating, and they ended up getting a divorce. She was a stay-at-home mom, so when he left, she didn't have any skills to get a job right away and ended up having to move in with her twenty-year-old daughter Tisha, who also had a three-year-old daughter. They picked me up and took me back to Tisha's two-bedroom apartment in Colton. The plan was for me to only stay there temporarily until Tisha and her daughter's father, Jeff, who was her high school sweetheart, got their place together, but that all changed in the blink of an eye.

Jeff had rented a nice car and was headed over to his boy's house. As he opened his car door to dial the code to get into the apartment complex, he was approached by two armed carjackers. They told him to get out of the car, and as he pleaded for his life, they shot him in the head, killing him instantly. Tisha was beyond devastated, and before they could even bury his body, she found out she was pregnant with their second child. I had never seen someone in that much pain. She could barely get out of bed and was crying every day. I felt so helpless and tried to help out as much as possible, like watching her daughter while she got some rest. I would dress her up as my little mini-me and take her to the park and pretend she was mine even though I was only twelve years older than her. And just like that, my temporary home became my permanent, at least for a while.

I got my first job at Baker's fast food right across from Fiesta Village. I was only fifteen, but it felt amazing to start making my own money. Ms. Bates was very religious and strict. She forced me to go to church and didn't allow me to listen to or watch any secular music videos. I couldn't even watch certain cartoons because she felt like it was witchcraft, so I spent a lot of time outside.

I usually would sit on the steps and talk on the phone with Tatiana most of the time. As I was having one of my daily conversations with her, I saw two cute boys walk past. There were many cute guys in that neighborhood, but after this one boy tried to talk to me and his girlfriend wanted to fight me over it, I wasn't fuckin' with any of them. Luckily, I had my little niece with me, which prevented the girl from fighting me. But these two boys caught my attention since I had never seen them around there before, and they were wearing matching referee shirts. When I told Tatiana about them, and she told me to call them over, so I whistled.

They turned and looked around, then noticed me sitting on the steps smiling, so they walked over. "Hey, what's up? Was that whistling at us?" one of them asked.

"Nah, you must be hearing things. I didn't whistle," I said, playing dumb in case they had girlfriends.

"You live here? I never seen you here before," he asked while the other one just stood there quietly behind him.

"Yeah, I moved in a few months ago. Do you live here?" I asked.

"Nah, but my cousin here does. We just got finished refereeing a game and was headed back to his house until my mom picks me up," he said, sitting down next to me.

"Hey, I'm gonna head to the house so I can change my clothes," his cousin said walking off. I told Tatiana I'd call her back. He introduced himself as Devin and we talked until his cousin came back and told him his mom was here.

We exchanged numbers and really hit it off. A couple of weeks later, we became official. I was so mad at Smokie for stealing my mom's gun that I didn't want to talk to him or Cornell ever again, so Devin became my second real boyfriend, but this time I was in love for the first time. He was tall, light-skinned, medium built, and so different from every boy I'd ever talked to. He was so sweet and seemed to genuinely love and care about me for who I was and not just for the sex, which we didn't even have until a month after becoming official.

We both wanted our first time to be special, so we waited for the perfect time to ditch school and not worry about anyone coming in and catching us. It was such an incredible feeling to finally make love to someone instead of just fucking them. I know it sounds crazy being only fifteen talking about making love and fucking, but that's how I truly felt at that time. I just wished he had been my first for everything, but I gave him my heart as if he was.

His parents liked me and would even pick me up to take me to his basketball games. Even Ms. Bates loved him, and she didn't like anyone. She said I needed a nice boy like him in my life. He was always polite, got good grades and was an all-star basketball player. He motivated me to want to do better in school, and for a while I did. We celebrated Valentine's Day and birthdays together. Everything was going great, but nothing great lasts too long—at least in my life it doesn't.

Everything came to a blow-up when he had a huge fight with his dad and ran away to my house. When his mom came over and asked if he was there, I lied to her and said he wasn't. Ms. Bates knew he was a good kid, so she let him stay the night after he begged her. She agreed, but only for that one night, so he slept on the couch. The next morning, he decided to go back home, and his parents were furious. Not only did they ground him, but they told him they no longer wanted him to see me anymore for lying to them.

He assured me it wasn't going to stop him from calling or seeing me, but with them taking his car and phone privileges away, it was hard for him to keep that promise. Weeks felt like months, and a month felt like years. He decided to sneak out to see me but got caught and put on a longer punishment. This time they threaten to take away basketball if he contacted me again. After I didn't hear from him for a while, I figured it was over and started dating Romeo, who I met when he came up to my school looking for his younger brother. Romeo was this very charming, short sexy chocolate boy with chinkie eyes that made him look Blasian, like Tyson Beckford, who was my number one crush growing up. I was instantly drawn to his bad-boy persona. He was three years older than me and had just graduated. He had a nice car and told me he was working the set of music videos from Snoop Dogg to Tupac.

I thought I had hit the jackpot when he showed interest in me, but he had other girls and wasn't ready to settle down anytime soon. I knew I had to step up my game if I wanted to be his girl, and I didn't want him to think I was too young for him, so whenever he asked me to ditch school and hang out, I would. We were fucking like rabbits. Back-to-back, every day all day. No matter where we were, we would find a place to fuck. At my school, at the park, even on the freeway. I rode him while he was driving, and we laughed as cars slowed down to watch.

After Devin got off full punishment and got his car back, the first thing he did was call me, but I was too sprung off Romeo, so I blew him off. Romeo and I had been seeing each other almost every day for months. He even introduced me to his mom, who quickly became like a second mother to me. She only had two boys and had always wanted a daughter, and I always wanted a mother I could connect with, so our bond was instant. Sometimes I would come over and just hang out with her without Romeo. We would go shopping, take pictures, and go out to eat together. We even dressed alike and did our hair the same way. I had started to miss so much school to hang out with Romeo that I got suspended again. Ms. Bates was so mad. Not only did she ground me, but she made me go with her to Bible study. I hated going to church especially bible study. I felt like the people there were always so judgmental and phony, but my girl Misha was there with her cute ass brothers, which made it fun to go. She told me she had gotten into trouble too for skipping school and had to be homeschooled.

While at home being suspended, Tisha told me I had to watch the baby and pick my other niece up from the bus stop after school around 3:30 pm while Ms. Bates was working at the church. I tried to call Romeo so he could come over, but he didn't answer the phone, so I called Misha to come over instead. She got dropped off by some guy and brought over a bottle of gin and juice. We sat on the bed, getting drunk and talking shit about how we couldn't wait to turn eighteen so we could do what the fuck we wanted to do. I was so drunk I gave the baby, who was only like six months old, a sip but sobered up enough to calm her down when she began to cry. I stumbled into the living room to grab her diaper so I could change it.

"OH SHIT," I yelled as I looked at the clock that had just turned to 3:50 pm. "OMG, can you please change her diaper while I run to the bus stop and pick up my niece?" I said as I rushed out of the house and up the street so fast, only to find an empty bus stop. I shook my head as I walked back to the house, knowing I was going to be in so much trouble.

When I got back, the phone was ringing off the hook. I picked it up, and it was Tisha screaming on the phone that the school just called her and said my niece was never picked up and she'd had to leave work early to go get her. I told my girl she should leave before Tisha got home. She arrived about forty-five minutes later with my niece and Ms. Bates following right behind her who had been at church. I was still drunk, but I felt so bad.

"Angie, why did you forget to pick her up?" Tisha while she checked on the baby, who was sleeping in the crib.

"Nothing, I had just dozed off and forgot," I said, slurring my words.

"Oh my God, have you been drinking? And why is my baby's diaper on backwards?" she yelled.

"Noooo, I haven't been drinking, and that was an accident." I slurred even worse than the first time.

"Okay, this is not working, you're going to have to find somewhere else to live," Tisha yelled. I knew I had fucked up this time, so I grabbed up all my things and left.

I tried calling Romeo from the pay phone again, but he still wasn't answering. I had no idea where I was going to go.

The first couple of nights, I slept in an empty apartment I had known about through my friends. I was a pro at unlocking windows and would sneak in at night and sleep in the closet. During the day, I would hang out at Taco Tia, looking for handouts to get some food. Someone must have seen me sneak in, because on the third night there was a new bolt on the window that I couldn't get open.

I sat on the curb, trying to figure out where I could go. After about an hour, I still had no clue, and it was getting late. I was so tired, so I decided to walk over to the laundry room and just sleep in there. As I walked over, Thomas who was the stepdad of one of the boys at my school, was outside smoking a cigarette. I'd seen him around the neighborhood a few times before, but never really talked to him because he always gave me creep vibes.

"What are you doing out here wandering the streets so late?" he asked.

"I got kicked out my house, so I'm trying to figure out where to go."

"So you ain't got nowhere to go? No family, no nothing?" He threw down his Newport and stomped it out with his shoe.

"No," I replied.

"So where you about to go?" he asked.

"I don't know." I said putting my head down, feeling embarrassed but was hoping he would help me find a solution.

"Meet me on the corner of Orange Street. I'll pick you up in a few minutes. I have somewhere you can stay." About thirty minutes later, he pulled up in a tan Oldsmobile Cutlass. "Get in," he said, opening the passenger door from the inside. "I'm going to talk to my cousin tomorrow and ask if you can stay at her house, but it's too late to go there now, so I'm going to get you a room at the Motel 6 for the night, so you are not sleeping on the streets. It's not safe for a pretty young thing like yourself walking alone at night. You hungry?"

I exhaled a sigh of relief. I was starving and so happy when he said that. *Maybe he wasn't as bad as I thought.* We got some food and checked into the room. As we were eating, he asked me if I was dating any boys at school. I told him I didn't date boys at my school anymore because I liked older guys like this boy Romeo. After we finished eating, he asked if I minded if he smoked. Even though I hated cigarettes, I said no since he was doing all these nice things for me. I was expecting him to pull out his pack of Newport's, but instead, he pulled out a pipe and a ball of foil. He opened it up, and there was a small brown rock inside. He lit the bottom of the foil up with a lighter and inhaled the smoke through the pipe.

"You ever smoke this before?" he asked coming over and sitting next to me on the bed.

"No, what is it?" I replied.

"Something that's going to make you feel a whole lot better. Here, just take a small puff." I took the pipe, inhaled it, and I lay back on the bed. I closed my eyes, and for a split second I thought I was in heaven. My body instantly felt like it was floating. All of my problems seemed to magically vanish. I had no more worries, or fear about my mom, a place to stay, school, or anything else in this world. But that fantasy world disappeared the moment I opened my eyes. This wasn't heaven at all because the devil was feasting between my legs, and I realized nothing in this world is free.

I don't remember much after that except waking up to an empty room and the phone ringing. When I answered it, the man asked me if I would be staying another night because it was check-out time. I told him no, gathered all my things, and walked outside. I sat on the steps trying to figure out what had happened the night before and what I was going to do now.

"Hey, baby girl. You thought I forgot about you, huh? You know I can't forget about you." He smiled, flicking his cigarette out the window of his car as he pulled up. "Get in. My cousin Mona said you could stay with her and her husband. They just had a baby, so I told her you would help her out."

I was still foggy about last night but didn't saying anything about it when I got into the car. When we got to their apartment and walked in, she looked shocked to see me. Almost like she was excepting someone else. She looked at her husband, who had a big smile on his face. She nudged him and said, "I didn't realize you were so young. Thomas told me you were having problems with your mom. I didn't get along with mine either, so I understand how it goes. You can sleep on the couch until you can find another place to stay. I put fresh blankets and pillows out for you, and you can put your stuff over there in the corner. If you need to take a shower or anything, the bathroom is down the hall, first door on the right. I put a towel out for you as well."

"Thank you so much. I really appreciate it," I replied. "Please let me know if there's anything you need me to do."

I had been there for a couple of weeks helping her around the house and with the baby. I spent a lot of time watching my nieces, so I was really good with kids. Minus that one time I got drunk. Her baby loved me and once she saw that she slowly began to love having me around too. I even took the baby out for walks so she could get some rest. I could tell by the way her husband looked at me inappropriately that I should avoid him at all costs so I would never stay in the house with him alone. If she left, I made up an excuse that I had to go and would just hang outside or with Romeo until she got back.

One night they had sex, and it was so loud it woke me up. He knew I could hear them and made it a point to fuck her even harder than he usually would. After they finished, he walked to the kitchen half-naked to grab some water, dripping with sweat and still hard. I was pretending to be asleep, but I could tell he knew I wasn't by how he accidentally dropped his towel as he walked past.

The next morning was a little awkward, but luckily, he had to rush off to work, so he didn't stay long. A few days later she said she had to visit her mother, and I would have the place to myself until she got back. After she left, I cleaned the kitchen. I went into the living room and started watching

TV. Around noon I heard the keys at the front door and thought she must have forgotten something since she'd only been gone for less than fifteen minutes, but it wasn't her. It was him. He had never come home during lunch before, so I was surprised to see him, but he said he had forgotten his wallet and had to come home for lunch to get it. Normally I would have made up an excuse to leave but since he was only staying for lunch, I figured he wouldn't be there that long. He went into the kitchen, heated up some leftover chicken and cracked open a beer.

"So how you like living here so far?" he asked, sitting in the chair across from me.

"It's cool. Your wife is so great. I love helping her with the baby. And he's so cute."

"That's good. I know she adores you and loves having you here. I know we don't talk much, but I like having you here too. It's nice to see a pretty face around the house. And you know, having you here has really helped spice things up in the bedroom too."

I was caught off guard when he said that and didn't know how to respond, so I started staring at the TV pretending like I didn't hear that part, hoping he would change the subject.

"Don't get me wrong; before the baby, we use to have some real good freaky sex, but after she got pregnant, everything changed. Having you here has made it feel like the good old days."

I felt so uncomfortable that he was telling me all this and just tried to focus on watching Ricki Lake.

He continued about how lucky Romeo was. "Have you ever been with an older man before? Not like Romeo but older." he asked, opening up his second beer and sitting closer to me.

"Umm, I almost forgot. I told my homegirl I'd meet her at the mall," I said, getting up and heading to the counter to grab my backpack. I could tell this conversation wasn't going to lead anywhere good, and I didn't want to mess up this living situation, so I was going to leave until she got back.

"I'm sorry, did I say something to make you feel uncomfortable? It's just I could tell by the way you look at me that you're attracted to me just as much as I'm attracted to you. Plus, I thought since you and Thomas got a room, you'd be down," he said, grabbing my waist and kissing me on my neck. I'm not going to lie. He was very attractive and kind of looked like Ginuwine. I probably would have messed with him if I didn't love Mona, and the baby but I just couldn't do that to her.

I pulled away and said, "I don't know what you're talking about," trying to play dumb. He backed me up, and I fell back on the couch. He grabbed my face with one hand and pulled me in for a kiss, and with his other hand, started rubbing on my breast. For a split second, I enjoyed it, but the guilt snapped me out of it, and I pushed his hand away.

Just then the front door swung open, and Mona stood there boiling with rage. She dropped the baby on the couch and started hitting him. "Valerie called and told me she saw your ass come back to the house as soon as I left. And I knew your dumbass would be over here doing some bullshit again," she said smacking him on his face.

"Baby, baby, please listen. I came home because I forgot my wallet, and we were just talking," he said, grabbing her hands to prevent her from hitting him again.

"That did not look like y'all was just talking!" she said.

I was starting to have flashbacks of the fight with Lil Scrappy. I went and grabbed the crying baby, hoping that by holding him it would prevent her from lashing out at me.

"Baby, you know after the last incident I said I would never cheat on you again and haven't. I swear we were just talking. Matter of fact you know she fucked Thomas," he said.

"What do you mean she fucked Thomas? My cousin Thomas?" Mona asked.

"Yeah, he told me they had gotten a room together right before she came to live with us and to watch out for her because she likes older men, but I didn't say anything to you about it because I knew you needed help with the baby and that you liked having her around."

"Wait, what? Did you fuck my cousin? You know he's like thirty years older than you AND married. Why would you do that?" Mona said snatching the baby out of my arms and handed him to her husband. *Oh shit it's about to go down*, I thought.

"No, that's not true. He's lying. Thomas got me a room because I had nowhere to go, but we didn't do anything," I pleaded.

"I should have listened to my gut. I knew you were going to be trouble the moment I saw you. I know my cousin. He doesn't do anything for anyone unless he knows he's getting something in return. So if I call him right now, he's gonna tell me nothing happened between you two?" she asked reaching for the phone.

My heart dropped to the pit of my stomach. I didn't know what to say. Tears started to fill my eyes, as I looked down. "Okay, look when we got into the room, he gave me something weird to smoke and I passed out. I honestly don't remember anything that happened after that, I swear! Mona, you have to believe me, I would never do that to you."

"What do you mean you don't remember? Wow, I know if you messed with Thomas, you would mess with my husband. You know what. Just get out of my house," she said, grabbing me by my hair and throwing me outside. I don't know why everyone always went for my hair, but it felt like déjà vu. I cried for her to believe me, but it seemed to be falling on deaf ears. She then grabbed all my clothes and belongings and threw them over the balcony. Everyone was outside watching, including some kids from school, so I knew this would be on the front page of the school gossip.

I grabbed as much of my stuff as I could fit into my bag and left the rest. I ran around the corner and into the laundry room, where I hid and cried myself to sleep. I waited until the coast was clear and knew no one was outside. I decided to pop up at Romeo's house. As I was walking to the bus stop, a dark two-door Ford Mustang pulled up next to me with two guys in it. The guy on the passenger side asked if I needed a ride somewhere.

"Yeah, I'm heading to my girl's house." I lied because I knew if I said it was a guy's house, then they probably wouldn't take me.

"Aight well get in, we'll take you. I'm Blaq, and that's my boy Blaze," he said getting out the car and letting me in the back seat.

"So what your girl look like? Is she as fine as you?" Blaze asked. I had them take me to Romeo's mom's house, but his little brother answered the door and said he'd gotten into trouble and got kicked out, and they didn't know where he was. I don't know why I just didn't wait for his mom to get off work and ask her if I could stay there. I guess I was embarrassed because she always viewed me as this sweet little angel, and I didn't want her to know the truth of who I really was.

I went back down the stairs and told them she wasn't home. "If you want, you can come chill with us. We about to hit up this house party tonight," Blaq said with his Tyrese Coco-cola smile. I stared up at Romeo's bedroom window wishing this was a fairytale. He would look out yonder, see me in distress then rush down and save me like I was his Juliet, but the lights never came on, and I had no choice but to go with them.

I had a bad feeling I shouldn't go, but at this point I didn't give a fuck anymore what happened to me. I felt like I was always fucking up and deserved whatever I got. I had lost everything I ever loved. I felt like no one wanted me or even cared if I died. Part of me was hoping it would all end like it did for Tina.

What's the worst that can happen that hasn't already? I thought. "Fuck it, let's go," I said. I hopped in the back seat, took a puff of the blunt Blaze handed me as we listened to "So Many Tears" by Tupac and drove off into the starless night.

"Trapped in a beautiful mind, her tortured soul was drowning in the tears her eyes could not shed." – Black Butterfly

Chapter IV
Shattered Chrysalis

WE PICKED UP THEIR OTHER. homeboy and drove to San Bernardino. I could hear, "*If it Don't Make a Dollar, It Don't Make Sense*" by DJ Quik bumping outside as we pulled up. When I walked in, everyone turned around and looked to see who I was. They could tell I didn't belong there, and I could see everyone whispering to each other about me. Blaq asked me if I wanted to dance, but I told him I wasn't much of a dancer and just wanted to hang out outside instead. He grabbed us both a drink, and we sat on the side of the house and talked about our lives for almost an hour. I told him about all the trouble I had gotten into and how I had no place to go. He told me about his rough upbringing with his mom and how she was on drugs. He said his boyz initiated him into their Crip gang a month ago and that they had become his family.

We had two completely different backgrounds, but somehow related to each other on so many levels. He was tall, skinny with a dark chocolate complexion, and his smile lit up like the stars in the night sky. When he saw that I got upset talking about my mother, he leaned over and kissed me softly with his big juicy lips and said he understood exactly where I was coming from. And as long as he was around, I would never have to worry about anything. He was like my ghetto prince. It was such a bittersweet moment, like finding a sunflower growing in the middle of a junk yard. Everything around us seemed to be tuned out, and for a short moment we were in our own little world.

"You're different than most girls I met around here," he said, smiling.

"So this is where y'all snuck off to," a big, husky guy said as he came around the corner, sipping on a 40. "So who's ol girl?" he asked.

"Oh, dis Angie. Angie, this is Mad Dogg. She just got kicked out of her people's house, so I told her she could chill with us," Blaq said, putting his arm around my neck and kissing me on my cheek.

"Is that right? Hey, Blaq, let me holla at you real quick," he said. He licked his bottom lip at me and put his arm around Blaq's shoulders as they both disappeared around the corner of the house. A few minutes later, Mad Dogg came back without Blaq and said, "Hey, shorty, we outta liquor so why don't you run wit me real fast to the liquor store?"

"Ummm, where's Blaq at? Is he coming?" I asked, standing up, looking around the corner to see if I could see him, but all I saw was a group of people smoking and drinking on the porch.

"Nah, Blaq is handling some business for me. He's gonna be awhile, so you might as well come, so you not sitting out here by yourself." A few gunshots went off in the far distance, and I realized he probably was right even though I knew I shouldn't go without Blaq.

I hopped in his Chrysler Imperial, put on my seat belt, and watched him squeeze his fat ass into the driver's seat. We drove past two liquor stores before I asked where we were going. "Oh, I gotta make a quick stop first," he said, looking down at my legs and licking his bottom lip again. I started to have this sick feeling in the pit of my stomach that made me feel nauseous. He popped in a cassette and started playing

"Ain't No Fun" by Snoop Dogg. We drove for what seemed like twenty more minutes before he pulled up on a hillside that overlooked the city.

"What are you doing?" I asked.

"So you going to give me some or what?" he said, leaning over and grabbing my chest.

"What? NO!" I yelled, pushing his hand away.

"Well, if you not fucking then you get out!"

"Okay, fine ... fuck you!" I said as I reached for the handle to get out, but it was locked. He then opened his door, leaned over, pulled me across to his side, and threw me on the ground. Then he grabbed me by my neck as he opened up the back seat and pushed me inside. I screamed for him to get off me, but he just continued to rip off my clothes.

He put one hand on my throat that was squeezing so hard I could barely breathe, and with the other hand, he unzipped his pants, pulled a condom out of his pocket and ripped it open with his mouth. Then he put it on as he forced his way inside me. He was so big and fat I couldn't even move my arms to even attempt to get him off me. The more I tried to fight back, the harder it was to breathe, so I finally just gave in as tears streamed down the side of my face. After he finished, he took the condom off and threw it off the side of the cliff and got back in the driver's seat. As he was backing the car up, we locked eyes through his rearview mirror, and he saw the tears pouring down my face.

"Why you bitchez always started crying afterward like you ain't want that shit?" He never even stopped at the liquor store as we drove back to the house. When we got back, he got out of the car and went to the crowd where Blaq was standing on the porch. He gave him a dap, pulled him in close and whispered something in his ear. Blaq looked back at me and handed him the blunt he had been smoking. Then he walked over to where I was still sitting in the back seat of the car, crying.

He opened the back door and asked, "You good?"

"Noooo, he just fuckin raped me," I cried. I was shaking so bad you would have thought it was in the middle of winter.

"He just told me you were with it."

"Nooo, I wasn't," I screamed.

"So why would you leave with him then?" He looked at me as if it was my fault.

"He asked me to go to the liquor store with him and said you were busy handling business and would be awhile and that I shouldn't be out here alone. Then I heard gunshots and didn't want to sit outside here by myself. I mean, why would you leave me out here like that? You said you would look out for me. I just want to go home," I cried.

He got in the car and closed the door. "Look, these aren't the type of niggaz you want to fuck around with, and I don't want to see you hurt. If you leave right now, he might think you about to snitch and go to the cops or something and trust me he won't let that happen. So just calm down. I promise I won't let nothing else happen to you again. I swear I was only gone for like ten minutes. I wasn't going to leave you out there like that." He put his hand on my leg to stop it from shaking and hugged me.

I knew after what happened to Tina I had to calm down and play it cool. "Okay, but can we just please not stay here long?" I said, looking back up at Mad Dogg, who was still on the porch laughing and smoking with his boys like nothing ever happened. "Yeah, we'll dip in like fifteen. Let's go inside and find Blaze. I'm going to take you to my cousin's house. I'm sure she will let you stay there."

We walked in, and I struggled not to slap the smirk off Mad Dogg as we walked past him. We saw Blaze dancing with some girl, and while we waited for him to finish, I went into the bathroom to wash up. Once the song was over, Blaq walked over and whispered in his ear. Blaze grabbed the girl by her hand, and we all walked out together. Blaq gave him another dap and hugged Mad Dogg and told him we were going to his cousin Diamond's house.

When we pulled up to her apartment, he left me in the car to explain to his cousin how I needed a place to stay. About ten minutes later, he came back and said she said it was cool and that he gave her some money so I could stay there. Blaze and the girl drove off, and I grabbed my backpack of clothes and headed inside.

She came out of her room with a blanket and pillow and said, "Hi, I'm Diamond. It's not much, but you can sleep on the couch."

"No, it's more than enough. Thank you so much for letting me stay here," I said, taking the blanket and pillow from her. I made up the couch and laid down. I was so exhausted I fell asleep with my clothes still on, and Blaq fell asleep sitting up next to my feet.

It was still summertime, so I didn't have to worry about going to school yet. I stayed there over the next couple weeks and would just tag along wherever Blaq went, even when he was selling drugs on the corner. One day he was getting ready to head out to the block and pulled out a silver Smith & Wesson revolver hidden in one of his shoeboxes.

"You ever seen one of these?" he asked, handing it to me.

"No, but I've seen people on TV play Russian roulette with it. Have you ever played?" I asked, looking down at the gun.

"Hell nah."

"Why? You a pussy boy?" I taunted.

"Man, you ain't gonna play that shit either," he laughed.

"How much you want to bet?" I said, taking all the bullets out of the chamber except one and spun the cylinder around just like I had seen in the movies. I didn't care anymore about living and was hoping it would go off the first round so I could finally be put out of this misery. I placed the gun to my head, and before he could lunge over and snatch it away, I pulled the trigger.

"What the fuck! Are you crazy or something? What the fuck is wrong with you? I thought you were just playing," he said, snatching the gun out of my hand.

I smiled and played it off like I was joking around, but inside I was mad I was still alive. I was tired of worrying about the next day. I felt like I was walking around like a zombie, dead to the world, and just wanted it all to end.

Another Friday night came. Blaq and his boys decided to hit up a pool hall. I sat in one of the highchairs and watched them get a couple of rounds of pool in. In the middle of the last game, a few guys wearing red came in. They all locked eyes, and one of Blaq's boyz said, "Dats dat nigga right there?" Blaq and his boyz started rushing toward them, yelling out curse words left and right. Before they could make it to them, staff rushed over and told them they had to leave.

Blaq signaled for me to come on, and we ran back into the car. Blaq and I got in the back seat, and Blaze and another guy got in the front. The guy was talking about how they should smoke the whole place up. Blaze popped open the trunk and pulled out a MAC-10 and handed it to him. He started the car and sped around in a circle. Blaq told me to put my head down, so I lay across his legs. The next thing I heard was tires screeching, gunshots spraying out, glass breaking, and people screaming. Then the car sped off, and we headed back to Blaq's cousin's apartment, which was the normal hangout spot for everyone.

I was so scared, but the adrenaline rush made it feel like I was in a movie like "Boyz n the Hood" or something. When we got back to the apartment, I sat outside on the stairs and just listened to them brag to some other guys about what had just happened.

"So was you scared?" the guy who shot the gun asked me.

"Nah, I wasn't scared," I said playing it off like I was cool with it, but inside I was scared shitless. I didn't want them to think I was going to snitch or anything. "Oh, shorty a G, huh. You ever had Cisco before?" he asked, handing me a bottle.

"Of course, I drink this shit all the time. It tastes like a wine cooler to me," I said, taking the bottle and a big sip, but the truth was I had only sipped it once before.

"A wine cooler, huh? Aight, I dare you to drink the whole thing then." He smirked. Everyone looked at me, and I didn't want to seem like a punk, so I drank the rest of the pint. "Daaaaaaamn, she did that shit." He gave me a pound and I felt like I was the man. Blaq was standing in the back looking down, not saying anything. He had this look on his face almost as if he knew something bad was about to happen and there was nothing, he could do to stop it. When I closed my eyes and looked back at him, he began to become a dark blur and disappeared into the shadows. The more I sat there, the more I started to feel like I was on a roller coaster. My world was spinning faster and faster. I grabbed on to the railing, struggling to keep myself up.

Then, I heard one of the boys say, "Let's get her inside."

He reached for my hand and I stood up, falling face-first down the concrete stairs. When I woke up, blood was pouring down my face, and everything was a blur. When I started to come to, I realized we were in his cousin's bedroom, and I was lying on her bed naked with a room full of guys surrounding me. I tried to get up, but my body was paralyzed, and every time I blinked my eyes, there was a different guy on top of me.

As another one was getting ready for his turn, I rolled over and fell off the bed and tried to crawl to the door, but there was a guy in a wheelchair blocking it. I grabbed at his legs, tried to pull myself up, and asked him to please help me. He reached down and unzipped his pants. One of the other guys picked me up and turned me around as he placed me on his dick. The up and down motion began to make me feel sick, and I threw up all over myself. He then let me go, and I fell onto the floor.

I was lying there in my vomit when the door opened, and his cousin came barging in. "What the fuck is going in here? Oooooh, hell no. You need to get this girl out of my house right now. Blaq, come in here, clean this shit up and get her out my house!"

He walked in from the living room and dragged me into the bathroom, where he started to clean me up. He sat me on the floor but I couldn't even hold myself up and fell backward hitting my head on the side of the tub. I threw up a few more times until there was nothing left but air. He put my clothes back on and as he carried me out to the car, I got a glimpse of myself in the bathroom mirror. That vision still haunts me to this day. I was unrecognizable. I had never seen myself that broken before. My hair was matted and tangled and stuck to the dry blood on the side of my face. My eyeliner was smeared all over my face, and my eyes were so puffy, they were almost swollen shut.

When we got to the car, I passed out again, then woke up to Blaze saying, "Aight, now throw that bitch outside."

"Come on, man, we can't just leave her on the side of the road like that," Blaq pleaded.

"Look, she ain't staying in my car, so you either take her out or I will." He got out and moved the seat up to let Blaq out.

"Fine, but I'm staying with her," Blaq said, pulling me out.

"Hahaha, nigga, all in love n shit. Aight, nigga, stay here with that ho all you want." Blaze slammed the door and sped off.

When they left, Blaq laid me on the grass and started walking down the street, trying to open up random cars to see if any were unlocked. When he finally found one, he picked me up and carried me to the car and put me in the back seat.

Once I realized he was laying me down on the back seat, I had a flashback of Mad Dogg and all the others and began to fill up with rage. I started hitting Blaq and taking all of my anger out on him. "You fuckin' liar. You said you would protect me. I thought you were different, but you're just the rest of them. What do you want? You want to take it just like they did? Here take it. Go ahead, everyone else did. Go ahead, take it, you fuckin' bitch!" I said, taking off my clothes.

"I'm not taking shit. I haven't fucked you yet, so why would I do it now, especially wit you drunk like this?" he said, holding my hands from reaching in his pants.

"Oooh, so now you don't want to fuck me? What I'm not good enough for you? I know you want to fuck me just like the rest of them. Don't fuckin' lie!" I snatched my hands away and reached to unzip his pants, but he pushed my hands away, so I jumped on top of him, kissed on his neck, and stuck my hands in his pants until his dick got hard. "See, I knew you wanted this," I whispered. Then I pulled his big dick out and rode him until he came. "I knew you were just like the others," I said right before I passed out again.

The next morning the sun woke us up. Blaq told me we were going to walk over to his auntie's house. It was a far walk, and my head was throbbing. I felt like I was going to die of dehydration the whole way there, but an hour later we finally made it. When he got there, his aunt was sitting at the dining room table, talking to some other older church ladies. He told me to sit in the living room on the couch and asked his auntie if he could talk to her in the other room. Moments later, she came out and asked me why I couldn't go home. I told her everything that happened between my mom and me. She had a very comforting soul about her, almost like a grandmother. She began to pray over me and told me these streets were no place for a young girl like myself and that I could stay with her, but I had to go to church and school, which had already started last week.

I agreed and she took me in, bought me new clothes, fed me, and mentored my soul back to health. Whenever I did something bad, she talked it out with me instead of calling me names or telling me hurtful things. I started to want to be on my best behavior so that I wouldn't disappoint her. I even decided to put boys to the side, including Blaq, to focus on school. She was able to enroll me, but the school said they needed my papers for me to be able to stay there, so she told me she would be taking my mom to court to get custody of me.

A couple of weeks later, I was in court standing there before a judge with my mom on the other side from me. Before he made his decision, the judge wanted me and my mother to go into the other room and talk things out to see if we could resolve our issues. When I got into the room, my mom sat there with my baby brother Chris. Looking at him made me so emotional. I missed him so much, but I still had so much anger toward my mom and blamed her for everything.

"So you're willing to leave your little brother for some stranger you barely know? You know she's only taking you in for the child support money. She doesn't care about you," my mom said with a smirk. I knew that wasn't true, and that she was only saying that to hurt me.

"Please come home Angie," my brother cried. My heart melted. I wished so bad that I could take him with me.

"I love and miss you, Chris, and I promise I'll see you again, but I can't live with Mom. I want to stay where I am," I cried.

"Well, you're not going back with her because I refuse to pay her a dime in child support." We went back and forth, but nothing was resolved, so we headed back into the courtroom. Then the judge asked me where I wanted to live. I told him I loved my brother, but I was doing so much better in school now and wanted to stay with her.

He only thought it over for a few seconds, then said I had to go back with my mother. I screamed out no, and we both cried as we gave each other our last hug goodbye. That was the last time I ever saw her. Still to this day, I can't remember her name, because everyone called her Auntie. All I know was that she was the one guardian angel I got to meet in person, and I'll never forget how she saved me.

I WAS SO DEPRESSED WHEN I GOT BACK TO my mom's, and to top it off, I was starting to feel really sick. I had the sharpest pain in my stomach that was getting worse each day. It got so bad I could barely walk, so my mom took me to the hospital. After an ultrasound, the doctors admitted me right away. About thirty minutes later, the doctor came in and revealed that I had PID, pelvic inflammatory disease, which is an infection from having untreated chlamydia. He said the infection was so bad that it was the size of a baseball, and they would have to do surgery to remove it. He also said there was a high chance I would never be able to have kids after this. When I heard that I began to weep uncontrollably, and looked to my mother for comfort, but she was so disgusted in what she had just heard, she couldn't even look at me.

When the doctor left the room, she said, "I can't believe you been out here hoeing around like this. At least now I don't have to worry about you getting pregnant anymore." Then she walked out, leaving me in that cold empty room where I cried myself into the next morning.

After the surgery was over, I was completely shattered and felt worthless. I hated who I was. I hated that I was always getting into trouble. Everything was always my fault. My dad left because he didn't want me. My mom, my family, and everyone at school hated me. I had been raped multiple times and felt like I had deserved it for putting myself in those situations. I'd had sex with countless guys, and now I could no longer have kids. No man would ever love me. I fell into a deep depression and contemplated suicide more than ever.

The only thing I couldn't decide on was how to do it. I wanted it to be quick and painless. I finally decided to take a bunch of pills that my mom had in her medicine cabinet and swallow them down with a bottle of vodka. Right before I took them, I told my brother Chris if anything happened to me to know that I loved him more than anything else in this world, and that I wished I could have been a better sister to him. He got scared and started asking me what was wrong. I told him everything was going to be okay as tears flowed down my face and I closed the door to my mom's bedroom. I wanted her to come home and find me lying dead in her bed, so she would be reminded of my death every time she went to sleep.

As I slowly drifted into unconsciousness, I kept hearing my brother Chris banging on the bedroom door. Eventually, he was able to get in by unlocking the door with a butterknife. He tried waking me, but when I was unresponsive, he called the police. I was rushed to the hospital, where they pumped my stomach. When my mom got there, she was so piss she told me she didn't want me to come home after I got out the hospital. She signed some paperwork admitting to a mental hospital and left me there.

I went to the mental hospital with a bad attitude, mad at the world that I was still alive, and my mom had won again. I ended up being roommates with this really pretty brown-skinned girl who was there because she had overdosed on alcohol. She told me she didn't try to commit suicide or anything and that she had just drank too much at a party. She hated this place just as much as I did and was just passing time until she got out. She even told me she was fucking one of the White guys on staff. Before she even told me who he was I already knew by the way he had looked at me when I first checked in.

When I first arrived, I thought I was going to get sucked up into her world and start getting into more trouble again, but once I started doing the therapy sessions, something in me began to change. For the first time, I felt like I had someone I trusted enough to open up to about everything I had gone through and not feel judged. There was something about her that seemed genuine, like she really cared for me.

She explained to me that the statutory rape was not my fault and that even though I was fully aware of what I was doing, he was the adult who took advantage of me and he deserved to go to jail. She also said just because I put myself in bad situations didn't give anyone the right to touch or force themselves on me. "I promise you; those rapes were not your fault. All of them should be in jail right now. You did not deserve any of that. You are such a strong person. I know you can get through this," she assured me.

After hearing that, I started to think maybe I wasn't this horrible person I thought I was and that I wasn't this lost cause. I was just lost, and as long as I was still breathing, it was never too late to turn my life around and find my way in this world. I even wanted to work out things with my mom, but she would never show up for any parent therapy sessions.

The only person who ever came to visit me was Romeo's mom Keri, who said I could stay with her when I got out. She said Romeo had joined the Army but had gotten kicked out and was back home, but she would make him sleep on the couch so I could stay there. Now I was even more excited to get out and have this fresh new start. When I completed all of my sessions, I was able to leave, and Keri picked me up. When I saw Romeo, he made it evident he missed me just as much as I had missed him.

"Okay, you guys, there will be none of that or any other stuff going on while she's living here. You listening, Romeo? I'm serious! I want her back in school and focusing on her homework, not you," she said, pulling me away from him. I wanted to be good this time. I tried so hard to resist all of my urges to be with him even when he begged me to sneak out and have sex with him in the car like we used to.

Eventually the temptations became too unbearable. It was like I was Christina Ricci in "Black Snake Moan." The desire was so loud, it was consuming my every thought. Keri and his brother had gone to bed, and I was in the living room watching TV since Romeo was gone. I thought he would stay out all night like he normally did on weekends, but this night he came back around midnight. I got up to go to his room, but he told me not to and to finish watching the rest of "Coming to America" with him.

It was one of my favorite movies, so I came back and sat on the opposite side of the couch from him. Every time he smiled at me, I would think about how good his lips felt kissing all over my body and how fat his dick was, which always made me cum. He was so sexy. It was so hard to be around him, and I couldn't even focus on the movie anymore. I knew he was feeling the same way because every time he laughed at the movie, he somehow ended up getting closer and closer to me until he eventually was sitting right next to me.

"You know one day I'm going to make you my Queen, right?" he said, moving my hair behind my ear to expose my neck. He knew my neck was my weak spot, and once he started kissing on it, there was no way I could resist his touch.

"Is that right?" I said, moving my hair back, covering up my neck, and hurrying over to the end of the couch.

"What you are scooting way over there for? You scared of me now, huh?" he said, moving closer to me.

"No, I'm not scared of you, but your mom is in the next room, and I don't want her thinking we out here doing something."

"You know she be knocked out when she sleeps. You know how many times I came home drunk knocking over shit, and she never woke up, so trust me, she is not going to wake up. Plus, if she does, you know she is only going to get mad at me and not you, anyway." He moved my hair back and softly kissed on my neck. "Tell me you didn't miss this," he said, kissing me down to my nipples and sucking on them until I couldn't take it anymore.

My pussy felt like it was on fire, and like a firehose only his dick could cool it off. I grabbed his head and stuck my tongue deep down his throat. He started sucking on it, which he had never done before, and it turned me on even more. He grabbed the blanket off the couch and threw it on the floor and placed me on top of it. I was wearing a T-shirt and pajama shorts. Instead of taking them off, he just moved it to the side and placed his dick inside me. His dick was so big and fat I couldn't control my moans. He tried covering up my mouth with the pillow, but the deeper he went, the louder I got.

"What the hell are you two doing?" his mom shouted. We both jumped up as the lights turned.

"I'm sorry, I'm sorry," I cried.

"I'm sorry, Ma, it was my fault," Romeo said, zipping his pants up.

"I knew this was going to be a bad idea. Romeo, you need to leave, and Angie, you need to go to bed."

I looked out his bedroom window and saw him getting into his car with all his belongings and driving off. He ended up moving into an apartment with his cousin, which worked out even better for us. Now we had a place to have sex without worrying about getting caught. After school, I would head over to his house for a couple of hours before going back to his mom's. Some days I would get there before he got off work, and chill with his cousin until Romeo got home.

Like normal, I was waiting for Romeo to get home, and talking to his cousin, when the phone kept ringing back-to-back. Every time he answered, he would say things like, "No, he's not home yet." Or "I don't know, you need to talk to him about that."

So I finally asked, "Who keeps calling?"

At first, he acted like he didn't want to tell me, but I knew he had a secret crush on me, so I sweet-talked him until he finally told me that it was some chick Romeo was talking to. I was so hurt and pissed that I wanted to burn all of his clothes but decided to throw them all in the garbage outside instead and write on this bathroom mirror *cheater* with my red lipstick.

As I was waiting for the bus, which was around the corner, I saw him run over toward me. "What's going on? Why did you write that on my mirror?" he asked.

"Your cousin told me you were cheating on me, so we're done," I replied.

He grabbed me by the arm when I tried to walk away and said, "It's not like that. I don't fuck wit dat ho anymore. He only told you that shit because he likes you. That was just some bitch I was talking to before we got back together but that bitch is crazy and now, she's claiming she pregnant."

"Pregnant? I can't. I can't go through this shit with you. I just got out of the hospital. I'm trying to get my life together. I'm already walking on thin ice with your mom. This is just too much drama for me right now." I snatched my arm away and got on the bus that had just pulled up. Hearing that he might have gotten another girl pregnant was just too much for me, and I didn't want to sit around to find out if it was true or not.

He kept calling his mom's house asking for me, and I knew I couldn't stay there anymore, so I called Ms. Bates and begged her to let me come back. I told her that I had changed my life around, and I was ready to focus on school and even go to church. She said as long as I went to school, continued my therapy sessions, and went to church and Bible study, I could come back. I agreed, and she picked me up.

The next day we made an appointment with my therapist, and that week they put me on Paxil. I hated it. I didn't feel like myself, but I was no longer angry at everything, and Ms. Bates was happy with the change, so I stayed on it. We had a meeting with my school, and at first, they said since I had missed so much school, the only way for me to graduate would be to get my GED. I begged and pleaded with them for any other option than that. They said maybe if I worked hard at continuation school and took night classes as well, I could possibly catch up enough to graduate on time, and I did just that.

THAT YEAR I DID EVERYTHING I SAID I was going to do. I worked my ass off and got caught up in school. I was even enjoying going to church. It was like everything he preached about was directed toward my life, and I loved who I was starting to become. I went from listening to Tupac, Mase, and Notorious BIG all the time to listening to nothing but Kirk Franklin. Every time I started thinking about my past and getting all depressed about it, I would just put on one of his albums like "God's Property" and listen to songs like "More Than I Can Bear," "Love," "Sweet Spirit," or "The Storm Is Over Now" until I could feel God's grace consume my body and wash away all of my sins. I started to have faith that God would never put more on me than I could bear, and my sweet spirit could make it through any storm with his love.

It seemed like my life was really turning around. I was so focused on school that I wasn't even hanging out with my friends as much anymore. I used to hate going to church, but now I was anxious to go every Sunday. And this Sunday was no different than the rest. The pastor told us to pull out our Bibles and turn to Matthew 7:15 and read "Beware of false prophets, which come to you in sheep's clothing, but inwardly they are ravening wolves." I clung to every word like a sloth to a tree, and tears flowed down my face as I started to think about all the people that came into my life and tried to destroy me. The collection plate was being passed around, and as I was throwing in a couple of dollars when I felt a tap on my shoulder from behind. I turned around and this cocoa, brown-skinned man with permed-out hair and long fingernails looking like a young Terrance Howard said "Hi, how are you?"

"Fine thanks," I replied, trying to keep it short.

"So what's your name?" he asked, but I pretended like I didn't hear him and just kept listening to the choir, which Ms. Bates was singing in.

He came around and sat next to me. "I'm Kovas," he said with a devilish smile.

"Kovas, is that your real name?" I replied.

"No, it's Kovert, but everyone calls me Kovas because all I drink is Courvoisier." He laughed. I rolled my eyes. "So what's your name?"

"Angie," I said, never taking my eye off the choir.

"Well, Angie, nice to meet you. I couldn't help noticing how the word touched you like it was touching me. I have been through so much lately so that I could really relate." He leaned over, exposing a wad of cash in his hands. He pulled out a couple twenties and threw it on the plate behind us. I just gave a half-smile and nodded to make it obvious I wasn't interested in anything he had to say or how much money he had.

"I'm sorry, I don't mean to bother you. It's just that I'm new to the area, and you seem like a nice girl, and I was hoping we could be friends."

Something about him just rubbed me the wrong way, but I couldn't put my finger on it.

"Honestly, I'm just trying to get my life together and focus on school, so I'm sorry but I'm not interested in making any new friends right now. But maybe I'll see you around church sometime." I got up and headed to the front, where Ms. Bates had just finished singing, and she handed me her purse. She hugged me and told me to wait for her in the car, and she would be out shortly.

As she was approaching, I could see her talking to the same guy that was trying to talk to me earlier. I looked at him and rolled my eyes again.

"Angie, I want you to meet this nice young boy who just moved out here. Maybe you can take him to teen Bible study and introduce him to everyone."

"Yeah, we already met," I said, giving him the same half-ass smile I had during service. Ms. Bates give him our number and the whole ride home, she just kept talking about what a nice guy he was and that he seemed like someone I needed to be around instead of guys like Romeo. I didn't see it, but I started to think maybe she was right and perhaps I just didn't see it because I was so used to being with bad boys. *Maybe he was the good boy I needed. I mean she did love Devin and he was one of my best relationships,* I thought. So when Kovas called on Tuesday and asked Ms. Bates if he could take me out to a movie that Friday, I agreed to give him a chance. Especially since I hadn't been allowed to go out since I'd moved back.

As I was getting dressed, I still had a bad feeling about going, but I thought, *What's the worst thing that could happen?* It was just the movies. He knocked on the door and had a bouquet, which he handed to Ms. Bates. He took out a single rose and handed it to me. He was only eighteen but seemed much older than he was. He came in and talked to her for a few minutes. Then we left for the movies. He was such a gentleman and opened up my car door to let me inside his blue Buick.

As soon as we got on the freeway, he said, "Okay, I have a confession."

Oh God, I thought. "What?" I asked.

"I'm not taking you to the movies. You can't really get to know someone at the movies, so I'm taking you somewhere else, but it's a surprise. I just really wanted to get to know you, and I knew this was the only way I could get you alone." I started to freak out and thought *I hope he doesn't try and rape me or something.* "Don't worry. You're going to love it. And I promise I'll get you home on time. We're almost there. I just have to make one quick stop." I hated hearing those words and was starting to feel déjà vu again. I was preparing myself for the worst and planning my escape when he stopped the car.

He pulled up into a motel, and I was ready to run as soon as he tried to get me to go inside, but he told me to wait in the car and he would be right back. He went to the door, knocked, and one of the girls from my church answered it. Then a White man came to the door behind her and handed him something. He then got back in the car, and we drove off. I was so confused and asked what that was all about and how he knew Nikki. He told me he'd met her at church a few weeks prior to meeting me and was just helping her out but not to worry about it. A couple of minutes later, we pulled up to Fleming's Steakhouse. I'd heard about this place but had never been.

"I wanted to take you to a nice restaurant," he said, exiting the car and coming around to open my door. I was shocked he had planned this nice fancy dinner and even more surprised about how easily our conversation flowed once I let my guard down and relaxed. He told me how he'd just gotten out of jail for selling drugs, and he'd come to church looking to turn his life around. Nikki was one of the first ones he had met, and since she was so nice to him, he was helping her get back on her feet since she had just had a baby and was having money problems. After he opened up to me about his life, I felt comfortable enough to open up to him about some of my experiences, but I only shared the problems I had with my mom and told him how I bounced from home to home.

It was starting to get late after dinner, so I told him we should start heading back home before I missed curfew. "I know you have to get back, but I'm enjoying our conversation, and I don't want this night to end. It's been a long time since I've been able to open up like this," he said.

"Yeah, I'm enjoying myself too, but I'm not trying to get into any more trouble, so let's just hang out again next weekend or something. Plus, I'll see you at church on Sunday."

"Next weekend? That's a long time from now. And I won't be able to talk to you like that at church. Look, we still have a little bit more time left. Why don't we just hang out and talk a little bit more, and then I'll take you back."

I thought about it and let out a big sigh and said, "Fine, thirty more minutes, but that's it!"

We pulled back up to the motel, and I was expecting to see Nikki there, but when we walked in, they were both gone. I sat on the edge of the bed, and he sat in the chair by the window and asked, "So tell me a little bit more about you bouncing from home to home. Has anything bad ever happened to you?" I hesitated at first about sharing everything, so I just told him about the rape with Mad Dogg. He then shared how his mother had been on drugs his whole life and that his grandmother had eventually taken him in after he bounced from family member to family member. We both related to the fact that neither one of us knew our father. He also said his mother was prostituting when he was conceived, so she didn't know who his father could be.

I couldn't believe he was telling me all this on our first date. Usually when I met a guy, they had never gone through anything major, so it was always hard to find someone I could relate to. We had so much in common and I had never shared these things with another person other than my therapist. I felt so comfortable talking to him that I shared the story about the statutory rape, but I was still too ashamed to tell him about the gang rape, so I never brought it up.

The next thing I knew, it was after 11 o'clock. "Oh, shit, I'm going to be in so much trouble when I get home. I was supposed to be home at ten."

"You should just stay the night. You are going to be in trouble regardless, so you might as well enjoy the rest of your night."

I had never met a guy like him before. He was so charming and had a way with words, and I didn't want the night to end either, plus after thinking about it, Ms. Bates was the one that forced me to go out with him in the first place, so she shouldn't be too mad. "Fuck it, you're right. I'm going to be in trouble regardless, so I might as well stay."

He smiled, jumped up, and lunged on me, pushing me back on the bed. I thought he was going to kiss me, but he just moved my hair out of my face and stared into my eyes, softly stroking his thumb across the side of my face. The more he stared at me, the shyer I became.

"What?" I finally asked.

"You're just so beautiful. I love looking at you. We could be great together, you know." He stroked his thumb across my lips and then softly kissed me. With every kiss and every touch, he slowly took his time like he was savoring the moment. "Have you ever made love before?" he asked.

"Yeah, I've had sex before with this boy I loved," I replied.

He kissed me again, this time sticking a little tongue inside, but pulled away before I could stick mine in his.

"No, I'm not talking sex. I'm talking about making deep passionate love. Every time I look you in your eyes, you look away. Every time I kiss you, you close your eyes. When you make love to someone, you keep your eyes open. You take your time. You taste every inch. You smell every scent. You feel every part of their body." He rubbed his fingers across my neck down to my nipples, then my stomach, and rubbed my pussy a couple of times, then came back up, leaned down, and softly kissed me again.

This time I kept my eyes open and locked them on to his. It was making me feel so vulnerable. I wanted to just hurry up, rip his clothes off and fuck, but he put my hands back down every time I tried.

Finally, he started to take my clothing off one piece at a time. The anticipation was killing me. I'd never wanted anyone so bad like this before. He sat up and took off his shirt, revealing abs. He stood there long enough for me to notice the small mole on the middle of his chest and stretch marks on the inner part of his arms. I was noticing every inch of his body like he said. He stood up, unbuckled his belt and his pants, pulled them down to his knees, and kicked them off. His dick flung out, and he stood there like a Michelangelo sculptor. He walked over to the window, and I noticed how nice and firm his ass was as he opened up the blinds so the streetlight from outside could shine down on me when he turned the lights off. He opened up my legs like a gynecologist examining every inch of me.

He started kissing the inner parts of my thighs down to my pussy, then he put his nose in it and took a deep breath. I felt so vulnerable. I had never been this exposed before. He took another deep breath as if he was trying to memorize my scent and then began to softly kiss it as he exhaled. I could feel his breath blowing chills down my spine. I wanted him so badly to dive right in, but instead, he kissed around it, teasing me until it almost became unbearable. Just when I couldn't take it anymore, he kissed it softly like he had done my lips the first time. Then began French kissing it, sticking his tongue in and out and sucking on my clit like it was my tongue.

He then flipped me over, raised my stomach up, and began eating my ass. I was damn near in tears from it feeling so good. He crawled on top of me, grabbing my breast and kissing me up my back to my neck. He then grabbed my hair, pulled it back until he could reach my lips, and kissed me passionately.

"How do you taste?" he whispered. I flipped over, and he rubbed his dick all around my pussy.

"Umm like strawberries," I whispered back. I begged for him to put it in, but the more I begged, the more he teased. He stuck just the tip in, and when I tried to force it all the way in, he pulled it back out and rubbed my juices all over my clit. I was at his mercy. I clawed at his back, anxious for him to put it back in. This time when he did, he stuck it deep, and I moaned in ecstasy. I felt our souls intertwine.

"Oh my God, I love you!" I screamed. The more I said I loved him, the deeper and deeper he got.

"This pussy is mine. You hear me?" he asked aggressively.

"Yes, it's yours!" I moaned.

"I mean that shit, you better not ever give this pussy away. It's mine now." He passionately kissed me again.

"It's your pussy, baby, I promise," I screamed, as I climaxed.

Shortly after he let out a loud moan and said, "Dammmn, baby ... yeah, you ain't going nowhere." He rested his head on my stomach, and I could feel the veins on his dick beating against my leg like a heartbeat.

The next morning, he woke me up with soft kisses on my forehead. "You ready to go back?" he asked.

"Noooo," I said, covering my face up with the sheets.

"Come on, get up. I better get you back before the police come looking for you."

I got dressed, and we drove back. My heart started to race as soon as we pulled into the apartment complex. We stood outside his car for a few minutes until he convinced me everything would be okay. We walked up to the door, and before I could even knock, it swung open, and Ms. Bates shouted, "Where have you been, young lady?"

"I apologize, Ms. Bates, it's all my fault. My car broke down last night, and by the time we got it fixed, it was extremely late, and I didn't want to wake you all up, so I decided just to bring her back the next morning," he said with a charming look on his face.

"Do I look like a fool to you? I wasn't born yesterday. Since you make all the decisions for her, then she can be responsible for her from now on. I already packed up all her things," she said, grabbing my things and placing them on the porch.

"Wait, you're the one who forced me to go out with him in the first place. It's not my fault his car broke down. Please don't kick me out again. I need to finish school," I begged.

"Well, you should have thought about that before you stayed out all night. You could have at least called, Angie. I was worried sick. I told you, I'm too old to keep going through all this with you. It's time for you to leave," she said, slamming the door in my face.

I turned to him like *What am I going to do now?* He pulled me in close and wrapped me into his arms. "Don't even trip. I got you. Everything is going to be okay, I promise," he said, giving me a kiss on my forehead as we walked back to his car. And just like that, I belonged back to the streets–trapped in the devil's cocoon.

Chapter V
The Devil's Cocoon

KOVAS TOLD ME HE HAD BEEN STAYING off and on with some chick in Baldwin Hills who had been giving him money since he got out of jail. He said if she asked any questions to tell her that I was his little sister and our grandmother had just kicked me out. He said we would only stay there until he could find us another place. She answered the door in lingerie and a silk robe as if she had been waiting for him all night. When he introduced us, she looked me up and down, doubting every word he was telling her.

"Your sister, huh?" she said, crossing her arms and giving me the side-eye.

"Yeah, my sister. We have the same mom, but different dads, and our grandma was tripping again. I was over there all night trying to convince her not to kick her out, but she just needs time to cool off. So she just needs to stay with us just for a little bit until things calm down," he said, grabbing one of her breasts and squeezing it as he pulled her in for a kiss.

"Get a room," I said, rolling my eyes as I walked in between them to step inside the house.

She showed me to the couch, and they walked into her bedroom together to "talk," but it didn't take long for me to realize they were doing more than just talking. I heard her moans when I went to the bathroom. I could tell the way he was fucking her was nothing how he had made love to me. It was rougher, and the way he was talking to her sounded like a completely different person, but it still made me sick to my stomach knowing he was in the other room fucking her.

I went back into her nice living room and sat on her nice couch, staring out the window to her nice neighborhood that looked like something out of Beverly Hills. I'd never seen a Black woman live like this before. I envied her and sat there wondering what she did for a living to have her own place like this. *She was probably some prominent executive or something. She wasn't pretty enough to be a model*, I thought.

I got startled when I felt him grab me and turn me around. He quickly grabbed my face and kissed me. I could taste his sweat and smell the scent of her expensive perfume. "I'm sorry you had to see that, but I'm doing this for us. I promise she doesn't mean shit to me, and we won't be here for long." He kissed me again before she came back out.

"Let me show you where your room is," she said, pointing upstairs.

It only took a few days for her to start suspecting that we weren't really brother and sister. Maybe it was how he always looked at me or how we both looked at her when she came in the room like we were hiding something, or perhaps it was how he would always come into my room late at night when he thought she was sleeping.

I was still being homeschooled, which made things a lot easier, but I was serious about wanting to graduate on time. So no matter what I was going through, I always made sure I did my homework. Occasionally, I would have to go in to turn in my work and pick up new assignments. When I got out, he would pick me up, and we would go back to her house and make love before she pulled up in her white Range Rover.

On the last day we were there, we were in the middle of having sex on her guest bed when we heard the front door close. She had come home earlier than usual. I got up and ran into my room. She must have smelled the scent of sex or something because they began to argue. A few moments later, she came barging in.

"You both must think I'm stupid or something. Tell me the fuckin' truth, you're not his real sister, are you?" she said, getting closer and closer in my face until she had me backed up against the wall.

He came over and grabbed her by her throat and threw her against the wall next to me. "Don't you ever get in her fuckin' face again, you hear me?" His grip was so tight she couldn't even answer back.

I grabbed his arm and told him to let her go. She fell to the floor and reached for her throat. "Get the fuck out my house. Both of you. NOW! Before I call the cops."

He grabbed me by my hand, and we grabbed our stuff as we left.

We went to his boy Rim's house, who said we could stay there. "Damn, you got any homegirls?" he asked as soon as I walked in.

"Yeah, I actually have a homegirl named Tatiana," I responded.

"What she look like?" he asked.

"She light-skinned with long hair," I said, pulling out a picture from my backpack that we had taken together.

"Oh yeah, hit her up and tell her to come thru." I called her and told her about Rim and put them on the phone together.

When he got off the phone with her, he said he was going to go pick her up. I hadn't seen her in a while since we went to different schools, so we embraced with a long hug as soon as she got there. When the guys got up to go into the kitchen to talk, Tatiana and I started catching up. She started telling me about Romeo and how he was blowing up her phone looking for me. He told her to tell me that he was sorry and that he loved and missed me. We had no idea Kovas was listening in our whole conversation.

"Hey, let me talk to you real fast in the other room," Kovas said, grabbing me by my arm from the couch and dragging me into the bedroom. As soon as he shut the door, he turned around and smacked me so hard with the back of his hand that I flew across the floor. I sat there looking up at him with my hand on my face, so confused about what had just happened. He grabbed my hair and pulled me up.

"What the fuck are you trying to do? Huh? Embarrass me in front of my boy?" he yelled.

"What are you talking about?" I cried.

He smacked me again and said, "Don't you ever talk about another man like that again. What the fuck I look like?"

He went to smack me again, but I blocked it and began hitting him back as hard as I could, but he quickly overpowered me. He put me in a headlock, then dragged me to the bed, where he held me down with one of his knees, and then covered my mouth with his hand as I tried to scream out.

"Shut the fuck up before I kill you. The more you fight back the longer I'm going to hold you down like this," he said, pinching my nose closed so I couldn't breathe. But I didn't care. I would have rather died than to give in again and not fight back.

"Everything aight in there?" his boy asked at the door.

"Yeah, we good. We just talking. Give us a minute," he said, pushing even harder down on my mouth as I tried to gasp for air. I kept hitting and scratching at him, but his grip was so tight that I eventually passed out.

When I came to, he had one hand loosely around my throat, and the other one was smacking me on my face to wake up.

"See what you made me do?" he said, kissing me all over my face and resting his head next to mine. "Look I'm sorry. I just love you so much. I lost it when I heard you talking about another man." He kissed me again. I was so pissed but, in a daze, so I just lay there quietly, thinking about what the fuck I'd just gotten myself into. The crazy thing was, I wasn't even scared. I was just pissed that he was stronger than me and I couldn't fuck him up the way I wanted to. I moved my head away when he tried to kiss me on my lips.

"Please forgive me?" he said, kissing me on my cheek instead.

This time he stuck his finger in his mouth and reached down to pull my panties to the side and inserted his finger inside me, which he knew I loved.

"You forgive me?" he asked, going in and out until I became wet enough for him to lick my juices off his finger. "You forgive me?" he asked again, unzipping his pants and putting his dick so deep inside that I thought he was fucking my soul.

I couldn't help but to moan "Yessss, I forgive you!" I tried so hard to stay mad, but once inside me, all of the anger left my body. After we finished, he gave me another kiss and helped me up so we could head back to the living room. When we got out there, we noticed Rim and Tatiana had left. About forty minutes later, he came back by himself, and I overheard them talking in the next room. Rim said he was still on probation and couldn't afford to be wrapped up in any domestic shit, especially with some minors, so we couldn't stay there anymore and had to leave.

We had no choice but to check into a motel that night. "Maybe I should get a job. We need our own place," I said.

"I just need to hustle harder and get some more girls."

"What do you mean, more girls?" I replied.

"I used to have a lot of girls working for me but ended up going to jail and losing everything, so now I have to start over from scratch. I got Nikki working for me, but we need a lot more." He sat down at the small table and started rolling up a blunt.

I was so naïve. I didn't know what he meant, so I asked, "So what do you mean by working for you?"

He licked the blunt, lit it up, took a couple of puffs, and handed it to me. "I mean they work for me and do whatever the fuck I tell them to do. I usually just get a room and the clients meet them there or wherever, but I want to make this shit bigger than it was before. I got the right people this time to go in on it with me. I fucked up last time by trusting the wrong ones, but that shit won't happen again," he said.

I took a couple of puffs and passed it back to him. The weed was starting to make me feel like I had the balls to say anything. "You not trying to have me out there fucking anyone, are you?" I asked.

"Fuck no, I told you this pussy is mine, but I do want you to be my bottom bitch."

"Bottom bitch? Shouldn't I be your main and only bitch?" I asked.

"Look, I deal with a lot of hoes, but it's all business, they don't mean shit to me, and I need that one bitch I can trust to hold shit down, and really rely on like on some Bonnie and Clyde shit. You still have a long way to go. But watch, by the time I'm finished with you, you're going to be one of the baddest bitches in the game. As pretty as you are, you could be having niggas buying you all kinds of shit without even fucking them. We can be setting these niggas up at Freaknik and make a killin' but you got a lot to learn before we can do that shit."

Damn, that would be dope, I thought. I was so tired of men using me. I wanted to learn how to use them back, and to do it without fucking or getting emotionally involved was precisely what I wanted to learn how to do. I was such a sucker for love that whenever I would try to use a guy, I would always either feel guilty or fall for them. I wanted to be a cold-hearted bitch and not give a fuck anymore, so I took notes and did everything he told me to do.

Over the next few months, the motel became our new home, and I watch him get new girls one by one. A couple of them he had met at a strip club. He would always attract the prettiest women who had the biggest problems or nowhere else to go. My job was simple—sit back and watch. He never tried to pimp me out and would beat the shit out of me if he thought I was even looking at another guy. I thought this was what unconditional love felt like. I thought he really wanted me to learn the game so we could be this power couple, but now I know he was just grooming me, and this wasn't love at all.

Sometimes the girls would stop by our room in between clients. I was always curious about what made them get into prostitution, so I asked a lot of questions. Every story was a sad one. Most of them had been sexually abused at an early age, some even by their family members, and most were either on drugs or alcoholics or both.

The most heartbreaking story was Cynthia, who they called Cyn for short. You could tell that before the drugs she used to be beautiful. She told me her father had been molesting her since she was three, and when she told her mom, she blamed her for it and ended up selling her for drugs when she was around seven. I couldn't believe a mother would do that to their child. She was starting to make my mother look like Mother Teresa.

Then she said she was trafficked in prostitution around twelve after dealing with an older boy who pretended to be her boyfriend. She said that was the roughest time of her life. She was beaten almost every night. Men would torture her just for their sexual pleasure. The scariest thing about it was some of these men were police officers, politicians, or married men with kids. Men you would never think would do something like this. One guy even knocked her front tooth out when she begged him for help after finding out he was a schoolteacher. Luckily, after a sting operation she was rescued when she was eighteen, but the damage was done, and she fell back into a life of prostitution.

I started to cry when she told me this, but when she noticed she started laughing and said, "Save your tears, baby girl. I cried enough for three lifetimes. Crying doesn't get you anywhere. It's a useless emotion. Trust me, I'm good now. I get to decide on who I want to fuck. And if I don't want to do it then I don't have to so I'm good." I could tell by the pain in eyes she didn't mean that.

She began to say how much she loved working for Kovas because he never hit her, and he let her work on her own terms. Kovas used to always say you catch more flies with honey, so he let them call the shots on who they wanted to fuck. He provided most of the clients so they would pay him first and then the girls would get their cut afterwards. Kovas was so charming. He knew a lot of people and could talk anyone into anything. He was the type that could sell a red popsicle to a lady wearing white gloves.

After hearing all these stories, it made me feel like no matter what you go through there's always someone who's been through something worse. Our stories may not have been the same, but I saw a piece of myself in each one and could see my future in their eyes. I knew in that moment that this was not the life that I wanted but I felt like I was in too deep to get out. I don't know what it was, but Kovas had this possessive hold on me. Usually when I didn't like where I was living, I would just run away, but there was something about him that always made me stay.

Part of me hated him, but the other part loved the way he made me feel. He made me feel like the most beautiful girl in a room filled with beautiful women. People had put me down my whole life. My mother, kids at school, guys I dated, and I was constantly beating myself up for the mistakes I made, so to hear something positive about me became like a drug, and I had to keep coming back for another hit to feed my insecurities. Everyone in my life had left me, but there was nothing I could do to make him leave me, and he would rather see me dead than to be with anyone else.

I STARTED WORKING PART-TIME AT McDonald's so I could start making my own money. When I got my first paycheck, the first thing I wanted to do was get my hair done. I even dyed it the first time and was looking extra cute, so I called up Tatiana and told her Kovas and I would pick her up so we could go to the Carousel Mall in San Bernardino and take some pictures. We both had on matching outfits from Rainbow that we wore to the BSU Magic Mountain trip.

As we walked through the mall, I saw this cute boy walking toward us from the opposite direction but quickly turned away so Kovas wouldn't notice me checking him out. I looked at Tatiana to see if she had noticed the guy, too, and as soon as I turned my head back around, I felt a hard slap across my face.

"You want to go talk to him, then go ahead," he said, pushing me toward the guy, who just stood there in disbelief about what had just happened. I was so embarrassed I just continued walking toward the picture place like nothing had happened. He stared at me the whole way there like he was waiting for me to say one word. I used everything I had in me to fight back the tears, and it showed in the photos.

After we dropped Tatiana off, he said he had to make a stop at his baby mama's house, who lived not too far from the mall. I was caught completely off guard because he'd never mentioned having a kid before.

"I didn't know you had a son," I said.

"Yeah, he's two, but his mom is a bitch and makes it difficult for me to see him unless I give her some money." We pulled up to a nice house, with a rose garden and a white picket fence. He knocked on the door while I waited in the car. A beautiful woman came out who had a short bob haircut and looked like a video vixen. She was wearing sweats, but I could tell she had a nice figure.

As soon as she saw him, they began to argue and went inside the house. About an hour later, all three of them came out, and she seemed to be in a better mood. He kissed his son on the top of his head and told him he'd be back soon. As he headed back to the car, she noticed me sitting there and stared at me until he got in the car and we drove off. I couldn't help but wonder what she was thinking. She looked at me almost as if she felt sorry for me and wanted to warn me about something.

"She had so much pain in her eyes and a sadness that burned a hole through my heart. I wanted to wrap my wings around her and tell her to hold on. The best of you has yet to come." – Black Butterfly

After we left there, we picked up Nikki from the motel where she had just finished up with a client. As we were about to get on the freeway, his car started jerking, then stalled out on the roadside. Smoke started to come out of the hood and fill the inside of the vehicle, so we all got out. He popped the hood open and checked the engine, realizing it was a lot more severe than just overheating this time, so he had to get it towed to the mechanic shop. About an hour later, the mechanic told him he had a blown gasket, and it would cost more to fix it than the car was worth.

"FUCK!" he yelled, hitting the top of the hood of the truck. He stood there for a few moments with a stern look on his face, contemplating what to do. He noticed a used car dealership next door. "Come on, let's go," he told us.

The owner came out looking like Cal Worthington from the car commercial with his flashy cowboy suit, boots, and hat. I couldn't help but to giggle inside when I heard, "If you need a better car, go see Cal," playing in my head.

"What can I help y'all good folks out with today?" he said, raising his cowboy hat, exposing his eyes, which were obviously looking at Nikki's breasts spilling out of her crop top. Nikki had a way with men, predominantly White men. They loved her dark-skinned complexion and White body. She was skinny with big breasts and a small ass with a long weave down her back that made her look like a Barbie doll.

Kovas gave Nikki a side nod, and she started twisting her hair and being more flirtatious. "My car just broke down, and I'm looking for another one," Kovas said.

"Well, you came to the right place. Let me show you around so you can see what I got."

We walked around, but Kovas wasn't interested in anything until he got to the white 1990 Chevrolet Caprice with a red interior. "How much for that one right there?" Kovas pointed.

Nikki walked over to the car and looked inside. "This is nice, real nice," she said, bending over, so her butt cheeks could show even more out of her tiny shorts. She turned and smiled back at the owner.

"Oh yeah, she's a beaut. We just got her in yesterday, and she only has 60K miles. She has new tires and purrs like a kitten," the owner said as he looked at Nikki, who purred back at him with a wink.

"Well, let's go in and talk numbers," Kovas said, putting his arm around the owners' shoulder as he whispered something in his ear. "Ang, you stay outside. We'll be right back," Kovas said as they all went inside.

About forty minutes later, they all came back out, and the owner handed him the keys and said, "Congratulations on your new car. It was a pleasure doing business with you." They shook hands, and we got inside.

"We'll see you in a couple hours to drop off that deposit," Kovas said as he started it up. We drove around for a couple hours and got something to eat from In and Out, then we went back up to the dealership and parked across the street.

"What are we doing back here?" I asked.

"Waiting for him to give us a signal," Kovas said, biting into his burger. We started to see employees walking out one by one. Fifteen minutes after the last person left, the light in front of the building flashed on and off three times. Nikki got out of the car and headed back inside. Thirty to forty minutes later, she came back out, and we dropped her off at her apartment.

A few nights later he said his friend owed him some money, and we were going to meet him in a West Hollywood at a club called Peanuts. As we were walking to the club, I noticed nothing but hot sexy Black men everywhere. I was like, *Damn, my girls would love this place*, but then I noticed none of them even looked my way. I knew I wasn't the hottest girl in the world, but damn, you would think at least one of them would look my way, but they were all looking at Kovas. Since I was only seventeen, I couldn't go inside, so I waited for him on the sidewalk. I was so surprised he would leave me alone with all these hot men walking past, but then realized it was because we were at a gay nightclub.

After we left the club, we drove to this big Beverly Hills Mansion, and parked across the street until a black Mercedes pulled into the driveway. "Let's go," Kovas told me as we got out and met the guy at the front door. When we got inside, Kovas told me to sit on the couch and wait while they went upstairs. About an hour later, Kovas came down with a stack of money in his hand. Years later, I found out from his boy Rim that Kovas occasionally fucked other men for money. So I'm sure this was one of those times. But at the time, I had no idea.

I thought with all this money he was making, we would be able to afford our place soon, but he said he was saving it all for his new business plan, and still needed to make a lot more. About a week later, he got a part-time job at a gas station. Next thing I knew, we were eating at fancy restaurants all the time and going on shopping sprees. *He must have gotten a manager position*, I thought.

He told me he had a few important business meetings coming up, and it didn't matter what he wore, as long as he had on an expensive watch and some nice shoes. He bought some Stacy Adam and a nice Movado watch. He even took me shopping at my favorite Bebe store and said I could get whatever I wanted.

He wanted to show me how far having a nice watch would get you, so we went to the Marriott hotel, and he asked to see the manager. He told him he was looking for a penthouse to use for an upcoming event and wanted to make sure there wouldn't be any issues with security. When the manager asked what kind of event it was, Kovas rolled up his sleeve and placed his arm on the counter. The manager immediately noticed his watch and complimented him on it. Kovas leaned over and whispered something to him, and they both smiled. After that, his whole demeanor changed, and he treated us like celebrities, showing us around the hotel, introducing us to staff, and taking us up to the penthouse.

"Yeah, this is perfect … We'll take it," Kovas said, shaking his hand and slipping him some money.

We then drove to his friend Marcus's hair salon which was also half barbershop. When we walked in, he and Kovas immediately hugged like it had been a long time since they'd seen each other.

"Man, it's good to see you. Is this your old lady?" he asked, looking down at me.

"Yeah, this is Angie. Angie, this is Marcus. We go waaaay back." I moved in closer to shake his hand.

"You remember my girl, Tamika," he said, pointing over to a tall, light-skinned girl doing hair who looked like Charli Baltimore. Kovas went over and kissed her on the cheek then introduced us. She was so tall she looked more like a model than a hairstylist, but I could tell she also modeled by all the photos of her on the wall. "Hey, Tamika, why don't you hook Angie up while Kovas and I go back into my office and discuss some business?"

"Sure, thing baby," she said, giving him a kiss then showing me to another girl who sat me down and began washing my hair. After she washed my hair, she placed me under the dryer, and my heart dropped when I noticed Devin walking in. I put the magazine over my face to prevent him from seeing me, but he noticed me right away as soon as she took me out the dryer and moved me over to Tamika's chair. I was so embarrassed. I hadn't seen him in years, and now here I was seeing him for the first time with my hair in a big-ass afro.

He stared at me like he wanted to say something, and I was so afraid he would and Kovas would see it. I knew if I got caught talking to him, he would flip the fuck out especially being in his boy's place of business. After he finished his haircut, he headed out but stopped in the doorway and turned to look at me but quickly changed his mind and continued out. I let out a big sigh of relief. As much as I wanted to run out to him and tell him how sorry I was for blowing him off, I knew it wasn't the right place or time.

Not too long after I finished getting my hair done, Kovas and Marcus walked out, shaking hands. When we got in the car, Kovas told me Tamika had been looking for a new roommate so that I would be moving in with her, and he would be staying with Marcus in his high-rise condo. I was so excited about moving out of that dirty ass motel, I didn't even care it was with someone I barely knew.

The next day I moved in and we clicked immediately. Surprisingly we had a lot in common, even though she was a lot louder than I normally hung out with. But I was the type that could get along with anyone once they got to know me. Over the next couple of months, we grew closer and closer, and she even confided in me that she thought Marcus was cheating on her after seeing a few texts on his phone. I already knew he was cheating on her because I had been at his house with Kovas and seen him there with other females, but as much as I wanted to tell her, I knew that I couldn't.

That weekend I was over Marcus's condo and Kovas hung up the phone and said, "Aight, everything is booked and ready to go." He told me he was going to buy me a sexy dress and wanted me to bartend at the event in the Marriott penthouse.

"I don't know how to bartend," I said.

"If you know how to pour a drink, you know how to bartend," he said. He also said there were going to be a lot of important people there like celebrities and people from Jet Magazine, and that I needed to be on my A-game so that the word would spread, and they could have more events like this.

He bought me a tight sexy satin black dress with some red pumps. I wore my hair straight with red lipstick looking like Aaliyah in her "We need a resolution" video. We got there early so we could set up. The first ones to start showing up were some of his girls and a few strippers, who I had never met before. He showed them to one of the bedrooms in the back and said this was their dressing room.

Later on, men started showing up one by one. I took their coats and asked if they wanted anything to drink, then escorted them to the living room area where they stood around listening to music and conversing. He told me which ones were the VIPs, and I would show them to a separate room that had gambling tables, girls and a minibar.

When the room filled up, Kovas announced, "Aight, aight, fellas the moment you have all been waiting for," then the music started playing "Touch It" by Monifah as the lights flashed around and one of the strippers came out. She worked her way around the room as the men threw money at her. Then each stripper came out one by one, and they all had their special tricks that got more and more impressive as each girl came out. Like sticking bottles inside them and squirting out the liquids or blowing bubbles out their pussies and doing all kinds of splits and flips. But all of them were nothing compared to the last one that came out, whose name was Jade. "Hot Like Fire" by Aaliyah started playing as she walked in. Everyone's eyes lit up like it was Christmas morning. Even Kovas was mesmerized by her, and I'm not going to lie, so was I.

She had a perfectly shaped body like a Coca-Cola bottle with an ass so phat I couldn't take my eyes off it. I had never seen an ass that big in person, and the way she danced had everyone hypnotized. She wore a bright pink panty and bra set with fishnet stockings. There was so much money on the floor you couldn't even tell what color the carpet was anymore.

On one of her tricks, she grabbed Kovas and sat him down on a chair and did a flip where her pussy landed right in his face. I could have sworn I saw him stick his tongue out to get a taste as she moved her ass around. My blood became hot like fire, and a jealous rage came over me. I felt so sick to my stomach like I had just caught him cheating. I knew we was always around pretty girls, but it had never been thrown it in my face like this before. I couldn't take watching her all over him, so I went back to the bar and downed a few shots of Goldschläger. He told me not to drink anything that night but I didn't care anymore.

Then I walked into the VIP room and started flirting with some of the guys, not giving a fuck what Kovas thought. One of the guys called me over and asked me to blow on his dice before throwing it and winning. He said I was his good luck charm and gave me a hundred dollars. Everything was starting to get blurry, but at least my mind was off Kovas. As I got ready to kiss his dice again, I felt Kovas grab me by my arm and ask me what the fuck I was doing in there.

"I fuckin' saw you. I saw what you just did to her. How would you like it if I started sucking dick in here, you fuckin' asshole?" I must have had some liquid courage because I never would have talked to him like that sober.

He didn't want to make a scene, so he quickly took me out the room and pushed me in the corner by the bar where no one could see us. "What the fuck are you talking about? It's business. I'm working. I knew you weren't mature enough for this shit. I shouldn't have just left your ass at home. You need to sleep this shit off." He grabbed me by my arm and took me to the strippers' room that smelled like Victoria's Garden and pushed me on the bed.

"Make sure her ass stays in here," he said, closing the door.

"Aww, did baby have too much to drink?" one of the strippers said, stroking my hair until I passed out. I woke up the next morning to an empty room and a pounding headache. I walked into the living room, where I saw Jade and Kovas being extra cozy on the couch.

"Look who's finally up," she said, standing up and kissing Kovas on the cheek. Then she walked pass me giving a "Yeah, I fucked your man," smirk. When she got to the front door she turned and said, "Thanks again, baby. I'll call you later."

I was so nervous that he was going to be mad about me getting too drunk that I didn't even pay attention to the shade she was throwing. The way he got up, I thought he was going to smack me, but instead handed me five hundred dollars and said, "This is for doing a good job last night. I got a lot of compliments about you, so I'm gonna forget about that little stunt you tried to pull."

Kovas was in such a good mood from all the money he'd made. He picked me up and sat me on the couch with my legs wide open and started throwing the wade of cash he had all over me. If felt like it was literally raining money. Then he started eating me out until his dick got hard enough to slide in.

Now that he had all this money, the first thing he wanted to do was go to Vegas and gamble. I had never been before, so I was super excited to go, but it didn't turn out to be anything like I thought it would be. We didn't even go sightseeing. We went straight to the Bellagio to check-in, then headed to the casino, where I sat and watched him gamble every dime he had away.

"I'm gonna need that five hundred dollars back that I gave you," he said to me.

"No, I'm not going to give you any more money so you can lose it all again."

"Well, I guess we stuck out here then, cuz we don't have enough money to get back home."

After realizing we would be stuck, I reluctantly gave him everything I had and watched him lose it all again in a game of Craps. I was so pissed, especially after I kept telling him to stop when he was on top winning.

"What are we going to do now?" I asked.

He looked around and saw the White guy he had been chatting with earlier. "Hey, how are things going?" the White guy asked.

"Oh, I hit big and was about to cash out," Kovas said.

"That's great. I wasn't that fortunate, so I think I'm going to call it a night. I was going to go back up to my suite. You both are welcome to join me, if you like."

When we got to his suite, he pulled out a bottle of Dom Perignon and poured us a glass. After we finished the glass, they began whispering, and I saw the White guy give him a bunch of chips, then Kovas said he would be right back. When he left, the old White guy poured me another glass and asked what my name was. When I told him, he came behind me and started rubbing on my shoulders. I pulled away and asked what the fuck he was doing.

"You know what I'm doing. Kovas told me all about his girls and said you were his best one," he said, trying to reach for my hand.

I smacked his hand away. "Fuck you. I don't do that shit," I said, running out of the room. I searched all over the casino and found Kovas getting ready to gamble it all away again. "Why would you leave me in the room in there like that? Why would you tell him I would have sex with him?" Everyone at the table turned and looked at us. "I didn't. I just told him you would give him a massage," he said. "We'll, we need to leave right now because he said he was going to call the cops," I lied.

"Aight fuck, I'ma cash out so we can leave." When he did, it still wasn't enough to get back to Cali. I ended up having to call Romeo's mom Keri to wire us enough money to make it home. I was so embarrassed and really starting to resent Kovas for everything he was putting me through.

A couple of weeks later, Tamika and Marcus got into huge fight about another woman. This time she said she was fed up and asked me to go with her to LA to some music producer's house that she used to talk to. As we were driving in the car, she vented, "These niggas out here ain't shit. I know you love Kovas, but you should watch out. Him and Marcus are a lot alike."

"Why, do you know something?" I asked.

She hesitated like she wanted to tell me something but then said, "No, I'm just saying you are too pretty for a guy like Kovas. You could be out here dating athletes or entertainers or whatever. My ex is working with this upcoming R&B singer who's staying at his house to work on his new album. I'm going to introduce you two. He's so cute too. Trust me, you're going to like him."

I told her there was no way I could do that because Kovas would kill me if he ever found out. She promised me that he would never find out and that I didn't have to talk to the guy if I didn't want to but just to keep him company while she handled business. I agreed, but I had another bad feeling and was nervous the whole way there.

We drove to downtown LA to a lavish building that looked like a fancy hotel. She parked her black Mercedes in a parking garage that was full of other luxury cars. Once inside, the guy at the front desk called the producer, and then showed us to the elevator once he confirmed it was okay for us to come up. A nicely dressed, chubby guy answered the door and gave her a long kiss. He introduced me to his artist, and I sat on the couch next to him as they went into the bedroom.

She was right. He was extremely cute. He was medium built, brown-skinned guy with a diamond earring in both ears and a million-dollar smile. As cute as he was, I still had no interest and just wanted her to hurry up so we could get back before Kovas found out. My lack of interest must have sparked his because he started asking me all kinds of questions like where I was from and what school I went to, but I tried hard to keep things short. He then started telling me how he got discovered by singing on the streets and just wanted to make it big so he could get his family out the hood. He seemed like a really nice guy, and I would have been interested in him if I weren't so scared of Kovas.

He played some of his music for me, and it was just as great as the music on the radio, if not better. I was pleasantly surprised and could tell he was going to be a star. Even though I had just met him, I was proud and hoped he made it.

Tamika came out with her hair all sweated out and said, "Let's go."

The artist stood up and shook my hand and said, "It was nice meeting you, Angie. I know you have a man, but here's my number. Call me sometime."

"Okay," I said, taking the number and placing it in my clutch.

When we got in the car, she pulled out a wad of money and handed me a hundred dollars. "That's for coming with me. See now, this is why you need a nigga with money."

As soon as we pulled up to her apartment, I saw Kovas waiting outside in the parking lot. It was like he had a sixth sense whenever I was doing something I had no business doing. "Remember, don't tell him shit. We were at my auntie's house all night," she said.

My heart sank to the bottom of my asshole, and I felt like I was about to shit all over her front seat. I took the artist's number out of my clutch and threw it on the floor outside the car.

"Where you been all night?" he asked.

"Oh, we were at her auntie's house," I nervously said.

"This late?" he asked.

"Yeah, I had to drop some money off and didn't want to ride out there by myself, so I asked her to come with me," Tamika jumped in.

"Is that right?" he suspiciously asked. When we got into the house, he followed me to my room. "Take your panties off," he said, shutting my bedroom door.

"What, why?" I asked.

"Just fucking do it."

I took them off, and he snatched them out my hands. He smelled my panties like a bouquet of flowers, then told me to lay down on the bed and open up my legs. I had no idea what he was about to do. He then reached down and stuck his middle finger inside me and smelled it again.

"You better not lie to me. You know I can tell if you've had sex. So where did you guys really go?" I knew since I hadn't had sex, he didn't smell anything and was just trying to scare me into telling him something, so I stuck to my story, and he finally seemed to believe me.

The next day he took me over to Marcus's house. As soon as I walked in, Marcus and Kovas started grilling me. "I heard you went to Tamika's auntie's house last night. How is she doing?" Marcus asked.

"I don't know. I didn't go inside. I just waited in the car," I replied.

"Oh really, cuz she told me you guys went downtown and you went inside to meet her auntie." *How did he know that,* I thought unless she really did tell him that? I didn't want to contradict what she said so I said "No, I didn't go all the way inside. I just stayed in the lobby area."

"So you just said a minute ago you stayed in the car. Now you only stayed in the lobby. Which one is it?" Kovas asked.

"Wait, so you were in the lobby downtown?" Marcus asked.

"Yes, I stayed in the car, but it was too hot, so I sat in the lobby and waited for her. I met her auntie when she walked her out," I nervously said.

"That's funny because she doesn't have an aunt that lives downtown. Her aunt stays in the Valley. The only person she knows downtown is that bitch ass producer she used to fuck with. Is that where y'all went?" Marcus asked.

Kovas grabbed me by my face and said, "You better fuckin' not lie either."

I was so scared and confused about what to say. I didn't want to snitch on her, but they already knew I was lying, and I didn't want to get punished for it. "Okay, fine, we did go to his house, but I swear we didn't stay there that long. She just went there to pick up some money, and we left. That's it, I promise." He pushed me down on the chair at the dining room table. My heart was beating a mile a minute.

"That's all I needed to hear," Marcus said, picking up the phone and calling Tamika. He went off on her, but she didn't believe I had told him all that and asked to speak to me. I told her I had no choice, and they forced me to tell them.

"I can't believe I fuckin' trusted you, you bitch. I want you to come to get all your shit and get the fuck out my house before I toss it on the streets," she yelled.

After she hung up, Marcus went back to the Salon. I could tell Kovas was so mad that I lied to him, but he wasn't saying anything. He went into the kitchen and grabbed a butcher knife, which he knew I was deathly afraid of since I was stabbed with one as a kid. He then slowly grabbed an apple and started slicing pieces and placing them in his mouth, all while never taking his eyes off me or saying a word. My heart was beating so fast I could hear it pounding out my chest. He then walked behind me and wrapped his arm around my neck with the knife close to my skin.

"So what should I do about you lying to me and being at some niggaz house doing who knows what?"

"I swear I had no idea she was going to some guy's house. At first, she told me we were going to her aunt's and I didn't find out until we were halfway there," I pleaded.

"See, I may have believed you if you would have just told me that in the first place, but you lied, so how do I know you not lying now? How do I know you weren't over there fuckin' some nigga?"

I didn't want to respond and make things worse, so I just stayed quiet, hoping not to piss him off even more. He wrapped his arm tightly around my neck as he cut and ate another slice. "I'm gonna tell you what. I'm going to make sure I teach your ass a lesson about lying to me." He then set the knife and apple on the table and dragged me into the room with his arm still wrapped around my neck. I didn't make a sound as he threw me on the bed. "Take your pants off," he said.

I quickly took them off, thinking he was going to fuck the shit out of me to teach me a lesson, which I sometimes loved. But this time, he grabbed me by my hair and turned me around and bent me over the bed. He spat on his hand and rubbed it on his dick until it became wet and hard. Then he rubbed it on the back of my pussy and then pulled up and then shoved it in my ass. I let out a bloody scream, and tears instantly poured down my face. I was in so much pain I couldn't even scream the second time.

He covered my mouth with his hand and started fucking me so hard. The pain was so intense it felt like he had shoved the butcher knife in my ass instead of his dick. After a while, he didn't even need to cover my mouth anymore because my cries could no longer come out. I had never felt pain like that before, and after he finished, I crawled into a ball on the floor until the pain stopped enough for me to crawl into the bathroom and wash the shitty blood away.

The pain was so bad, I lay on the bathroom floor for hours until he came in and carried me back to bed where I stayed until the next morning. The next day he took me over to Tamika's house to get all of my belongings and said I would be staying with him at Marcus's house. I was so sore.

I was walking like I had just been hit by a truck. When we got there, I was thinking she would be at work, but she was there crying on the couch with her two sisters. As soon as I walked in, she yelled that thanks to me, Marcus had fired her from the Salon. Kovas yelled back that she was a cheating ho, which was probably the only reason she didn't beat my ass on sight. She just gave me the direst looks as we grabbed all my things. When Kovas went to the car to load up some of my items she locked the front door and came into my room where I was grabbing my clothes out the closet. Her sisters waited for her in the hall. I thought for sure they were going to jump me.

"I can't believe you told them. I really looked at you like a little sister and thought I could trust you, but you fuckin' stabbed me in the back, and now Marcus kicked me out of the salon and cut me off. Kovas has you so wrapped around his thumb, and for what? He doesn't do shit for you. He's been cheating on you the whole time y'all been together. Marcus even told me he fucked some stripper while you were passed out in the other room at that event. He also fucked that chick Nikki you always be hanging with, and one of the chicks at the salon," she said, laughing.

Kovas started banging at the door and ringing the doorbell, but they all ignored it. "If I was such a little sister to you, then why the fuck is you just telling me all this now?" I yelled back.

"Because you are so blind that even if I had told you, you woulda still stayed with him," she said crossing her arms.

"Well, since we're being all honest and shit now, Marcus has been cheating on you too with multiple women. He was also at the party all boo'd up with some stripper, and I heard he even had a threesome, so I wasn't the only who was blind. You really shouldn't be taking all your anger out on me when he's the one that fucked up. He was looking for something to use against you so he could break up with you and used me to do it. They had me cornered and wouldn't let me leave until I told them something. And I'm the one who had to pay the price for trying to cover up your shit. But you know what, thanks for letting me know all this. Trust me, I won't be blind anymore."

I grabbed my last box and headed outside. "You okay? I thought y'all was in there fighting. I was about bust down the door," he said.

"Nah, I'm good. It must have gotten locked by mistake," I said, not telling him shit about what she had told me. He took me back to Marcus's house, but I knew after everything that I had just heard I wasn't going to be staying for long. Today was the final straw that broke the camel's back.

I waited for the right moment when Marcus was going to stay at one of his chicks' house for the weekend. After he left, I snuck into his bedroom and called my mom while Kovas was taking a nap on the couch. I told her I had caught up in school, and since I was about to go into my senior year, I wanted graduate at Redlands High School with all my friends. I could tell she missed me by the way she didn't hesitate for me to come back home.

I knew Kovas didn't know where my mom lived so there would be no way he would be able to find me there. I then called Romeo and asked him if he could pick me up at Carl's Jr. around midnight. I told him I couldn't talk and would explain everything to him once he picked me up. I then went into Marcus's medicine cabinet in his bathroom and grabbed a few of his prescription sleeping pills I knew he had.

Later that night, I fixed Kovas his favorite drink, Courvoisier XO and acted like where were going to have one of our nasty drunk sex nights. I crushed the pills up and mixed them into his drink until I could no longer see any traces. I must have put too much in because it didn't take long for him to pass out. I packed up as much of my stuff as I could carry.

Before I was getting ready to walk out the door, a crazy thought popped in my head. I wanted to get him back for all the shit he put me through over the last year and a half. And also, to let him know how serious I was about it being over. I went into the kitchen and grabbed the super glue we used to fix my shoe once. I first checked to make sure he wasn't waking up by rubbing on his dick like I was about to give him head. When he didn't budge, I super glued his dick to his stomach and wrote "Checkmate!" in lipstick on his chest since I knew Chess was his favorite game to play.

I got to Carl's Jr. around 11:30 pm, but luckily Romeo was already there waiting for me. He got out the car, and I dropped all my things as I ran into his arms. I felt overwhelmed with so many emotions like a kidnapped child who had just been rescued. He could tell immediately I had been through a lot. It was written all over my face. I looked like I hadn't slept in years.

He grabbed my things and placed them in the trunk of his red BMW. He said he was going to take me back to his place, where he was living with a friend. I told him everything I had gone through since I had last seen him. He said Tatiana had told him how we got into it over him and how he'd smacked me in the mall. "I can't believe you stayed with someone like that. Thank God you're okay. My mom has been missing you like crazy and asks about you all the time. She's going to be so happy to see you." He pulled me over to his side of the car and kissed me on my forehead. I rested my head on his shoulders and let out a big sigh of relief.

WHEN I FINALLY GOT TO HIS PLACE, I felt so safe and at ease that I wanted to make love to him all night. I put on some music by Rome. I teased him by taking things slower than we usually did. I slowly took off my dress and let him take a good look at my body before I started kissing him all over his. I sucked on his nipples and made him look me in my eyes when I sat on his lap and rode him on his couch. I asked him if he missed my wet pussy as my juices dripped all down his dick and his balls, leaving a wet spot on the cushion. The more I talked, the more excited he got until he could no longer control himself. He let out a loud moan as he pulled me close to him, preventing me from continuing to grind the nut out of him.

"Damn, girl, when you learn how to ride like that?" he said, picking me up and carrying me into his bedroom, where I lay in his arm's until we fell asleep.

The next morning, he took me to see his mom then dropped me off at my mom's house. I couldn't wait to see my baby brother Chris, who was no longer a baby anymore. I was even happy to see Ryan, who had doubled in size. I knew I could no longer beat him up like I used to, so I kept my distance from him. I came back just in time to enroll in Redlands East Valley High School, which had just finished being built, and we were going to be the first class to graduate from it.

I thought this would be another chance for me and Romeo to get back together, especially after seeing his mom again and feeling like old times, but Romeo was still Romeo. He always had a lot of girls, and after one of them called to tell me that, I realized things would never change, and we were better off just being friends. Once again, I just wanted to focus on school and stay out of trouble as much as possible. There were so many rumors about me when I got school, people didn't know what to believe. Some of them thought I was even dead since I had been gone for so long.

For the first time, I loved being back in Redlands. Tatiana was there, even Cornell was there, and we became friends again. I wasn't interested in dating anyone at school, although one boy I rode the bus with did catch my eye, but he was a sophomore and way too young for me. So I looked at him as just eye candy. He was tall, skinny, and light-skinned and played basketball. He had some of the sexiest lips I've ever seen on a guy, like a young Chico DeBarge. We always flirted with each other on the bus but acted like we didn't know each other once we got to school.

One day he sat next to me on the bus and asked if I could do him a favor. He made me promise not to tell anyone what he was about to tell me. He said he was still a virgin and wanted me to be his first and that I didn't have to worry about him because he wasn't looking for a relationship or anything. He just wanted to lose his virginity and had heard so much about me that he knew I'd be the perfect one to do it with. I didn't know how to take that. I wasn't sure if he was complimenting me or calling me the perfect slut. Now I know I said I just wanted to just focus on school, but he looked too good to pass up and I couldn't resist taking another virginity, so I told him to come over on Wednesday after school when I knew my brother Ryan had baseball practice and would be home late. After that, I could tell he was so nervous because he barely made eye contact with me anymore.

Wednesday came, and he got off the bus with me. He was quiet the whole way to my house. I told Chris to stay outside and play as we went in. "Are you sure you ready for this?" I asked.

"Yeah, I'm sure," he replied.

When we got to my house, I grabbed a blanket and laid it on the living room floor and blasted Jon B. from the stereo. He lay down, and I got on top of him and started kissing him all over his bony chest. He was so skinny I could feel his hip bones while I was on top of him. I was so used to fucking older men that it felt weird to fuck someone younger than me, so I told him to get on top. He pulled out a condom, which took a few minutes for him to put on, and then slid inside my wet pussy. After two and a half strokes, he stopped and said, "I think I did something!"

"What do you mean think?" I said as he pulled out, and the condom was filled with fifteen-year-old sperm. It took longer for him to put the condom on than it was for him to be inside me. After that, I realized I never wanted to fuck a virgin again.

A few months later on a Saturday afternoon, I was home watching TV with my brothers while our mom was at work when there was a knock on the door. Chris got up and answered it. Before I could even look out the window to see who it was, I heard a familiar eerie voice.

"Is Angie here?"

My heart dropped. My brother looked at me and said, "Yeah, she right here."

Kovas walked in and said, "So this is where you been hiding, huh? This must be your brother Chris. Is there somewhere we can talk?"

I was frozen like the time I saw Curtis chocking my mom, but I wanted to remain calm, so I wouldn't scare my brothers. "Umm yeah, let's go outside," I said.

As soon as we got outside, he yelled, "Did you really think you could just do that shit to me and run off like that? Did you really think I wasn't going to find you?" He walked toward me, but I backed up and made sure to keep my distance from him. "Look, Tamika told me everything. She told me how you were cheating on me the whole time we were together. How you fucked Nikki and that stripper while I was passed out in the room. You're lucky I didn't do anything worse."

He had this blank stare on his face that was hard to read. "Do you know how long it took me for me to heal from that shit? I still have a scar. And how you gonna believe that bitch instead of just asking me first? She was just mad because you snitch on her. And you dumb enough to fall for that shit. I thought you were smarting than that."

"Well, I don't give a fuck anymore. I'm done. I'm tired of all the bullshit you put me through. Plus I'm happy where I'm at, so there's nothing you can say to get me to come back," I said, slowly making my way toward the front door.

"What did I tell you before? You belong to me and you ain't going nowhere. I rather see you dead before I let you leave me. You think I'm playing with you?"

We both stood there like a Mexican standoff. When I looked at the front door, he rushed toward me, but I managed to slip by and run in the house. I screamed as I tried to close the door, but he busted in before I had a chance to lock it. I ran into the kitchen and picked up a butcher knife. Ryan came out his room to see what all the noise was about.

"Now, don't be stupid. If you come at me with that knife, you'll only have one chance, and if you miss and I get that knife, I'll slice your fuckin throat right here in front of your brothers, and then they'll be next."

My brothers stood there terrified. They didn't know what to do. I didn't want anything to happen to them, so I put the knife back in the drawer. As soon as I shut it, he quickly came over and put me in a head lock and tried to drag me out of the house, but Ryan stood in front of the door and told him to let me go. Kovas laughed as he tried pushing him out the way, but Ryan jumped back, did a twist in the air, and kicked him on the side of his face, which caused him to let me go. Blood poured down the side of his mouth.

He licked some of the blood off with his tongue and wiped the rest of it off with the back of his hand. "Oh, you all must want to die today," he said, lunging toward Ryan.

I grabbed the back of his shirt, which slowed him down enough for Ryan to give him another Jean Claude Van Damme kick to his chest, causing him to fall on the floor this time. He turned his rage toward me, and Ryan snuck behind him and put him in a choke hold. I knew Ryan had a black belt but never knew he could fight like this. Kovas somehow got loose from his grip and flipped him over on his back and punched him in the face. I jumped on his back and began hitting him as hard as I could, but he backed into the wall, which knocked the wind out me, and I fell to the floor. Ryan got back up and tried to kick him again, but this time Kovas grabbed his foot and flipped him into the ground. He then jumped on top of Ryan and started choking him so hard I could see the color fade from his face. I was trying to catch my breath and find something around the house to hit him with when we heard a loud bang at the front door.

It caught us all off guard when we heard, "It's the police, open up." Those words were like music to my ears. Chris had called the police while all of this was going on and ran to the door to let them in. By this point Kovas had let go of Ryan and was trying to clean himself up.

"What seems to be the problem?" one of the policemen asked.

"Nothing, Officer, we just had a little disagreement, and I was just about to leave," Kovas said, trying to walk pass the officer to the front door.

"Hold up, not so fast. That didn't sound like a little disagreement. Let me see your ID," the other officer asked.

"Umm, I don't have it on me," he said.

"Turn around and put your hands behind your back," the officer said as he grabbed him and placed him in handcuffs. As officer was patting him down, he came across Kovas's wallet in his back pocket. He then put him in the back seat of his car while he ran his name in the system where he found a warrant out for his arrest and took him into custody. I told the other officer his car was at my house and I wanted to make sure he didn't have a reason to come back to get it. He told me they would have it towed and not to worry about that. He then asked me if I wanted to press charges, but I didn't want anything to happen to my brothers when he got out, so I said no. I was hoping whatever he was being arrested for would keep him locked up long enough for me to find another place to stay. When they left, I went into the house, hugged Ryan, and thanked him for helping me.

"No problem. I couldn't just stand there and watch him put his hands on you like that. I'm the only one that can do that," he said, and we both laughed. Chris came over and I gave him a hug too. "And thanks, Chris, for calling the cops. I don't know what would have happened if you didn't."

A couple of weeks later, I received a call from his lawyer who explained Kovas was looking at some hard time and needed me to testify for him. He said since Kovas was twenty-four and I was only seventeen and still a minor that I would only get probation, which would be expunged off my record when I turned eighteen.

"Wait, what? Kovas is twenty-four? I thought he was nineteen. And what do you mean I would only get probation? Probation for what?" I asked.

"For the stolen credit cards. He said that you were the one that used them to purchase all the clothing and jewelry."

"I don't know anything about any stolen credit cards. All I know is that when he got the job at the gas station, he started making a lot of money and he was the one that was taking us out on shopping sprees, not me. I thought it was because he got promoted to manager or something," I explained.

The truth was, I did know about the stolen credit cards. He left one in the car one day and when I noticed a different name on it, I asked him about it. He told me he would ask to see the customer's id when they used their cards to make a purchase. Then he would distract them in conversations but only hand them back their id's. Some of them wouldn't even notice he didn't hand them back their credit card. When I told him how fucked up that was, he said not to even trip because as soon as they reported their card stolen the bank would give them back their money.

"Well, like I said, with you being only seventeen, you would only get probation, which is nothing but a slap on the wrist, but if he gets convicted, he's looking at some real time due to the three-strike law. Do you want him to go to jail for a long time?" I sat there and thought about everything he had put me through and what he did to my brother.

"He can go to hell for all I care," I said, hanging up the phone. The lawyer called back a few times, but I never answered. Kovas called collect twice, but I never accepted. I knew by me not helping him get out of jail, I was signing my own death warrant. I wasn't afraid to die, but I was afraid of something happening to my family and I knew I couldn't stay at my mom's house for much longer.

"Battered and bruised, like an oak tree that survived a hurricane, she weathered the storm, proving you could ride through hell, come out smiling, and ready to set the world on fire." – Black Butterfly

Chapter VI
Turning Leaves

I WAS SO RELIEVED WHEN I FOUND OUT Kovas would be in jail long enough for me to finish high school, but I knew it would only be a matter of time before he got out and came looking for me. I was sitting on the couch contemplating about what I was going to do after I graduated when an Army commercial came on, and for a limited time only if I called, I could receive a free pair of dog tags. *Oooo, free dog tags*, I thought. I immediately called them up, and the recruiter said he would be by the next day to bring me over more information.

A very handsome White guy who looked like young Brad Pitt came knocking on my door in his Army formal uniform. He explained to me all the benefits the Army had to offer. I started asking about the Air Force since my grandfather had served with them and I wanted to do something in the air.

"Oh well, you can go airborne. The Army has a great airborne program. Matter of fact, are you hungry? Let's go grab a bit to eat, and I can tell you all about it." He took me out for lunch and even took me next door to Mervyns and bought me a cute school outfit. "See, the Air Force wouldn't do all this for you. Plus, if you join with me, I can get you an enlistment bonus of up to twenty thousand dollars."

"Wow, really?" I was so intrigued when I heard that, but I still wasn't ready to commit four years of my life to the Army. I was the type that like to test things out before I made a commitment. Plus, I was just looking for a temporary solution until I could get a nice job and my own place. Then he told me I could join the Reserves and would only have to go in one weekend a month and two weeks during the summer. After hearing that I was sold. Money, getting out of California, and jumping out of planes, I was ready to leave the next day, but I still had to graduate.

Later that night, he came back and talked to my mom after she got off work and got her on board. I had never seen her so proud of me and felt like one of those Army commercials. Then the next day, he went to my school and talked to them about transferring me to Orangewood High School, which was a continuation high school, so I that could graduate early and leave for boot camp in April.

Months went by, and I did exactly that. I worked my ass off and was able to graduate early. I even managed to stay out of trouble for the most part. My mom and I occasionally still bumped heads, but we were starting to get along a lot better than before. I decided to celebrate with my friends by going to this club called Metro aka "Meet a Ho," which is what I did. I met this hot guy named Tony who was medium built with a bald head. All my girls and I were checking him out, so I felt extra special when he walked over to me and asked me if I wanted to dance. I wasn't the best dancer, but after taking a few shots that we had snuck in, I thought I was Mya on the dance floor. After we finished dancing, he told me he was from San Diego and asked if I had ever been, which I hadn't. I told him I was getting ready to leave for the military, and he offered to take me to the beach down there the following weekend. I thought this would be a perfect way to leave Cali.

The weekend rolled around, and he was five hours late. Every time I called him, he kept telling me he was on his way.

When he finally showed up at my mom's house, he was with three other guys. "What the hell, you were supposed to be here this morning. It's almost 4 o'clock. How are we going to be able to go to the beach now?" I yelled.

"I know, I know, my bad. I had to pick up my boys, and they were taking forever, but I promise I'll make it up to you. We can still hit the beach tomorrow. I'll even take you to a nice fancy dinner tonight to make it up." He smiled. He was so sexy, and I really wanted to go to San Diego, so I agreed to still go even though I had another gut feeling I shouldn't.

I went around to the passenger side to get in, "Uh, can you sit in the back? There won't be enough room if all my boys sit back there," he said, opening up the back door so one of his boys could get out and let me sit in the middle. Everything was screaming for me not to go. You would think I would have learned my lesson by now, but I was so worried about him making that long drive for me than I was for my own safety.

About a quarter of the way they started blasting the music even louder and lighting up a blunt. He passed it to me, and I took a few puffs, but I could tell immediately this didn't feel like a normal blunt. "Damien" by DMX was playing on the radio as a dark cloud came over us like it was about to thunderstorm, and I started to hear a deep voice tell me this was my last chance. "After this there will be no more," the dark voice said. I was so scared and wanted to scream and jump out the car.

"You all right, shorty?" Tony asked, looking at me thru the rearview mirror, which only made me have a flashback of Mad Dogg.

I started to feel like I was hyperventilating. "Can you roll down the window? I need some air," I asked. The fresh air started to bring me back down to earth. I looked back at him in the mirror, and I could have sworn I saw horns coming out of his head. I rubbed my eyes, and next thing I knew I was sitting in the front with only one of his boys left in the back seat. "Where's your boys?" I asked.

"Uhhh, they got dropped off like ten minutes ago. You sure you okay?" he laughed.

We dropped his last boy off, and I was so relieved. Then he drove over to a building that looked like some apartments. "Where are we going?" I asked.

"Man, I'm exhausted with all this driving. I just want to check into our room and relax. We'll go to the beach and dinner tomorrow, I promise." I was so pissed, but what other choice did I have now? We checked into our room and sat on the bed. I was trying to get to know him more, but he didn't seem interested in anything I had to say. As I was telling him about myself, he leaned over to kiss me. I pulled back, thinking how rude he was for not letting me finish my sentence. He then reached over and tried unzipping my pants. *Here we go again,* I thought.

I pulled away and asked, "What are you doing?"

"What do you think I'm doing?" he said, still trying to unzip them.

"We just got here, plus I don't want to do anything tonight. I'm tired and just want to go to sleep," I said, getting under the covers with all my clothes still on.

"Tired? You gotta be fuckin kidding me. If anyone should be tired, it should be me. I'm the one that's been driving all fuckin' day. And for what?"

I could tell he was getting pissed, and I didn't want to say anything else to make things worse, so I just closed my eyes and pretended like I was going to sleep. I actually did doze off and was awakened to him going through my purse. Then I heard the door open and shut. When I got up, I noticed he had taken my Dallas Cowboys jacket and my wallet. "Oh, fuck!" I thought. I ran outside but couldn't see him anywhere, so I went back inside, hoping he would call or come back. Ten minutes later the phone rang.

"Hello," I answered.

"So are you fuckin' or not? I didn't drove all that way for nothing."

"What, why would I fuck you just for taking me to the beach?" I shouted.

"Do you know how many females wish they were in your spot right now? I could have any bitch I want and you over there acting like a damn tease. So are you fucking or what?"

"Fuck you! I'd rather walk home than to fuck your bitch ass," I said, slamming the phone down and hanging up on him. I was expecting for him to call back and apologize for being such a dick. But he never did, and now I was stuck four hours away from home with no idea on how to get back.

I spent the whole night calling everyone I knew, even people I hadn't spoken to in years, but no one could come through, so I had no other choice but to call my mom. She was so pissed I lied to her about staying the night at Tatiana's. Instead of coming to get me, she told me I had to get out when I got back.

The next morning the phone rang, and I was hoping it was someone who could come pick me up, but it was the guy at the front desk telling me it was check-out time. I started to panic as I desperately made my last few calls. Finally, a guy I used to talk to said he would come to get me but needed gas money, so again I called Keri, who agreed to give it to him. I sat on the curb for hours waiting for them to finally show up. When they did, I was so grateful and made a promise to myself I would never ignore my instincts again.

When I got home, I picked up all my things while my mom was at work and stayed at Tisha's house until it was time for me to leave. The ironic thing about all of this was, I ended up having to go back down to San Diego to take the Armed Services Vocational Aptitude Battery test before I was shipped off to Fort Jackson, South Carolina for boot camp.

FLYING TO SOUTH CAROLINA WAS THE first time I had been on a plane. I was so excited about finally getting the fuck out of Cali. It felt like I was getting another chance to start over and make something out of my life. When I got to reception, everyone started talking about all the stories they had heard about what was going to happen at boot camp. It was like hearing an urban legend, no one knew what to believe.

After we processed our paperwork and got issued our uniforms, we took our infamous Army photos. Then all the boys went to the barbershop for haircuts, and all the girls went to the salon to get their braids and weaves removed. Like Coco Chanel used to say, "A woman who cuts her hair is about to change her life." So I decided to cut my hair off like I was G.I. Jane, but the black version. I wasn't that crazy to shave my head bald, so I got a bob cut instead.

When reception was over, we all got on the bus and headed over to our barracks. Everyone was so happy and joking around. They even started singing cadences like we were in summer camp. When we pulled up, we saw a line of drill sergeants standing in the rain, and before we knew it, they were screaming in our faces to get off the bus. Everyone was scared shitless. Some even began to cry. I thought it was funny and tried so hard not to laugh.

"You think this shit is funny? You think this is a game? You better wipe that smile off your face right now. This ain't no game, White," he said, calling me by my last name and getting so close to my face I could smell his tart breath. I squinted as spit flew in my eye. It seemed just like the movies and reminded me of *Major Pain,* and I couldn't stop giggling. "Since you think this is a joke, White, you can be the first one to drop and give me twenty."

It was such a struggle to do twenty pushups, but after I finished, he then said, "Now, everyone else can drop and give me twenty, and you can thank White for that." I could see the steam coming off everyone's heads as they dropped to the cold wet grass. *Maybe this wasn't the best way to start,* I thought. After they got up, I quickly wiped the smile from my face, but it was too late. I was now on the drill sergeant's radar.

Once we got to the barracks, we had to empty everything out from our personal bags. "White, did you think you were coming to a resort or something? How many beauty products did you think you would need? Well, I'm going to tell you. You only get three items, and the rest goes in the trash."

"What? That's not fair. Why does everyone else get five? I just bought all of this stuff."

"Say one more word, and everything will go in the trash." Some of the girls were smirking, and I could tell they were enjoying every minute of it. I knew now Drill Sergeant Mullins had it out for me, and shit was getting real. I only kept the shampoo, conditioner, and hair gel. I was so mad I had to get rid of all my perfumes, makeup, and body lotions. But when he wasn't looking, I was able to sneak back in my Herbal Essence bodywash. After that, we checked into our rooms, took a tour, and went to the Post Exchange. A couple of girls started crying and said they had made a mistake by joining, and the next day they ended up quitting.

It never felt so good to finally lie down in a bed after such a long day. "Lights out," someone yelled, turning them off. It felt like as soon as I closed my eyes, we were being woken right back up with loud sounds of pots banging and screams for us to get up and get downstairs. It was then I realized the guys' barracks was directly right across the hall from us, and we were co-ed.

One boy immediately caught my attention, and I knew I was in for some trouble. I had always dated Black guys, but when I saw this tall, sexy Italian boy with a New York accent he had me feeling like a Bronx Tale, and I wanted to kiss those sexy Ashton Kutcher lips of his. We both made eye contact but quickly snapped out of it when Drill Sergeant Mullins yelled for everyone to keep their eyes forward. After morning PT, we went to the chow hall for breakfast. I grabbed my tray and sat down across from Private Elinor, who was this small, cute girl that slept in the bunk bed next to mine. She was mixed with so many different races, I couldn't tell what her ethnicity was.

"Drill Sergeant Mullins has it out for you, huh?" she asked, laughing.

"Yeah, I guess so. He definitely has a major stick up his ass," I said.

"We should put eye drops in his drink. That will make him shit that stick right out," she said. We both laughed, and I knew when she said that she was going to be my partner in crime.

Over the next couple of weeks, we did a lot of physical training. One night it was my turn to stand guard while everyone was sleeping, and when I looked across the hallway, I saw Private Rizzo, the Italian boy who'd caught my eye the first day. He was also on guard duty. He smiled and pointed to the side of the building for us to go so we wouldn't be seen.

"What it do, shorty? Real talk I have been trying to holla at you since we got here," he said with his New York accent.

"I know, I've been trying to talk to you too, but it's hard to do anything around here without the drill sergeants all in my ass," I said,

"You can always write to me, na'mean?"

"Huh? I'm not mean," I said.

He laughed and said, "No, na'mean means you know what I'm saying!"

"Oh yeah, I know what you are saying, and I can write you." I bashfully smiled. I was such a White girl when it came to slang and always felt like I needed to carry around an urban dictionary.

"Well, we better get back before they catch us and start illin'," he said.

"Okay, I'll see you around," I replied. As I was about to walk away, he pulled me in and gave me a small kiss. I thought about that kiss all night and the next day I wrote him a letter while in the bathroom. I put it in my BDU's leg pocket and waited for the perfect time to give it to him.

We all got called into the auditorium to watch the movie "Saving Private Ryan." I sat next to him and slipped him the letter. In the middle of the movie, he got up to the bathroom so he could read it. The next thing I knew, the movie stopped, and the lights came on. Then I saw Rizzo with his head down, standing next to Drill Sergeant Mullins, who had my letter in his hand. *Oh shit*, I thought.

"Where's Private White? White, stand up!"

I slumped down in my chair, hoping he wouldn't see me, but someone pointed me out after he asked again. I stood up and my face was as red as a tomato. He told me to come to the front and handed me my letter.

"Since Private White likes to write letters, I think it's only fair we all get to hear it. Read it out loud!"

I was horrified but played it off like I didn't give two shits about it and even laughed as I had to describe how sexy he was. Once I finished reading the letter, he told me I lost my phone privileges for a week. I was so pissed. Phone calls were the only thing we had to look forward to each day, not to mention Rizzo didn't even get in trouble over the letter, and the shit was his idea. After that, he realized I was too much of a target for the drill sergeants, and he didn't want to be caught up again, so he moved his interest to another girl.

I was venting my frustrations out to Elinor on the balcony when we saw Drill Sergeant Mullins walk past. She looked at me and pointed, then hocked a big loogy over the railing that landed right on his hat. She had a very short haircut, so he thought it was one of the boys and smoked all of them until someone confessed. Since we were the only ones that knew, no one did, and they got smoked all day. It was the sweetest revenge, especially towards Rizzo.

Even though I was constantly getting in trouble from everything I did, like not shining my boots or making up my bed tight enough, I really enjoyed boot camp. Especially during weapons and combat training. During one of the training sessions, we had to throw a live grenade over a wall, and one of the females threw the pin instead and dropped the grenade by her feet. Luckily the trainer was standing right next to her and grabbed it in time to throw it over the wall before they were blown to pieces.

Another girl named Private Woodson freaked out in the gas chamber and started punching one of the drill sergeants to let her out. They were so mad at her. They made her do it twice. I had been through so much in my life that this was a piece of cake for me, and I passed everything with flying colors.

Toward the end, we learned how to set up tents, go on night patrols, and perform night operations. We ate MREs that were like catching fish in a barrel to get a good one, but the spaghetti was always my favorite. After our eighth week, things got intense. We went on a final three-day field march and performed everything we had learned over the last seven weeks. It felt like we were really going into war. We got shot at, tear gas was thrown at us, and we had to do the longest march ever while carrying a forty-pound bag on our shoulders and holding our M4 rifles.

My bunk buddy Webster was about to quit, but I made her hold on to my bag so I could pull her weight, which I instantly regretted as we struggled to make it up the hill. Just when I thought I was about to give up too, Drill Sergeant Mullins noticed and made her let me go. Luckily, we were almost there, and both made it to the finish line. That was one of the proudest moments of my life. Especially when Drill Sergeant Mullins said, "Good job, White. I'm proud of you."

Week nine was our final week and the graduation ceremony. It was such a bittersweet moment. I was so proud of myself for making it all the way through without getting kicked out, but I was also sad I didn't have any family there to celebrate with me. I had to stand there alone and watch everyone else embrace their families.

After graduation, we all exchanged phone numbers, took pictures, and said our tearful goodbyes. I was assigned to go to Fort Belvoir, Virginia, for AIT and took a bus ride up there with a few others I knew. Woodson ended up being one of my roommates. She was one of the girls that never liked me from day one because she thought I was stuck up and a troublemaker. Our other roommate was a girl named Williams, who came from another boot camp. Williams and I immediately hit it off, especially after we learned we were both from Los Angeles, California.

I don't know what it was, but drill sergeants always had it out for me. The first day I got there, I got called to the front again and dropped for not having my boots shiny enough.

No matter what I did, I could never get my boots as polished as everyone else's and was always getting dropped for it. I got dropped so many times my arms were starting to look like Angela Bassett's. So I decided to try something different and put some of my CarMax lip balm on my boots' tips. The next day Drill Sergeant Smith called me up to the front again, and I thought for sure he was going to know what I did. "Now that's what I'm talking about, White. This is how your boots should look every day. I want everyone in here to have their boots as shiny as White's. Good job, now get back in formation." I was laughing so hard inside when he said that.

After PT and breakfast, we headed over to our job training. On the bus was also the class before us that was getting ready to graduate. There was another White boy named Davis who caught my attention. I could tell he grew up around nothing but Black people by the way he was always clowning on everyone. He started going in on how lame it was for guys in his class to be all boo'd up with chicks in barracks.

"All this pussy we could be getting off base and y'all wanna risk getting caught, for what? These females here are lame as fuck. You would never catch me all boo'd up like some sucka." He laughed. I was the type that when I saw a sign that said stay out, I had to go in, or if it said don't touch, I had to touch it. I'm so glad I wasn't born in the segregation days because I know I would have been arrested or killed for sure for pissing in a "Whites only" fountain. I don't know what it was but always had this rebellious nature about me. So the fact that he said he would never hook up with a girl from AIT made me want him even more.

He usually sat alone on the bus, so the next day I wore my best perfume, did a cute zig zag line in my hair that was pulled back into a curly bun, and used CarMax to make my lips look irresistible.

"You mind if I sit here?" I smiled at him.

"This ain't the damn '50s. You can sit wherever you want." He and his boys laughed. *Damn, that was a little harsh*, I thought. Every time I tried to initiate conversation, he would keep it short and then go back to talking to his boys like I was annoying him. When we pulled up to class, I thought this shit did not go as planned, and maybe this was going to be more challenging than I thought. After class, I sat next to him again, and this time, he paid a little more attention, knowing I was sitting next to him on purpose, but he still kept things short.

"What happened right there?" I asked, grabbing his hand and softly stroking the scars on his knuckles.

"I lost my temper and punched out a window," he said, snatching his hand back.

"Oh, I have a scar too, right here on my stomach," I said, lifting my shirt and pulling down my pants just enough for him to see the top of my pussy line.

"How you get that?" He ran his thumb across it.

"My mom stabbed me on accident when I was five."

"Damn for real? That's crazy. How she stabbed you on accident?"

"I was acting up, and she hit me with her purse but forgot she had a knife in there. We lived in LA, so she carried it around for protection," I said, tucking my BDUs back in my pants.

"Oh, okay. I'm from Detroit so I get it. I punched the window out after I got home from school and seen the black eye my stepdad had given my mom." The look in his eyes after he said that seemed like it was something he rarely shared with anyone. He was about to say something else but looked up and noticed we were pulling back up to the barracks and got up without saying another word.

The next day I headed toward the back of the bus where he was sitting but decided to sit in the seat in front of him instead. "You can sit over here if you want," he said. His boys made a "Ooooo" sound, but he just told them to fuck off. We started talking some more about our families and what made us join the military. I made sure to look him in his eyes the whole time, which I could tell made him feel vulnerable.

"You want to know something crazy?" I said, leaning in so I could whisper something in his ear.

"What's that?" he asked.

"I've never been with a White guy before. I've always wanted to but just hadn't met the right one yet."

"Well, I love Black women, that's all I've ever messed with."

"Oh yeah?" I said, smiling. We sat there for a moment in silence and when he looked back at me, I decided to go in for a kiss. He didn't move his lips until I grabbed his head and pulled him closer. The whole bus went crazy when they noticed us kissing. His boys started talking all kinds of shit, but he just flipped them off as he continued kissing me until we got to class. He was such a good kisser, and I couldn't wait to continue where we left off.

After class, I sat next to him again, and we immediately went back to kissing like we had been thinking about it all day. I had just put lotion on my hands, so they were nice and slippery, so I reached down in his pants and started stroking his dick until it became hard enough for me to pull out.

"Damn," I said as I looked down at his big dick. "I didn't know White boys were packing like this."

"Not all White guys have small dicks," he laughed.

I really wanted to fuck him after seeing that. He had his back to his boys so they couldn't see anything, but they knew something was going down, especially after he yelled "FUCK" after busting all in my hand, which he wiped off with his brown undershirt.

"I see what you are trying to do. You a tease, huh?" he said, putting his dick back in his pants.

"I'm not a tease. I want it just as much as you do. Why don't you sneak into my room tonight and I'll show you how much I'm not a tease? I'll leave the back door unlocked after lights out."

"Hell nah, Drill Sergeant Johns don't play that shit, and she on duty tonight. Plus, what about your roommates?"

"No, I'm telling you I know someone that does this shit all the time. Just come around 0100. The back door will be unlocked, and all you gotta do is go up to the second floor. I'm the last one on the left. And don't worry about my roommates. I know a spot we can sneak off to."

"Aight, but if I get caught, I'm gonna be heated yo!"

"Trust me, you're not going to get caught," I reassured him.

That night I went down around 1250 and unlocked the back door, but 0100 rolled around, and there was no sign of him. Then 0200 came, and I figured he'd chickened out or changed his mind. The next morning when I got on the bus, he gave me the dirtiest look, and one of his boys was sitting in my spot. I could tell he didn't want to be bothered, so I sat in the front.

After class, the same thing happened, so now I was starting to get pissed that he was ignoring me. When we got off the bus, I tried to talk to him, but he told me to leave him the fuck alone, and I couldn't understand why. Later on, that evening, I noticed he had gone into the laundry room, so I followed in after him.

"What the fuck are you so mad at me for?" I asked.

"Man, just leave me alone," he said, trying to leave the laundry room, but I blocked him from going out.

"Look, we don't have to ever talk again, but the least you can do is tell me why you're so mad at me? What did I do?" I asked again.

"Because you got me out here looking like a fuckin' clown. I tried to come up last night, and Drill Sergeant Johns caught me just like I said she would. Then she made me sleep on the bare floor in the dayroom all night without shit. And everyone knows because she made me stay out there until they all woke up. Now I gotta hear them talkin' shit about it all day. I knew I shouldn't have been fuckin' with you. So don't say shit to me anymore," he yelled as he pushed me to the side and stormed out. The following week they all graduated, and I never got the experience with my white chocolate like I wanted to. After that, I decided to take his advice and only mess with guy's off base.

Since Woodson and I were roommates, it forced us to have to interact with each other. Once she got to know me, she ended up apologizing for judging me the way she did, but I couldn't even blame her. I did make a bad first impression and walked around like I had this massive chip on my shoulder. I was so immature when I first got there, but I felt like I had grown up so much over these last few months.

After we hashed things out, the three of us became tighter than infantry pussy. When we finally got our first weekend pass off base, we decided to go to Washington DC with this other soldier named Hendricks to do some sightseeing and parting. We looked like the original Destiny's Child with our color-coordinated outfits. When we got to DC, I was blown away to see so many Black people and knew exactly why they called it a chocolate city. I never knew Black people were out here living like this. There was chocolate everywhere, and they had nice jobs, drove nice cars, and lived in nice big townhomes. I felt at home like this was the place I was always meant to be. We went to the White House, checked out all the monuments, went to the African American museum, and even did some shopping at the Potomac Mall.

Later that night, we ended up going to a nightclub called the Ritz. I had just gotten through dancing when I noticed this very tall light-skinned guy who looked like a young Bizzy Bone except with a short fade checking me out at the bar.

"Can I buy you a drink?" he asked. He introduced himself as Kevin and bought me a Long Island Iced Tea. As we were talking, another guy I had been talking to earlier came over and handed me his number before he left. Kevin's friend thought that was rude and snatched the number out of my hand and threw it on the floor. I was so pissed that he did that, I didn't even want to talk to Kevin anymore and walked away. Kevin ran over to me and apologized for his friend and said he was just drunk, and he would never do anything like that. Then he handed me the number back.

He was so handsome, and since he gave me back the number, I decided to let it go. We went to the bar to finish our conversation. We talked and danced all night. When he found out I was from Cali, he got even more excited and said how much he loved West Coast music and always wanted to move out there. At the end of the night, we exchanged information. Since I was still in training, I didn't have a phone number for him to call me, so I gave him my address to write, and within a week, I received my first letter.

Over the next few weeks, we constantly wrote and saw each other on the weekends. I was falling fast and hard for him. He was a twenty-four-year-old churchgoing mama's boy. He was so sweet, caring, and everything I thought I needed in a man. He reminded me so much of Devin. So I tried my hardest to stay out of trouble and not lose my weekend passes, but me staying out of trouble was like telling a bird not to fly.

As I was walking down the hall, I passed Drill Sergeant Smith's office and saw his hat sitting on his desk. It was almost like there was a light shining from above on it for me to take it. I started to walk away, but the temptation was too great, and I couldn't resist the urge to grab it and put it on. I walked outside and started imitated Drill Sergeant Smith. Some of the soldiers who didn't know me thought I was a real drill sergeant especially when I told them to drop. I loved having this power. The ones that did know me started laughing their assess off. "White, you are so crazy. You better put that back before he catches you," Woodson said. I went back and put it back on his desk, precisely the way it was, and thought I was in the clear.

About thirty minutes later, I heard, "White, bring your ass down here now, front and center." Drill Sergeant Smith yelled from outside my barrack.

I ran downstairs and stood in front of him. "Sir, yes, sir," I shouted.

"Put your back against the wall, squat down, and hold your arms out. So you think you run shit around here, huh? You think you a drill sergeant now?"

"No, Drill Sergeant," I replied.

"Well, that's not what I heard. I heard you walking around here wearing my hat like you earned that shit. Do you think you earned that shit? You think you have what it takes to be a drill sergeant, White?"

"No, Drill Sergeant." My legs were beginning to shake. "Well, we about to find out if you have what it takes. If you can stay in that position for five minutes, I'll forget all about it and let you slide, but if you quit, you lose your weekend pass and are on cleaning duty for two weeks. That means I want every piece of trash picked up, and every inch of this lawn mowed. You got four minutes left."

A huge crowd had started to form outside just to watch.

Five minutes doesn't seem that long until you're doing this shit. Every second feels like a minute, and every minute feels like an hour. There was no way I was going to be able to do this, I thought. My legs were already starting to tremble uncontrollably, and I was slowly sliding down.

"Come on, White, you got this," Williams screamed from the balcony.

"Three minutes left!" Drill Sergeant yelled. I started to think about me not seeing Kevin and somehow got the strength to pull myself back up. Sweat was dripping all down my neck, and my thighs and ass were on fire.

"Keep going, White. Don't give up!" Woodson chanted.

Tears of pain started to mix in with my sweat, and my arms began to shake like I had Parkinson's. As soon as he yelled two minutes, I couldn't take it anymore and fell flat on my ass. The whole crowd sighed in disappointment. "Next time you put on that hat you better make sure you earned the right to wear it. Now grab the lawnmower and get to mowing. I want this whole yard done before I get back," Drill Sergeant said as he walked away.

I was so mad at myself for losing my weekend pass. I decided to take my anger out on the lawn, so I just grabbed the mower and started mowing everything in sight, including flowers, sprinklers, and rocks. I didn't care what it was. If it was on the ground, it got mowed, and sparks were flying everywhere. Williams laughed so hard she threw up on the stairs.

Over the next couple weeks, I had no choice but to stay on base, but that didn't stop me from seeing Kevin on the weekend Drill Sergeant Smith wasn't on duty. When he came up, we drove to an empty parking lot and talked until it was time for me to check in. He brought me a bottle of Alizé so I could at least party in the room with my roommates. We were so in love and hadn't even had sex yet. I loved the fact our relationship wasn't based on sex like all the others. We made plans for him to move to California with me after I graduated AIT and even talked about getting married.

When I finally got my weekend pass back, we checked into the hotel at the Ritz-Carlton in Pentagon City. He brought my favorite candy, Twizzlers, and some red roses that he spread all over the bed. He popped in the CD "Tonight" by Silk, and we sat in a warm bubble bath talking and giggling all night until our fingers started to look like little ball sacks. We kissed our way onto the bed, where he laid me down on my back and started kissing me all over my body. He kissed his way down to my nipples, then back up to my lips. He rubbed his dick against my pussy until it got nice and wet. Five minutes later he moaned, "Oh shit, I'm about to come … Sorry, it's been a while. Just give me a second, and I'll be ready again," he rested his head my chest, and I stroked the waves on his head.

A few minutes later, he kissed me until his dick became hard enough to finish the job. We made love that whole weekend and every weekend after that until it was time for me to graduate.

The last week of AIT, Drill Sergeant Smith called me into his office said sternly, "Shut the door." I thought for sure I was in trouble again and prepared myself to be smoked. "You're about to graduate in a few days, and I know you probably thought I've been harder on you than anyone else here, and I have been, but there is a reason for that." He cleared his throat like he was starting to get choked up.

"When you first came here, I saw this hardheaded rebellious kid who was constantly getting into trouble, and to be quite honest, I didn't think you were going to make it. But I also saw something special in you, and I knew you just needed some tough love and guidance. You remind me so much of my own daughter, and I want nothing but the best for you." Tears filled my eyes as I watched him fight back his own. "Over these last few months, I've watched you grow from this troubled little girl into a beautiful young lady, and I'm so proud of you. After you graduate, I want you to go out there and make something out of yourself. You have the potential to be anything you want. AND STAY YOUR ASS OUT OF TROUBLE!"

We both laughed, and he gave me a hard hug, then told me to drop and give him twenty. I initially joined the military to run away from my problems, but it ended up changing my life instead. It taught me discipline and gave me a sense of accomplishment. Before we got there, I used to wear so much makeup, trying to cover up who I really was, but since we weren't allowed to wear any, it forced me to take a good look at myself without the mask on. Now I barely wore any, even when I was allowed to, and I had more confidence in myself than I ever had. I was finally starting to love the person I was becoming.

ONCE GRADUATION WAS OVER, I FLEW back to Cali and stayed with Tisha and Ms. Bates again, but they were planning to move to Vegas since the cost of living was cheaper and was starting to pack everything up in boxes. So I decided to move in with Keri. She was the main one that wrote me when I was in boot camp and AIT. She even taught me how to drive and took me to get my driver's license. Romeo had his place, but once he heard I was back in town, it didn't take long for him to pop up. It felt good to see him, but I quickly made it known that I was in a relationship with Kevin and how he planned to move down as soon as I got a job and a place stay for us. He said he was happy for me and was okay with us just being friends, so we always kicked it. He even told me about some of the girls he was dating.

After a few weeks of job searching, I began to feel discouraged. I thought by being in the Amy Reserves, I would easily be able to find an office job or something, but they all required prior experience, which I didn't have. I couldn't even get a job at Walmart because I had no experience and refused to go back to working fast food again.

I had just returned from another lousy job interview and told Romeo how I felt and how I needed to hurry up and make some money fast before I went through all of my savings. "Why don't you dance? One of my homegirls works at Déjà vu in Redlands, and I know she can get you a job there," he said.

"Dance? Like as in stripping? Hell no. I'm not even a good dancer. I would look hella stupid up there. Plus, I have stage fright," I said.

"What, please, you don't even need to know how to dance like that. All you need is a sexy body and a pretty face, which you got, and you can make easy money. My homegirl make over a thousand a week."

"Wow, really?" I said.

"Yeah, and you can work during the day when it's less competition, so you don't have to worry about being up there in front of so many people." He smiled like he was picturing me up there.

"I don't know," I said. "Well, how about I take you up there, and we can just check it out. If you don't like it, then we can leave."

"Okay!" I replied.

That same day we went up there. Inside was a dark room with sexy red lighting. A cute Asian chick was dancing on the pole. She had no breast or ass and couldn't dance at all, but guys were still throwing money at her, so I knew I could at least do better than her. The owner came out, looked me up and down, then asked when I wanted to start. I hesitated, so he told me before I answered I could take a look around and talk to some of the girls. He signaled to one of them to come over.

Her name was Candy, and she took me to the back and introduced me to the others while Romeo sat by the stage. Everyone there seemed so nice and looked like they were having fun. Candy told me how nervous she was her first time, but after a couple of shots and dances, it got easier. Some of the others chimed in and confirmed how it got easier the more you did it. She also explained that many of the guys were retired or on their lunch breaks or just passing through town, and it was easy money, unlike the nights where it was a lot more girls, and most of them had regulars. I went back out to the front and told the owner I'd start the next day.

"Great, let's go to my office and fill out some paperwork. You can make your own hours and came in when you want. All you need to do is pick out a name," he said. My favorite car at the time was a Mercedes, so that's what I chose.

I was so nervous on the first day that I had to drink a few shots before I could get enough courage to get up there. The crowd was mostly older White men, and I could tell they didn't want to hear any rap or R&B, so I told the DJ to put on "Sweet Emotions" by Aerosmith. Going to a mostly all-White elementary school, I listened to a lot of rock & roll and alternative music, so I knew a lot of great songs that I could dance to. Plus, people used to say I danced like a White girl, so I fit in perfectly as I flipped my hair and rolled around on the stage. I could tell I wasn't doing too bad because a couple of the men who were sitting in the back got up and moved to the front.

"Open up those legs," one of the men yelled out.

"Come on, baby, take it off," another one said.

I unsnapped my bra but covered up my chest with my hand.

"Let us see," another guy chanted.

The crowd grew anxious as I finally revealed myself. *Okay, that's not so bad*, I thought. When I got up there, I thought I would feel humiliated and want to cry, but in a way, I felt sexy and desirable, and just like Candy said, after a couple of dances, I got used to it. When I walked off stage, one of the old White guys grabbed me by my hand and said, "Well, aren't you a pretty little thing. Can I get a lap dance?" The thought of me dancing on this old-ass man made me sick to my stomach, and I wanted to throw up all over his face.

"Sure!" I smiled, then pretended he was some rich celebrity that used to be hot back in the day.

After I finished my first lap dance, I made my way around the room and did a few more. By the end of the day, I walked out of there with almost four hundred dollars, and within the first month I had over three thousand saved up just working three days a week during the day.

I kept all my money in a jar and hid it under the bed in Romeo's old bedroom, where I was sleeping. I had just got home from shopping when I noticed eight hundred dollars was missing. I called Romeo and was screaming at him to give me back my money since I knew he was the only one that would take it. He came over and showed me the new stereo system he had bought with my money and said if it weren't for him getting me the job, I wouldn't have all this money, so I owed him at least that.

I was pissed he'd stolen it instead of just asking me, but he was right, I wouldn't have all this money if it wasn't for him, so eventually I let it go and just decided to put all my money in the bank. On the days I wasn't working, I still went on job interviews searching for an office job because I knew there was no way this church boy would be okay with me stripping. I never told Kevin I was dancing and lied to him about where I was working.

I'm not going to lie, though, part of me enjoyed dancing. I had always been this shy and insecure person but being on stage gave me this confidence I never knew I had. During the day shift there wasn't any drama like you see in the movies. Yeah, there may have been some jealously here and there, but we all had this sort of sisterly bond between us that no one else could understand unless you worked there.

A lot of them were working there to pay for college or were single moms who would do anything to provide for their kids. It's funny, because I had always assumed that strippers would fuck anyone for money, but I knew a few of the girls, including me, that never fucked with anyone at the club or had boyfriends that they were very loyal to. Working there really changed my perspective about strippers. I didn't look at them as just objects; these were women who were just trying to survive, and I respected them their hustle.

Now don't get me wrong; there are some gold-diggers that would fuck anything for money, but no little girl ever thinks *When I grow up, I want to be a stripper or a prostitute.* Nine out of ten times something happened to them that made them think their bodies were no longer worth cherishing. Even though I had always gotten so many compliments my whole life, I had the lowest self-esteem and never knew my worth. I'm not trying to glorify stripping or prostitution, but it just seems like the world is so focused on what they're doing instead of why they are doing it, and no one ever faults the men for their contributing factor in all this.

Halfway through my second month, I had just finished my shift and was packing up my things. I had worked later than usual since I had a job interview that afternoon. As I was leaving, the night shift was coming in. One of the girls smacked me on my ass as I bent over to grab my things.

"Hey, new booty. I haven't seen you here before. When did you start?" she asked with her almond-shaped green eyes and cocoa brown skin. She looked Brazilian and was so mesmerizing. I couldn't stop staring at her eyes.

"About almost three months ago, but I only work a couple of days a week during the day," I answered.

"Why are you working days? With that face and that booty, you could be making a killing at night." She sat across from me, opening her legs up, placing one of them up on the counter, exposing her phat pussy lips that was coming out of her shorts.

"I know, but I'm not the best dancer and don't even know how to swing on the pole like that."

"Oh, that shit is easy. Come with me, I'll teach you." She grabbed my hand, took me to the back room and showed me a few tricks, and she was right. It was pretty easy. She said I should practice after my shifts and come back on Tuesday for amateur night. I was very hesitant, and my palms were sweating at the mere thought of it, but she was so convincing, and eventually I agreed. I was a little curious about the night shift and wanted to see if it was really like everyone said it was.

I arrived on Tuesday as promised, and immediately felt like a small fish in a tank full of sharks. Some of these women were no joke. Like Sapphire, who could stop everyone in their tracks the moment she set foot on stage. "I don't think I can do this, and liquor isn't helping this time," I said to Jasmine.

"Follow me," she said, grabbing my hand and taking me into one of the bathroom stalls. "Here, sniff this," she said, putting some white powder on her hand.

"What is that?" I asked.

"Speed. It's going to make you feel so sexy and confident. You'll go up there and kill it. Trust me, I use it all the time, and you can't even tell."

She was right. I couldn't tell at all she was on anything, so I sniffed it and instantly felt a high like never before. It was like I was drunk but alert at the same time. Like I was aware of everything I was doing but didn't give a shit about what anyone thought. The DJ called out for all the amateurs to come to the stage, and I felt ready. I had him play "It's All About Me," by Mya. I could see Sapphire and some others around her start to giggle as I came out wearing a lime green see-thru dress with a matching thong.

I started off slow walking around the pole, leaned back, closed my eyes and took a deep breath like I was inhaling the spirit of my alter ego. When I opened my eyes, I imagined that there was only one guy in the room I was dancing for. I chose the guy Sapphire was sitting next too, which was one of her biggest clients. I never took my big brown eyes off him as I crawled seductively across the stage.

I stood up, grabbed the pole, and did the upside-down flip that Jasmine had taught me. It was my first time doing this in front of an audience, but I wasn't even nervous. Money was flying in from everywhere. I swung my hips from side to side and stroked the pole like it was his dick. He bit his bottom lip, and I licked mine. I could see Sapphire getting agitated as she snatched her hand from his.

I took off my dress and waved it around my head with one hand and with the other I held on to the pole as I slowly squatted down. I lay on my back with my legs straight in the air, shaking my ass while I pulled my panties off. I stood up and slingshotted my thong to his table. He picked it up and placed it in his suit pocket. I blew him a kiss and did my last flip around the pole. Sapphire got up and stormed over to the bar.

"Give it up for Mercedes. She's one of our newest girls," he shouted, and the crowd cheered as I got off stage and went to the back to change into a new outfit where I was greeted by Jasmine.

"Oh my God, you were so amazing. Everyone keeps calling you Mya," she laughed. "See, I told you, you would kill it. Hurry up and get dressed so we can make this money. There's a guy out there who wants to meet you and he's never tipped anyone besides Sapphire." She pulled me over to the guy I had been dancing for on stage. He was a well-dressed nice-looking White lawyer. He introduced himself and said he'd been coming here for a while but never wanted a private lap dance from anyone else until now. We went in the back, and I gave him a couple lap dances. It was rare that I got to dance for a nice-looking man, so I enjoyed every moment of it. He told me he had an early business meeting and had to leave but wanted to see me again. He handed me five hundred dollars that was wrapped around his business card. I smiled told him I would be back tomorrow night.

When we finished, Jasmine grabbed me and told me this other old guy wanted the both of us. It was a mixed crowd, and the nights had a lot more Black guys around my age, but Jasmine told me the young ones never wanted to spend any money. All they wanted to do was try to fuck for free, and we needed to stay where the money was at.

We went into the private room together and started dancing for this older Black guy. I was a little caught off guard when she came from behind and started rubbing on my breast. I went to move away, but she pulled me back and whispered in my ear, "Just relax and go with it. This is what he wants, and he's paying us double for it, so don't fuck it up." She continued to grab my breast, then took off my dress and turned me around and started kissing on my neck down to my nipples. She grabbed my hands and placed them on her breasts, and I did the same thing to her. Then we started kissing. This was the first time I'd ever kissed a girl with tongue. She then sat me down on his lap, where he began to rub on my breast as she pulled my panties off and started eating me out until his time was up. I was extremely high and drunk. My body was so numb like I was given an epidural. I couldn't even feel her down there.

After that we worked our way around the room, and I ended the night with over a thousand dollars. Since I didn't get off until late, Romeo agreed to pick me up. I was so horny and hopped on him as soon as I got in the car. I started kissing all over him and sucked his dick until we got back to his place. While we were having sex, I was telling him how much I missed and loved him and wanted us to be back together.

The next morning, I woke up feeling so sick like I had the flu. I had forgotten everything I had told him until he reminded me of it over breakfast in bed. He said was so happy that we were back together. I didn't know how to break it to him that I only said all of that because I was drunk and high on drugs. I felt so guilty for cheating on Kevin. I started to feel like I was losing control and getting sucked back into life I fought so hard to get out of. Jasmine was blowing up my phone, but I ignored her calls and called out sick for the rest of that week.

Romeo came over his mom's house every day to check on me. He would bring me food and rub my hair like he used to when we were together. The more he took care of me the harder it was to tell him the truth. I was still in love with Kevin and wanted to be with him.

"I wanna take you somewhere on Friday but it's a surprise," he said. I was sick for over week but was starting to feel a lot better and thought Friday would be perfect time to break the news. Friday came, and he picked me up and took me out to an elegant dinner. We laughed, talked, and ate some amazing food. It was such a nice place that I decided to tell him once we got back in the car. Plus, I didn't want to embarrass him in front of all these people. I figured since we were having such a good time it would make things a lot easier.

I could tell he was starting to get anxious about something but thought maybe it was just me being paranoid. When the waiter came over, I assumed he was bringing the check but instead he placed a slice of cake in front of me with the words "Will You Marry Me?" written out in chocolate. When I looked up, Romeo was down on one knee, holding out a black box with a small diamond ring in it. I knew I wasn't going to marry him, but there was a crowd, and I couldn't break his heart like that, so I said yes when he asked, and we kissed as people cheered around us.

When we pulled into the parking lot of his mom's house, he smiled, giving me a big kiss and calling me his future wife. I felt like shit. Like I was about to take a knife and stab it into his heart.

"Umm, yeah about that!" I said. "I'm sorry, Romeo, but I can't marry you." I put my head down.

"What do you mean? You just said yes!"

"I know, but I didn't want to say no and embarrass you in front of all those people. The truth is … I still want to be with Kevin, and we're still together."

"What about all that shit you told me last week?" he asked.

"Honestly, I didn't remember telling you all of that until you told me. I was so drunk and high that night. Jasmine gave me some speed so I would be able to go on stage and I did and said a lot of things that I didn't mean."

"So you just gonna play me like that after everything we been through? How you going to choose this guy over me? We've known each other for years and you've only known this guy for a few months."

"I know. I'm so sorry. I never meant to hurt you and still want us to be friends." I reached over and grabbed his hand, but he snatched it away. I handed him the ring back as I got out of the car and went back to his mom's house.

A couple days later, I called Kevin like I usually did every night, but this time I could tell something was off the moment he answered. "What's wrong?" I asked.

"Have you been stripping?" he replied.

It felt like the wind had just gotten knocked out of me, and the only response I could say was, "Huh?"

"You heard me. Have you been stripping?"

"Yeah, but I was only doing it for us so I could hurry up and get a car and a place so you could move down. I've been trying to get an office job since I moved down here, but no one is hiring. I'm so sorry. I know I should have told you, but I didn't want you to look at me differently," I cried.

"Did you have sex with your ex?" he said.

"No, why would you think that?"

"Because he called and told me you were. He also said you were living together and that he's been taking you to the strip club every day and that you told him y'all were getting back together."

"Noooo, he's lying. I've been staying with his mom because my second family is moving to Vegas, and she's like a mom to me. I still haven't even talked to my real mom in almost a year, so his mom all I have. And yes, he's taken me to work when I couldn't find a ride, but that's it. I never had sex with him, and he's only telling you this because he wants to be with me, but I told him I wanted to be with you. I mean, how else do you think he knew about you? I told him everything, and he was pretending to be my friend so he could break us up. You have to believe me. I love you and only want to be with you," I pleaded. I felt bad for lying but I didn't want to lose him.

There was a long pause and a deep breath. I thought he was going to say it was over and hang up, but instead he said, "Well, I'm not moving to California anymore. Sounds like there's just too much drama out there, and I don't wanna be caught up in anything, so if you want to be with me, then you're going to have to move to Maryland." At this point, I was sick of Cali, and since I loved DC, I agreed to move back and bought a one-way plane ticket.

Keri was visibly upset when I broke the news to her. When Romeo found out I was moving and that his plan to break us up backfired, he immediately came over while I was in the middle of packing.

"So did she tell you the truth on why she's really moving to Maryland?" he asked his mom.

"Romeo, what are you talking about?" Keri said.

"Mom, she's been lying to everyone. She's not this sweet innocent girl you think she is. I know you always say I'm the bad influence on her, but she's the one that's been playing everyone. She's telling me she wants to be with me then telling this other guy the same thing. And she's not a receptionist like she told you she was. She has been stripping."

They both looked at me. "Angie, what is he talking about? Is that true?" she asked.

"He's the one that took me up there to get the job in the first place," I said.

"Yeah, after you asked me to," he replied.

"So is this true? Have you been stripping?"

"Yes, but Romeo is the one that got me to strip. He's twisting everything around."

"Wow, I'm so disappointed in you. I can't believe you would lie to me like this and then try to blame Romeo for it." I tried to explain my side, but it just led into a heated argument, so I called Laneshia to come to pick me up and the next day they dropped me off at the airport. I understood why Keri was disappointed, but I couldn't believe she'd turned on me just like all the others. And once again, I felt like I'd lost another mother.

I LANDED AT DULLES AIRPORT AND WAS back in a chocolate city. All my sadness seemed to disappear the moment I saw Kevin. We were so excited to see each other we kissed and embraced like it was our first time again. He took me to his mom's three-bedroom condo where he was living there in Beltsville. His older brother Dwight had moved out when he started dating this girl named Havana, who had moved down from New Jersey to be with him. She was an Afro-Latina like me but with dark brown skin, and a big Brazilian ass. She had a daughter from a prior relationship and another daughter by Dwight. Since she and I had both moved down to be with these brothers and had no other family, we hit it off and instantly became like sisters.

They were a very Christian family and attended First Baptist of Glenarden with Pastor John Jenkins Sr. every Sunday. I was very skeptical about going back to church since I had lost my faith after meeting Kovas, but once I heard Pastor Jenkins preach for the first time, I was blown away. He was so funny and captivating. It was like being at a Christian comedy club. I didn't know pastors could even be this funny. Even though he was very entertaining, he also had deep messages that would bring tears to my eyes every time he preached the word.

I'll never forget the day I stood up and got saved for the first time. He told everyone to turn to Proverbs 24:16 and read, *"For though the righteous fall seven times, they rise again, but the wicked stumble when calamity strikes."* He started preaching that no matter what you have done or how many mistakes you've made, it's never too late to turn your life around. God's love for us is everlasting, and he's just waiting on us to confess our sins to him with an open heart. All we need to say is, *Lord, have mercy and forgive me*, and just like that, you're forgiven. Then the choir started singing, "We All Fall Down" by Donnie McClurkin. Then Pastor Jenkins asked for anyone who wanted to be saved to come up to the front and confess their sins.

I looked up at Kevin with tears pouring down my face. I let go of his hand, and then started walking toward the front. I fell to my knees, threw my hands in the air, and cried for God to forgive me for all my sins and for ever doubting his love for me. I cried and cried until I had no more tears left to cry. I felt God's mercy consume my body. When I stood back up, I felt as if I had left my old self down there on the floor, and I came up a reborn woman.

After church, we went to our favorite restaurant called Jasper's, that had the best stuffed shrimp with crab that I'd ever had. I could tell Kevin had something on his mind because he was quiet the whole car ride there. When we sat down to eat, and I asked him what was wrong.

"Nothing, just thinking a lot about what the pastor has been saying lately. Especially that we shouldn't be living together before marriage."

"So what are you saying? You don't want to live together anymore?" I asked.

"No, what I'm saying is I think we should get married." He smiled.

"Are you serious?" I asked.

"Yes, I'm serious. So will you marry me?" he grabbed my hand and asked.

"Yes, of course!" I shouted, jumping up to hug him and giving him a big kiss. His mom was so happy to hear that and gave us both a hug.

The next day he told his brother Dwight the news, but he didn't seem pleased about it at all and even made a comment about us rushing things. He then asked to see my ring, knowing I didn't have one yet. Kevin told him he was saving to get me one. Dwight just laughed at him and said we weren't ready for marriage.

Kevin and Dwight were very competitive toward each other and always had to try to outdo one another. A couple of weeks later, Dwight proposed to Havana, and she came over, showing off her brand-new ring. I was happy for them, but I could tell Kevin was pissed, and he ended up borrowing some money from his mom to get me a bigger ring than hers.

After months of being out there, I got my first real job as an assistant manager for a printing company, which I got because I had printing experience from AIT. *Finally, the military was starting to pay off,* I thought. I also bought my first car, a blue Chrysler LeBaron convertible, and loved it. Everything seemed to be falling into place until Kevin crashed my car a couple of months later, and I was stuck driving an old Ford Focus, but I didn't care. I was so happy to finally have my own car and a job where I wasn't flipping burgers or taking off my clothes.

My boss was from India and treated me more like family than his employee. I would occasionally eat dinner at his house with him, his wife and two sons. And he would bring me back souvenirs when they went to India. I loved learning about their culture and was astonished when I found out they still had arranged marriages.

Kevin would always get jealous over the littlest things but was nowhere near as crazy as Kovas, so I thought his jealous ways were cute at first. Like the time he got mad and called off our engagement because I said "Damn" when I saw Mel Jackson in Soul Food. Or the time he picked a fight just because I wanted to hang out with a girl from work. He said now that we were getting married, we were becoming one, and we should no longer be doing things separately, which meant no hanging out with friends unless we did it together. I believed him and thought that's what you're supposed to do to have a healthy marriage, so at first, I didn't mind doing everything together, especially after we got married on August 21, 2000, exactly one year from the day we first met.

We didn't know we needed a marriage license in Maryland, so we had to drive all the way to Virginia to get married in a small courthouse just so we could get married on the day we wanted. I still wasn't speaking to anyone in my family except my brother Chris, and my family in Vegas, so the only one that came to the wedding was Kevin's mom. Dwight said he had to work and couldn't get off, but I know it was only because they were still mad at each other over the engagements. We didn't have a lot of money, so we just took a dinner cruise around the Potomac River for our honeymoon, but I didn't care. I was so happy and in love.

Not too long after we got married, Havana and Dwight also got married, and the brothers started to get along again. We always hung out together, and our marriage was off to a great start. We were always traveling and doing new things together like horseback riding, sky diving, swimming with dolphins, and a helicopter ride over New York.

Word must have gotten to back to my mom that I had gotten married because I received a surprising package from her filled with wedding gifts. She sent dishes, candles, a picture frame, and a check for a hundred dollars with a wedding card signed *Love, Mom.* I was so happy to hear from her and immediately called to thank her. We hadn't spoken in almost two years, so things were a little awkward at first, but I could tell she missed me just as much as I did her.

While speaking to my mom, I realized she had turned her life around too. She was going to church and even started doing a lot of volunteer work and was donating to children in Africa. She also said Kovas had stopped by almost a year ago looking for me, but she told him I had joined the military and was stationed somewhere out of state. After that, she'd never seen him again.

We never spoke about the past and swept everything under the rug. I didn't want to bring it up and make this awkward conversation even more awkward. Our family was not the best at apologies, but I could tell by the way she was talking that she was sorry for everything she had said and done. Especially after she told me she loved me for the first-time. I knew it would still take some time, but we were finally on the right path of healing our relationship.

After we hung up, I was so inspired by my mom that I decided to start volunteering at a homeless shelter in Baltimore. I was there for almost a year, which was funny because at first, they all thought I was doing it for community service. I even called and apologized to Keri for lying to her and we were back on speaking terms. I just wish I had done the same to Romeo for hurting him, but sadly he died in a car accident while I was in the middle of writing this book, so I never got that chance. But I hope he knows how truly sorry I am for hurting him and will always love him for the significant role he played in my life.

On my twenty-first birthday, Kevin surprised me with a Himalayan kitten that I named Coco. It was the cat I'd always wanted since I was a little girl and watched the movie "Homeward Bound." When I was told I couldn't have kids, I was initially devastated because I thought that's what life was all about, getting married and having kids. But as I got older, I realized it was a blessing in disguise and that I didn't even want to have kids. Kids can be a blessing, but they can also be a nightmare, and I didn't want to go through the same things my mother and I went through.

Plus, I knew if I ever changed my mind about wanting kids, there were so many in foster care that needed homes. I also saw how kids changed so many relationships. It seemed like men would always cheat on their women when they were pregnant. And my biggest fear was being a single mom or staying in an unhappy relationship just for the kids. When I first told Kevin all this, he was even happier to get married because he didn't want kids either. He had a shitty relationship with his father and was such a mama's boy that he wasn't interested in the responsibility of taking care of a baby.

Part of my job at the printing company was to deliver printing supplies to various companies. One of the businesses I delivered to was an HOA management company. Every time I went in there, the people were always so nice to me, and I wished I could work there. It would be the perfect office job I'd always wanted. After delivering to them for almost a year, my prayers were answered when one of the administrators told me the administrative assistant was leaving, and she could talk to the owner about hiring me since they all knew and loved me. My eyes got so big like I nominated for an award. "Oh my God, yes! That would be sooo amazing," I shouted.

She told me to wait, and then went to the back of the office. A few minutes later, she came out with the owner. He told me he had heard so many great things about me and if I wanted the job, it was mine. I was so surprised it happened that quickly and immediately said yes. He then said he didn't want to ruin his printing relationship with my boss and told me he would call and speak to him himself.

By the time I got back to the office, I could tell by the hurt in his eyes that he had already heard the news. He tried to offer more money to stay, but I told him it wasn't just about the money. I had always wanted an office job, and now this was my chance. Two weeks later, I started my new position at the front desk, and within a year, I had worked my up to becoming a community accountant. The owner even paid for me to take accounting courses. I couldn't believe I was actually going to college.

I finally had everything I'd ever wanted. I was happily married with my fur baby and a job I was proud to have. I was even speaking to my whole family again and started to have a great relationship with my mother. Had I written this book back in my twenties, I would have thought this would have been my happily ever after, but life is not a fairytale. We don't have happy endings. We have happy moments, sad moments, blessings, struggles, and tribulations. Then the whole shit starts all over again.

SOMETHING THAT WOULD HAVE BEEN A blessing to most married couples turned out to be the beginning of our downfall. Whenever Kevin and I made love, I would always cum first and then him, but never at the same time except this once. I remember this moment because we had never cum at the same time before, and when it happened, it felt like this burst of energy was flowing throughout my body, almost like our souls were intertwining, and a miracle was being created.

About a month later, I was at the gas station, and the smell of the gasoline started to make me sick. It seemed like my sense of smell began to heighten, and all of the scents that I once loved were beginning to make me feel nauseous. I told this to one of my coworkers, and she suggested I take a pregnancy test, but I explained to her that it was impossible for me to have kids and there was no way I was pregnant. But after I threw up during lunch, she insisted and bought me one anyway.

"Fine, I'll take it, but I know I'm not pregnant," I told her as I went into the bathroom and peed on the white stick. I started to pace back in forth in the bathroom, anxious to see the results. When I looked down, there were two pink lines. I grabbed the back on the box and read two pink lines means you're pregnant. *No fuckin' way*, I thought. How could this be? I came out of the bathroom, looking like I had seen a ghost.

"Sooooo, what did it say?" she asked.

"It says I'm pregnant," I said.

I sat at my desk all day thinking about how I was going to tell Kevin. Our life had been going so great, and we were saving up to get our place. I knew having a baby would mess up our plans, and he would be mad about it. When I got home, I waited for him on the couch. He could immediately sense I had something to tell him. I put my head down and showed him the pregnancy test.

"How are you pregnant? I thought you couldn't have kids!" he said.

"Yeah, I know. I didn't think so either."

"So were you lying about it?" he asked.

"Nooo, I wasn't lying about it. I told you I had an infection when I was younger, and that's what the doctors told me. I'm just as shocked as you are."

"FUCK!" he said, punching the wall. I knew he was going to be mad, but I didn't think he was going to be this mad. I was starting to see a whole other side of him that I had never seen before.

We had several arguments about it, and I became so stressed and sick that I couldn't keep anything down. The only person that seemed to be happy about it was my mother. She was so excited to be a grandmother that she wanted to fly out right away, but I told her now wouldn't be the best time.

I called and made a doctor's appointment, but they wanted me to wait a few more weeks before coming in. In the meantime, my mom had mailed me a book on what to expect during my pregnancy.

Kevin and I weren't talking, and he even slept in the third bedroom. I felt like my biggest fear of becoming a single mother was already starting to come true. Don't get me wrong, I have nothing but respect for single parents, but I watched how hard my mother struggled to raise us and how the effects of her working so much affected me and my brothers. I just didn't want to go through all of that. Luckily, Pastor Jenkins gave one of his amazing sermons on Ephesians 5:25, which read, "For husbands, this means love your wives, just as Christ loved the church and gave himself up for her." This must have hit hard because Kevin began to have a change of heart.

After church, he apologized for the way he had been treating me since I told him I was pregnant and said he would be more supportive. He even told his mom and brother about it, who were even more excited about it than my mom was. Soon everyone knew and were even starting to pick out some names.

I still had mixed feelings. On the one hand, I was married and in a good situation to bring a child into this world, but on the other hand, I was so scared that this was going to change everything. I didn't want anything to change. Plus, I wasn't just having morning sickness. I was having all day and all-night sickness. Everything made me sick. I hated being pregnant and didn't understand why women wanted to go through all of this.

I was now in my second month and getting ready to head to my first doctor's appointment. Since the doctor's office was walking distance from my job, I went in alone without Kevin. The doctor came out in a very cheerful mood and seemed happier about it than I was as she placed the gel over my stomach for the ultrasound. I could tell immediately something was wrong the moment she looked at the monitor, and her smile turned into a look of concern.

"Do you see this oval shape right here?" she asked.

"Yes," I responded.

"Well, this is the amniotic sac where the baby should be. However, it's empty."

"So what does that mean? I wasn't pregnant?"

"No, you were pregnant. However, you are in the beginning stages of a miscarriage, and it should be passing through within the next couple of days. I'm so sorry."

Everything she said after that seemed to go in one ear and out the other. Then she left me in the room to get dressed and handed me some information on what to expect during a miscarriage on my way out. I felt numb, like this was a bad dream. When I was headed toward the lobby, I saw a little girl sitting with her pregnant mom, and reality hit. I burst out in tears. One of the nurses came over and asked me if I was okay. "Yeah, yeah, I'm fine," I said as I rushed past her to my car where I sat and cried for the remainder of my lunch break.

I didn't understand why I was so upset. I didn't even want to have the baby, so you would think I would be happy to find out I was losing it, but I couldn't help feeling like I had just lost a part of me. After a few moments, I pulled myself together and went back to work. I sat there at my desk, thinking again about how I would break the news to Kevin.

When I got home, I told Kevin and he seemed more upset that he had told his family and friends we were having a baby than he was about losing it or about how I was feeling. The next morning, I woke up with the sharpest pain in my stomach. When I pulled back the covers, there was a pool of blood in the middle of the bed. I screamed out to Kevin, who was in the bathroom, getting ready for work.

As soon as he ran in and saw all the blood, he looked like he was about to pass out. "Okay, okay, let's get you cleaned up and to the hospital," he said, grabbing my hands and helping me into the shower, where a big blood sac came out. It was so big it wouldn't go fit down the drain and I had to pick it up and flush it down the toilet. I felt like I was flushing away my child and it was so painful to watch. Once the blood stopped, I got out, and we headed to the hospital. When we got there, they admitted me into surgery and performed a D&C.

Once I came to, the doctor explained to us that even though I had scar tissue on my uterus from the infection that I could still get pregnant. It just might take a little help to get the eggs to stick to the walls, but with all the technology they now have we shouldn't be discouraged. However, once he said that the first thing, I asked about was how I could get on birth control. There was no way I wanted to go through that shit again. Within hours, I was out, and we were on our way back home. The next day I went to work like nothing ever happened. My manager tried to convince me to go home, but I felt better at work than being at home thinking about it.

After seeing how Kevin handled things when I got pregnant and not being there for me after I lost it, I started to look at him completely different, and everything seemed to start going downhill from that point on. Kevin's controlling ways got worse and worse, and I was starting to feel suffocated. Things came to a boil when he wanted me to stop being friends with Havana after she and Dwight had separated due to him cheating. He felt that since they were no longer together, there was no reason we should continue hanging out with her even though she was the mother of his niece and about to give birth to his nephew.

She had made me the godmother and wanted me to be there in delivery room with her, but Kevin had forbidden me to go. Whenever Kevin would tell me to do something that I didn't want to do, he would threaten to kick me out, and I would eventually cave in because I was so scared of being on the streets again and not having anywhere to go.

But this was something I wasn't going to budge on. I was sitting on the bed and told him I was going no matter what.

He started threatening me again with his favorite phrase, "Well, if you don't like it, then you can just move out."

But this time, I replied, "I don't care, I'm going to the hospital whether you like it or not." I had this *I don't give a fuck* smirk on my face, which infuriated him even more. He reached over and grabbed my legs and dragged me off the bed, causing me to hit my head hard on the ground. This was the first time he had ever put his hands on me, and all those old memories of Kovas came rushing back. I lost it. I jumped up and started throwing things at him and hitting him until his mom came out and broke it up.

Somehow the cops got called, and when they came, they explained to us that we both could end up in jail over what happened, and it was better we just let things cool off and work it out. With all the drama that went on, I ended up missing the birth of my godnephew. Havana was so mad at me, and I couldn't blame her, but I promised her that I would never let that happen again, and after she heard everything that had happened, she forgave me.

We didn't speak for over a week, and he slept in the third bedroom again. He must have gotten horny or something because he finally came into the room and apologized, which was a rare thing for him to do. For a while, things were good again, and he even let me go to Havana's house on the weekends to help out with the baby without causing any issues until I told him I was going to her birthday party.

I was driving us to his brother's house to watch the fight when I told him. He started saying he didn't want me to go because there would be drinking and probably guys there since she was dating again. I tried to explain to him it wouldn't be like that, but he wasn't hearing any of it and started talking his old shit again. I told him since I had missed my godnephew's birth, there was no way I was going to miss her birthday party. He got so mad when I said that he grabbed the steering wheel and yanked it while I was still driving, and we ended up running up on the curb in the center divider.

I pushed his hand off the wheel and yelled, "What the fuck are you trying to do, kill us?" He pushed me back, and we began fist fighting.

A man saw this happening, rushed over, grabbed him out of the car, and threw him on the ground. "What are you doing hitting a woman like that?" he said. The guy then asked me if I was okay and if wanted him to call the police, but I said no, thanked him, and sped off, leaving Kevin there in the middle of the street.

I was so mad when I got home, I packed up all my things and left not knowing where I was going to go. I didn't want to call Havana even though I knew I could stay there because she was living in a tiny three-bedroom apartment with three kids plus her brother and she was always complaining about how crowded it was, so I didn't want to add to her stress especially with a new baby.

I called one of my coworkers instead and asked her if I could stay at her house. When she told me no, I realized I had nowhere to go and felt like I was a kid all over again. I ended up staying in a hotel that night with my cat Coco and cried myself to sleep.

I woke up the next morning and decided I would no longer depend on him or anyone else ever again. I checked out and went back home and acted like I had forgotten something but was hoping he would beg me to stay so I could have enough time to figure things out. When I got there, he came out of the bedroom and did exactly what I thought he would do, beg for my forgiveness. I was trying so hard to be mad but couldn't help but to laugh when I saw the black eye on his face that he had tried to cover up with his mom's makeup.

"I know, I know I deserve this, and I feel so stupid how I lost my temper like that," he said. He thought I'd stayed the night at Havana's, which I let him believe because I didn't want him knowing I had nowhere to go and try to use that against me later. I told him I forgave him, but my mind was made up. I wanted to move out and get my own place. I just needed to save some more money to do it.

That's when I ended up getting a part-time job at CitiFinancial doing collections. At the HOA company, I was the only Black woman that worked in the office, and the rest were older White women, but at CitiFinancial, it was mostly Black, and a lot of people were around my age.

After orientation, we were assigned someone to train us on phones. The guy that was assigned to train me was named Darryl. He was a very attractive guy who looked just like TI. I could tell a lot the girls in the office had crushes on him by the way they would walk by and flirt with him, but he always blew them off because he had a girlfriend. Since I was married and only there to focus on saving money, we instantly became friends. Instead of training me like he was supposed to, we would talk and joke around most of the time. It felt so good to finally have a friend I could talk to and laugh with.

Over the next couple of months, our friendship grew stronger and stronger. All the girls were jealous because we were so close, and they thought something was going on between us, but there wasn't. He reminded me of my little brother since I was four years older than him. He told me how he and his best friend Rick would always ride dirt bikes and said they would teach me if I wanted to learn.

I grew up being the only girl in my family. I had two younger brothers, two male cousins, a godbrother and two uncles. The only women were my mom, grandmother and my grandmother's sister. I was more of a tomboy, than a girly girl. I hated shopping, or getting my nails and hair done so when he told me about riding dirt bikes I jumped at the chance. Saturdays were always half days, and they were closed on Sundays. But I lied and told Kevin they'd started being full days and was now open on Sundays just so I could meet up with Rick and Darryl.

The first time I tried to ride, I crashed into a bush and damn near broke my leg, but eventually I got the hang of it and was able to ride alongside them. They even surprised me by getting me my own dirt bike. We were as thick as thieves, riding and doing everything together.

"She wasn't the type of rider who waited for sunny days. She rode regardless of the rain. She knew that was the only way you could see the rainbow." – Black Butterfly

NOW THAT I HAD MY SECRET FRIENDS and a lot of money saved up, Kevin and I actually started getting along better. I didn't feel as smothered or controlled as I did before, so I decided to give our marriage another shot. We decided to celebrate our fifth-year anniversary in Hawaii. We even bought brand new wedding bands to get a fresh start.

We flew into Honolulu and were greeted by beautiful Hawaiian women who placed colorful leis around our necks as soon as we stepped off the plane. We learned to surf, went scuba diving, swam with sharks in a cage that in the middle of the ocean, and even went ATV riding. I thought since I had been riding dirt bikes, ATV riding would be a breeze, but I got too cocky and ended up driving off a small hill and crashing into a tree. Luckily, I wasn't hurt but that was the end of my ATV riding.

On the last day, we went to the Polynesian Cultural Center. It was so beautiful to learn and experience how the Polynesians lived. We saw how they danced with fire knives, fished, and climbed up a palm tree with just their bare feet, and we went paddling in a canoe which was so romantic.

Everything was going so great until one of the hot Polynesian men asked if I wanted to take a picture with him. Even though there was a hot Polynesian woman who wanted to take a picture with Kevin, he still got mad and said I smiled too hard when he put his hands around my waist. I couldn't believe how angry he was getting over something this small and thought it would blow over, but it didn't. He had an attitude for the rest of the day, even at the luau dinner, which was supposed to be an enchanting evening.

While they were showing the audience some Polynesian dances, I got called up to go on stage with a few others, but I refused to go, knowing that it would make Kevin even more mad. That whole night I felt like I was walking on eggshells around him. When we got back to the room, he went on and on about the man grabbing my waist. I knew at that point nothing was going to change and our marriage was over.

When he got back home, I realized I had bought us two tickets to a comedy club at "Jokes on US" in Laurel to see Huggy Lowdown. But I didn't want to go with him anymore, so I called Havana and asked her to come instead, but she wasn't able to find a sitter. I then called Darryl, but he wasn't able go either, so I ended up calling Rick, who said he would be down to go. Rick had been dating his high school sweetheart, but she was nowhere near as controlling as Kevin was and had no problem with him going with me since she knew we were just friends.

After the comedy club, I came home to find the locks had been changed. Kevin went to the door and opened it with the chain still on and said, "I know you didn't take Havana to the comedy club. I saw you there with some other guy when I drove by. So you can go back to him." Then he slammed the door in my face. I knocked a few more times, but it was late, and I was so tired, so I called Rick and went back to his place, where his parents let me sleep in the basement for the night.

The next day I went back and saw all of my belongings sitting outside the front door. I grabbed it and put it all in my car. Then I knocked on the door to get Coco, but they wouldn't let me in. So I had no choice but to call the police, who told them they had to give me a thirty-day notice before putting me out, which was good to know. But I told them I was moving out anyway and just needed to get my cat. It was Saturday morning, so I still had to go into my part-time job. I had planned on getting another hotel for the night until I could find an apartment since I could now afford one on my own.

While at work, I started telling Darryl everything that happened. Rick and Darryl lived at home with their parents, so I knew I couldn't stay with either of them. One of our co-workers named Corey overheard our conversation and said that I could stay at his place for five hundred dollars a month until I found my own place but had to sleep on the couch since he only had a two-bedroom townhouse that he shared with his cousin. I was so happy I didn't have to stay in a hotel. I didn't care about sleeping on the couch and agreed.

After work, I followed him to his house, and he introduced me to his cousin Eric, a handsome bald-headed guy with a beard that made him look older than he was. Corey told me he had a very jealous girlfriend, and if she asked any questions to say that I was friends with Eric. Eric started telling stories on how crazy she was, like when she slashed his tires when he stayed out too late with his boys. Corey just shook his head and handed me a set of keys to the house.

Sure enough, she came over that night, and the first thing she did was look me up and down and ask who I was. Eric came down and sat with me on the couch to make things less awkward. While she and Corey went upstairs, Eric and I began talking about my life and how I'd ended up in this situation. He didn't say much about himself, only the basics of where he grew up and what he did for work. After about fifteen minutes of them arguing, we heard the bed start to squeak and knew the coast was clear, so he went back upstairs, and I went to sleep.

Over the next few weeks, Kevin was constantly blowing up my phone, trying to convince me to come back home, but I ignored all his calls. One weekend Corey left with his girl to the Poconos, and it was just Eric and me at the house. I was sitting on the couch, watching TV when he came downstairs.

"You mind if I join you?" he asked.

"Sure. I'm just watching Boomerang. One of my favorite movies next to Purple Rain," I replied.

"Oh yeah, that's one of mine too," he said, sitting on the other side of the couch from me. We would occasionally look at each other during the funny scenes and laugh, but as soon as the movie was over, he got up and went back into his room. I'm not trying to sound conceited or anything, but I didn't understand why he wasn't trying anything. I was making it obvious that I was into him by giving him my notorious sexy eyes and smile, but he didn't seem interested at all. *Maybe he's gay*, I thought.

I hadn't been with anyone besides Kevin since I moved out here five years ago, and it had been months since we'd last had sex. I was so horny; the littlest things would turn me on. Especially since I could hear Corey and his girlfriend fucking almost every night. I decided to take matters into my own hands. I hopped in the shower, purposely forgetting my towel downstairs. After I washed up, I called out for Eric and asked him if he could bring me my towel. When he brought it up, I told him to come in, and as soon as he opened the bathroom door, I opened up the curtain to reach for it, standing there naked. He stood there, shocked.

"What's wrong, you never saw a naked body before?" I laughed, wrapping the towel around me. I walked up on him like I was going to kiss him but walked past him instead. Before I could make it out, he grabbed my hand and pulled me back in for a kiss. *Finally*, I thought. We passionately kissed back to his room. I dropped the towel and lay back on his bed. Then he crawled on top of me and kissed me all over my body. When I tried to reach down to unzip his pants, he grabbed my hands and stopped me.

"What's wrong?" I asked.

"I have something I need to tell you, but I don't know how to say it, and I don't want to freak you out."

I started to get nervous like he was about to tell me he had a disease or something. "What is it? You know you can tell me anything," I said, rubbing his back.

He hesitated and fought back the tears before answering. I knew it at that point it was serious and grew anxious to hear what it was. "About four years ago, I was on my way to my grandma's house, and as I got out of the car, another car pulled up on me and thought I was someone else and started shooting. I got hit in my leg with a shotgun, and by the time I got to the hospital, it was too late to save, and they had to amputate it." A tear flowed down his face. It took me a minute to realize what he was saying.

"Wait what do you mean they amputated it? Like they cut off your leg?" I was so shocked but curious at the same time.

"Yeah. I have a good prosthetic, which is why I don't have a limp or anything, so most people can't even tell unless I show them."

"Can I see?" I curiously asked. He got quiet again. "Trust me. I'm not going to be freaked out. I'm just glad you don't have a disease or anything," I laughed, kissing him on his shoulder. He reached down and took off his shoes, pants, and then snapped the prosthetic from his knee. Before he pulled it off, he gave me one last look for reassurance. "Go ahead," I said. He took a deep breath and pulled it off.

I'm not going to lie. It was weird as fuck seeing a man sitting there in his boxers pulling off one of his legs, but he was such a cool guy, I didn't care, so I pulled him on top of me. Surprisingly having only one leg made him more flexible, and he was putting me in all kinds of positions I had never been in before. We had sex that whole weekend, and when Corey found out, he didn't seem too surprised.

After a couple of weeks went by, we were lying in his bed one weekend after just having sex, when we heard loud banging coming from the front door and a girl yelling. He hopped over to his window that was right above the front door and looked down and said, "Oh, shit!" He hopped back to the bed and put back on his prosthetic leg then said, "It's my crazy ex I told you about. We broke up a couple of months ago, but she hasn't been able to let it go, especially since she pregnant with my baby but I'm not even sure if it's mine yet."

"Pregnant? You never told me you had a baby on the way," I said, putting my clothes back on.

"Honestly, I never expected things to happen between us the way they did and didn't know how to tell you. Look, I have to handle this. Can you please just stay up here and don't come downstairs until I come back?" He stood at the door, waiting for my answer.

"Fine!" I said, rolling my eyes.

When he went downstairs, I opened up the window to hear more clearly and get a peek at the pregnant girl still banging at the door. "Open the fuckin' door. I know you're in there. I saw your blinds moving," she yelled. He opened the door, and they immediately began arguing. "Is she in here?" she screamed.

"Who?" he asked.

"The girl I heard you were over here fuckin' with. Is this why you haven't been returning my calls?" I could hear her trying to make her way up the stairs and prepared myself for her to bust through the door.

"Yo, chill the fuck out. Ain't no one over here, and I ain't fuckin no one else," he yelled back. *What?* I thought.

"Well, whose stuff is all this and where did this cat come from?" she asked.

"It's a friend of Corey's. She's been staying here for a little bit until she gets her own place, but we not fucking. So I don't know where the fuck you got that shit from, but you trippin' and way out of pocket for coming over here like this."

"I'm sorry baby, but you haven't been returning my calls, and I want us to work things out," she said in a softer tone.

I had to listen to them go back and forth for over three hours. My blood was starting to boil the longer I was up there waiting. Things got quiet for a while, and I could have sworn I heard them down there having sex. Who knew a one-legged man could have this much drama? I was so pissed I wanted to storm down there and call him out, but I didn't want to put myself in another homeless situation, so I kept quiet until she eventually left. When he came upstairs, he tried to apologize, but I just pushed past him and left.

Over the next few days, I avoided him as much as possible. I knew it was time for me to find my own spot. I had more than enough money saved and finally located an affordable apartment right up the street from Darryl and Rick in Windsor Mills. However, I still had a few things at Kevin's house that I needed to get. I had Havana use her daughter's key to make me a copy so I could get the rest of my things while Kevin and his mother were at work. I called off work and got Darryl and Rick, who took off from school to help me rent a U-Haul and move out one of the beds and TVs that we had bought together.

Finally, I was all moved in to my first apartment, which was the second proudest moment of my life. I no longer had to depend on anyone else ever again and could do whatever the fuck I wanted to do. It felt so liberating and no one could tell me shit. I even bought myself another cat which Kevin always told me I couldn't do. She was a Siamese kitten I named Mocha to keep Coco company.

When Kevin came home and saw that I had moved the rest of my things out, he lost it. It finally hit him that I was gone and not coming back. He had Havana call me and beg to meet up with him. She said he wasn't mad and that after five years of marriage, he didn't want to end it like this and wanted to at least talk to me in person one more time. After some convincing, I agreed to meet with him at his favorite restaurant, the Cheesecake Factory.

When I got there, he was already sitting at the table with some white lilies, which he knew was my favorite. He gave me a hug and a kiss on the cheek. It was a little uncomfortable at first, but the more we talked, the more it started to feel like it did when we first met. With all the drama I went through with Eric, it made me appreciate how much Kevin really did love and care about me. I could tell he'd changed since the last time I'd seen him. He told me he had been going to counseling and realized how wrong he was for the way he treated me, and said it had a lot to do with how his father treated his mom growing up. That was the first time he'd ever share anything about his dad.

Part of the reason why I left him was because of his controlling ways. But I was starting to think maybe since I had my own place, things could work out this time since everything would now be on my terms. After dinner he walked me to my car and one kiss led to another. Next thing I knew we were back at my place christen every part of my apartment.

The next day we agreed to give our marriage another try. Darryl and Rick couldn't believe I went through all of that trouble to move out just to have him move right back in. But what they didn't understand was he wasn't my boyfriend. He was my husband. And when you are married you have to do everything you possibly can to make things work, and that's what we did.

At first, he seemed okay with everything including the fact that I had two guy best friends that I would occasionally go riding with. I decided to put things to the test and see if Kevin had really changed when Darryl invited me to a fight party his boy Wayne was having. Normally Kevin would freak out knowing it was a party with drinking and other men there. But surprisingly, he said he was okay with it and would be at his brother's house also watching the fight.

When I got to Wayne's apartment, I saw Rick, Darryl, and a few others I'd never met before were sitting around waiting for the fight to start. I immediately noticed this tall sexy chocolate man with dreads standing in the kitchen looking like he was posing for a Jamaican magazine. I could see him leaning over and whispering something to Wayne about me. I came in, said hi to everyone, then sat down next to Darryl and Rick.

I asked Darryl who he was, and he said that was Wayne's best friend, Bryan. When I looked back at him, he was still looking at me and smiled. I quickly turned back around, embarrassed he'd caught me checking him out. During the fight, we repeatedly made eye contact. I got up and went into the kitchen to make another drink, and Bryan followed in behind me.

"Hi, how are you doing?" He smiled. There was something about him I was immediately drawn to. I could tell by the way he smiled that he was a very charming man who probably had a lot of females like Romeo.

"I'm good, thanks!" I replied.

"So you live close around here?" he asked.

"Yeah, my husband and I live up street in Cedar Gardens."

"Oooh, so you're married?" He looked confused and down at my ringless finger. "Yeah, we just got back together. We've been married for five years and hit a rough patch, but now we are trying to work things out." I took a sip of my drink.

"Oh, okay, I can respect that. Well, I ..." Before he could finish his sentence, we were interrupted by everyone screaming from a knockout during the fight. We both rushed back in to see what happened. After the fight, I could tell Bryan wanted to finish talking to me, but he never got that chance. I said my goodbyes to everyone and headed back home.

When I got back, Kevin was still out with his brother, so I sat on the couch to watch some TV until he got back. Nothing good was on, so I flipped open the laptop that Kevin and I shared to check my MySpace account. When I opened it, a link popped up for BlackPlanet.com. At first, I thought it was porn site or something, so out of curiosity, I clicked on it and saw Kevin had a profile and had been messaging women for months. I wouldn't have been mad if these were before we started working things out, but some of the messages had been sent after he moved in and one was even sent earlier that day. I was so pissed and wanted to throw the computer out the window but came up with an even better idea instead.

I went back on there and created a fake profile to see how far he would go with it while we were in the middle of working things out. I knew he loved the Christina Milian type, so I searched the internet for look-alikes and found the perfect girl to use. He was a huge Pittsburgh Steelers fan, so I also added that to her page and clicked on his profile so he would see I'd checked him out. I didn't want to make it obvious, so I didn't send him any messages.

When I got to work on Monday, I checked the eighty something messages she'd received during my lunch break. Halfway through, I saw a message from him, and my heart sank. I was so nervous of reading what he wrote, but I opened it anyway and read him saying that he clicked on her profile and noticed she was a huge Steelers fan just like him and saw that they had so much in common and he would love to get to know her more.

I was so torn. Part of me was so hurt because I never thought this church boy would ever cheat on me and honestly thought we were working things out. But the other part of me was glad to know I could finally end this on-again off-again marriage and move on with my life. Before I broke the news to him, I wanted to have some fun and get a little revenge, so I messaged him back and told him I was the niece of Jerome Bettis who was the Steelers' best halfback. I knew that once he heard that his dick would instantly get hard. And I was right. He was so excited to hear that he kept messaging her all throughout the day.

Over the next few days, he messaged her back and forth, not even realizing we were sometimes using the same computer to do it. Sometimes I would mess with him by coming out in the living room to watch him hurry and click off the site. I did this multiple times just to fuck with him. I wanted to see if he would say anything to her about me, so I messaged him and asked if he was dating anyone or had ever been married. I told him my last ex had lied about being married, so I would never date anyone who lied to me.

The next day I received his response, and it started with "I have to be completely honest with you. I was married for five years, but we have been separated for over six months now and about to get a divorce. I caught her cheating with some guy she met at work, so I completely understand where you are coming from and would never do that to you. I'm like water, and she's dirt, and together we made mud. I'm just ready to start my life over with someone I can trust, and I feel like you're exactly what I've been looking for. I would love to discuss this more in person. Can we meet up?"

I couldn't believe how full of shit he was. I felt so stupid to think he was the type that would never do something like that to me. I didn't understand why he would move in with me and say he wanted to work things out if he wanted to be with other women. I tried so hard to pretend it wasn't bothering me, but deep down inside, I was heartbroken. I started crying at my desk, and some of my co-workers came over to check on me. I told them everything that was going on, and one of our other co-workers suggested I ask him to meet her at the Cheesecake Factory Friday at 8 pm and then stand him up. She said she and her husband were planning on going there, and she would go and report everything that happened. I thought that was a perfect idea especially since that was his favorite restaurant.

I figured if he was going to break my heart, I should do the same to his, so I sent him the message confirming their date. Later that night, my co-worker called me and said he came up there with flowers and a box of candy and waited for her for almost an hour. By the time she had sat down, eaten her food, and was getting ready to leave, he was still outside waiting. We had a good laugh over it, but inside I was still hurting, especially seeing his face every night like nothing was wrong.

A couple of hours later, I read angry messages from him talking about how he'd waited over an hour for her, and she could have at least called instead of wasting his time if she wasn't going to show up. Reading how angry he got did kind of make me feel a little better, and I wanted it to keep going, so I sent him a message saying she'd had a family emergency. Her grandfather was in the hospital but doing much better now. She apologized for not making it and asked if she could make it up to him by treating him to dinner tonight. He sent a smiley face and said he understood that family always comes first, and he agreed to meet her again.

Family first, my ass, I thought, rolling my eyes. Later that night, he told me he was going to his brother's house, and I gave him a half-assed smile as he walked out. As soon as he left, I went up to Home Depot and bought a new lock for the front door. Then I went to Staples and printed out all the messages he'd sent her and placed them in an envelope. I went back home, changed the locks, and put all of his shit in the hallway outside, then set the envelope on top of his shoe box with a big smiley face on the front.

When he came back, he started banging on the door. I looked through the peephole and saw him holding flowers that he had probably bought for her and was going to give to me. I then saw him grab the envelope and start to read all of the messages. He looked down and threw the flowers on the floor. He knew there was nothing he could say or do to make things right again. He grabbed all his things and left but not before taking the parking pass out my car, which he knew would end up getting my car towed. I had to call Rick and spend two hundred dollars just to get my car back. *I guess karma is a bitch.*

As soon as word got out that Kevin had moved out, Bryan immediately reached out to Wayne to hook us up, so Wayne threw another gathering and invited me over. Bryan was so funny and had me laughing all night. He even played the piano and made up a funny song about how he wanted to get to know me that had me laughing so hard I was in tears. After everything that had happened, it felt so good to be around someone who could make me laugh the way he did. We had such a great time. I didn't hesitate to give him my number when he asked for it at the end of the night. I knew he wanted to kiss me when he walked me to my car, but I heard he was a playboy, and I didn't want to make it that easy for him, so I turned my head when he leaned in for kiss and he settled for my cheek instead.

SINCE I WAS JUST GETTING OUT OF A marriage, I had no interest in jumping back into another relationship. This time I just wanted to date around and have fun. So when I heard Bryan was a player, it made me more interested in him since I knew he wouldn't pressure me for anything serious. The next day he came over, and we sat on my balcony and talked all night. He opened up to me about his family and how his dad was really abusive toward his mom growing up, but eventually left him, and has been with his stepdad ever since. He said that his stepdad has been the best father he could ever ask for. Hearing how great his stepdad was started to make me feel a little jealous that I never had a male role model in my life. Then it dawned on me, *maybe this is why I would always seek the love from older men. I am trying to fill that void of not having a father.*

I don't know what it was, but I always had a way of getting people to open up to me about things they never shared with anyone. Maybe it was because I never judged them for anything and was how I was always so open about my life and the mistakes I've made. I probably should have been a therapist or something. I even called my balcony the confessional since that's where people would open up to me the most. Plus, I had a red light that set the mood for deep conversations.

Bryan tried to kiss me again that night and the next night, but I was still playing hard to get, so I resisted. I had just bought my first vibrator and finally learned how to make myself cum, so I wasn't as horny for a man as I used to be, which was a great way for me to hold out. After almost a month of us hanging out, Bryan came over and offered to give me a massage. Besides Kevin giving me half-assed massages when he was trying to get some, I'd never had a real massage like Bryan was giving me. It felt like I was at a real day spa.

After he finished massaging my back, he went down to my legs and started rubbing up his fingers against my inner thighs, softly grazing my pussy, turning me on more and more. He worked his way down to my legs and then my feet. Then he told me to turn over. I was a little reluctant at first. I was small, so I hated how my breast disappeared when I was flat on my back, so I covered them with my shirt.

He started at my feet and then worked his way up my legs and back to my inner thighs. When he got to the top of my thighs, he started rubbing on my pussy. I wasn't planning on having sex with him when he first came over, but his damn massage was feeling so good, I knew my vibrator was no match for him. He started kissing my stomach and worked his way down to my clit and kissed it as if he was kissing my mouth. He stuck his tongue in and out like he was

French kissing it. It was so tough to make me cum, especially off head, but he said he wasn't going to stop until I did. Every time I tried pulling him up for some dick, he stopped me and kept going until I finally came, then he came up in the middle of my pulsating and stuck his massive dick inside of me, and I came again. He was the first one to ever make me cum off head and dick.

His dick was feeling so good it hurt. I was damn near in tears and wanted to scream his name, but my pride held back, and he knew it which only made him penetrate my guts even harder. I could no longer hold it in and swallowed my pride like nut as I screamed out his government name. Right after I said that he pulled out and nutted all over my stomach. I lay there in awe and was expecting us to fall asleep in each other's arms, but he got up and went back to eating my pussy until it became wet enough for him to slide back in. He then bent me over doggy style and was fucking the shit out of me until I almost couldn't take it anymore. "Okay, okay, it's yours," I moaned.

Just as I was about to wave the white flag, he pulled out again and nutted all over my ass. I'd fucked a lot of guys in the twenty-five years of living, but he was by far the best. He fucked me like Mr. Marcus the porn star, and I knew I had a lot to learn if I wanted to please him the way he was pleasing me. We finally dozed off, but a couple hours later I woke up to him eating my pussy again which led to us fucking against the dresser. I then got down on my knees and started sucking him off, but two minutes into it he picked me up and fucked me while walking across the room. Then he busted his third nut when he bent me over the bed.

Once we laid down, he asked, "How often do you give head?"

"Not that much, why?" I asked.

"I can tell," he said, laughing.

"Yeah, my ex-husband didn't let me watch porn at all. He felt like it was a sin, so I never really learned how to do it, but I want to be the best you ever had, so teach me how you like it."

He softly kissed me like I was his future prodigy then said, "You ever heard of Super Head?"

"No, who's that?"

"She's this porn star named Karrine Steffans who gives the best head, which is why they call her Super Head. So if you want to learn what I like, just watch one of her videos."

After he told me that, I watched all her videos and practiced with a cucumber his size repeatedly until I felt like I'd nailed her technique. When we had sex, I never went down on him. I wanted to perfect it before I tried it out again. He came over to watch a basketball game and sat on my couch as I went into the bedroom. When I came out, I was wearing some black lingerie. I walked over to the TV and turned it off, then bent over so he could get a good look at my ass while I turned on the stereo and started playing "Warmth," by Janet Jackson. He looked so shocked to see me since I had never worn anything like that for him. He stood up, but I pushed him back down on the couch and unzipped his pants, pulling them down to his ankles. I kissed all over his stomach and sucked on his nipples until his dick became as hard as the cucumber I was practicing on.

Then I put his dick so deep down my throat my eyes began to water and this thick saliva that looked like aloe vera slime started to form. When I used to suck dick, I didn't want to make a mess, but now I knew the messier and wetter, the better and I had to be nasty with it. I spit on his dick and watch this long thick trail wrap around the top of his head like icing to a cake. I sucked it back up and then wrapped both my hands around his dick and stroked it up and down in a rotating motion. Then I started sucking on his balls while still stroking his dick with one hand.

"Ahhhh shit," he moaned. I worked my way back up and sucked the soul out of his dick like a straw using both my hands until he yelled my favorites words, "Fuck, you're about to make me cum!" His nut shot so far down my throat I could feel it hitting my tonsils which started to make me gag. Instead of swallowing it, which probably would have made me throw up, I continued sucking his dick while letting his nut slide out the side of my mouth, down to his thighs until he couldn't take it anymore and pushed me off him. "I'm sorry. My bad. Damn, baby! I wasn't expecting that at all. You learned that shit quick," he laughed, pulling me up and kissing me on my forehead.

Even though I didn't want to fuck anyone else, I didn't want to jump into another relationship either. I still needed time to date and figure out what I really wanted. This was the first time I was single as an adult and I wanted to enjoy my freedom while it lasted. I told him he was free to hook up with other women just as long as he didn't lie to me about it, but he said he didn't want to fuck with anyone else either.

A month went by, and I received a call from some White girl talking about how they had just got through fucking when she went through his phone and saw all my messages. She said they had been dating for over a year, and he had just left her house. I told her we weren't together, and he was free to fuck whoever he wanted to. After we hung up, I immediately called Bryan and yelled at him for lying to me.

"Why would you lie when I said it's okay for you to be with whoever you want? All you had to do was be honest about it."

"I know, I know, but I swear that was my first time seeing her since me and you hooked up. I was only using that bitch for money, but once we hooked up, I cut her off. Then she called me this morning and said she had something important she needed to talk to me about. I thought she was gonna say she was pregnant or something, so I went over there, and she was wearing nothing under her robe. I tried to tell her it was over, but she was all over me, and I couldn't resist once she started kissing on me. She must have gone through my phone when I was in the shower, but I swear I was going to tell you everything tonight."

I sat there thinking about everything he said. I mean, I did tell him it was okay for him to be with other women, and he did say he was going to tell me everything tonight. I knew I couldn't be too mad at him even though I wanted to be, so let it go.

A couple of weeks later, I went to the doctor for my routine checkup, and I was caught off guard when the doctor came out and told me I had chlamydia again. I was so confused because I didn't have any symptoms and had just gotten checked before Bryan and I hooked up. After my first infection, I was always paranoid about catching something, so I constantly got checked. Since I hadn't been with anyone else since my last test, I knew that it was Bryan who gave it to me. The doctor informed me that sometimes people could have it, especially men, and not show any symptoms, which scared the fuck out of me.

This made me reevaluate everything I had told him about him fucking other women. I called him over and told him about the chlamydia and said we either need to start using condoms after he got treated, or he needs to cut everyone else off. He agreed this was a wakeup call for him as well and said he wanted to be exclusive. He even changed his phone number to prove it, and just like that, I jumped into another five-year relationship.

Chapter VII
Fly Black Butterfly, Fly

HAVANA HAD DIVORCED DWIGHT BY time Kevin and I separated. Since they had two kids together, I would occasionally see him at her house when he would drop the kids off after his weekend visits. I took my godmom-auntie duties very seriously and would pick my godnephew up once a month for the weekend. Sometimes I would even take him out dirt biking with Rick and Darryl.

Once Dwight heard I was dating someone, he started becoming an asshole toward me. He had to come by my job to drop off the car seat so I could pick his son up after I got off. As I was putting the seat in my car, he started telling me not to have his son around a bunch of niggaz. I rolled my eyes and tried to ignore him, but once he started calling me all kinds of hoes and bringing up the fact that I used to strip, I began to get pissed off. Especially since he was doing this right in front of my job. After I had enough, I snapped and called him a bitch, then started cursing him out until my manager came out and broke it up.

Later on that evening, while I was playing with my godnephew, my phone kept ringing off the hook from an unknown number. When I finally answered it, it was Dwight's new girlfriend who was threatening to beat my ass if I ever called him a bitch again. She was this tall, skinny, thirty-something-year-old African chick who looked just like a gremlin and was such a downgrade from Havana. But I didn't care, because I felt like she was exactly who Dwight deserved to be with.

After a fifteen-minute screaming match, I realized I was wasting my time arguing with her over some dumb shit which was taking away from the time I should be spending with my godnephew. I calmly told her the next time we saw each other we could just handle it from there. Then I hung up and ignored all her calls until they finally stopped ringing.

A couple of months went by, and it was the Fourth of July weekend. I was at Havana's house for a barbeque when she told me she was inviting one of her favorite co-workers over, who was this gay guy named Topaz. I had never met a gay guy before but had always wanted one as one of my best friends. I had a lot of female friends, but I never truly felt like I fit in with them. I hated doing all the girly things they like to do. And they were things I just couldn't talk to my boys about like how sexy another guy was so having a gay friend would be like having the best of both worlds. So when she told me he was coming, I got so excited.

He called and told her he needed a ride and asked if she could pick him up, but she had to finish cooking and asked if I could do it instead. She then handed me the phone so we could introduce ourselves. When I heard his voice, it was exactly how I imagined a gay man to sound and I said, "Oh my God, I can hear the gayness through the phone. I love it and can't wait to meet you!"

"Umm, put Havana back on the phone," he snapped. After I handed her back the phone, I could tell that I had offended him, by the way she kept defending me, and telling him I was not like that, and to please give me another chance. I felt so bad. My mouth constantly got me into trouble, which is why I'm usually very quiet and reserved when I first meet someone sober. But that night, I was tipsy and blurted out the first thought that popped in my head. After some convincing, he agreed to still let me pick him up. I thought it was going to be so awkward but as soon as he got into my car he said, "Oh my God, gurl you are so pretty."

"Thank you. I appreciate that. Hey, I really want to apologize for offending you. That was not my intention at all. I've always wanted a gay friend. So I got really excited, and it just came out wrong. I'm so sorry. I really do want us to be friends," I pleaded.

"Gurl, it's okay, I accept your apology. Being a gay black man, I have to deal with a lot of offensive comments, especially from black woman, so I thought you were like the rest of them. But I can tell you're not like that and Havana explained everything, so we're good," he said giving me a big hug.

That night we ended up having such a great time that we exchanged numbers and eventually he did become one of my best friends. Even Havana got jealous of our friendship and said I stole her friend away. After the fireworks was over, I dropped Topaz off at his house and went back to Havana's to stay the night. As I was chilling outside on the patio drinking, I saw Dwight's car pull up. When he got out to bring the kids inside, I noticed the gremlin sitting in the front seat. She looked back and we made eye contact. I quickly jumped up off the patio and ran towards her as she was getting out the car. We both met in the middle of the street and started fighting like wild cats. Somehow, she got loose from my grip and hopped back in the front seat of the car where she tried to lock it, but I opened it before she could and started punching her some more.

She then kicked me back, closed the door and locked it. I opened the back door and managed to get her in a headlock, but she bit me on the arm, going through the skin with her braces. Dwight rushed over and pulled me out of the car by my legs and then punched me in the face. I tried to go after him, but he ran around the car like a little bitch, got in, and then drove off. I had scratches all over my face and a bite mark on my arm, but it was worth it. She had been talking so much shit for months, that she deserved this ass beating. My boys wanted to beat Dwight's ass for putting his hands on me, but I told them not to do anything because karma was a bitch, and she would eventually get his ass back, which she did.

About a month later, I was at Cedar Point in Ohio with some friends for the weekend when I got a call from Havana saying that someone had keyed Dwight's brand-new Cadillac Deville, flattened all four of the tires, and poured bleach in his gas tank. This Cadillac was his dream car and something he had been talking about getting since Kevin and I first got together. I'm not going to lie. I was thrilled to hear that happened to him and wished I could thank whoever did it, with a meat lovers pizza from Pizza Hut or something, but I had no idea who it could be. He was an asshole who had a lot of enemies, so it could have been anyone.

Havana told me he blamed me for it and was going to be pressing charges against me for the car and the fight against the gremlin. Since I wasn't in town when it happened, I knew there was no way I would be charged for the car. But since they were pressing charges for the fight, I decided to do the same in return since she was the one that initiated it. As soon as I got home, I went to court and filed the exact same charges against them.

Two weeks later, two police officers came to my job and arrested me. The arresting officers were nice enough not to make a scene or put me in handcuffs until I got into the car. I told my job what happened as I was walking out, and one of my co-workers said she would pick me up from jail after work. Once I got there, the other officers started treating me like I had murdered someone. They were being such dicks and so rude. I took my mug shot, then they put me into a cell by myself next to the men's cell who kept trying to get my attention, but the officers quickly shut that down.

The good thing was the same happened to Dwight. He was arrested at his job, and she turned herself in shortly after. They hired a lawyer, but I always watched a lot of crime shows and knew they had no case against me, so I didn't bother to hire an attorney and went straight to court to defend myself. The judge called our case up and asked how we pleaded, which was not guilty. After a few minutes of reading through some papers, the judge told us the case was dismissed.

"Thank you, Your Honor," I said, smiling at them as they stood there, dumbfounded and pissed. I was confident I would get off but didn't know it was going to be that easy and gloated all the way back to the car.

Since I had no family in Maryland, except Havana and the kids, I desperately wanted my little brother Chris to move in with me after he graduated high school. Especially when I heard, him and my mom were having problems. I thought this would be a perfect opportunity for us to make up for lost time. He agreed to come out for a visit which was just in time to attend court with me. I wanted him to like Maryland so much that he would want to stay. So I decided to welcome him to Baltimore the best way I knew how.

As soon as I picked him up from the airport, I asked him if he wanted some Baltimore head. He looked so confused and asked what I was talking about. Rick, Darryl, and I just started laughing as we drove him over to this chick's house that Darryl was talking to. Darryl had broken up with his girlfriend a couple of years prior after he caught her cheating on him. She tried to win him back by tattooing his name on her chest, but he had so many groupies waiting in line to take her place that he decided to play the field instead of giving her another chance. He never admitted it, but I could tell she really broke his heart because he had no interest in being in another relationship after that.

I don't know what it was, but women wanted to be with him so bad they would do anything just to impress him. Especially this one. She was so in love with Darryl she did anything he asked her to do. He told her my brother had just flown in from Cali, and he wanted her to welcome him to Baltimore, and she agreed. She took my brother into her apartment while we waited for him outside.

Actually, I take that back. I do know what women saw in him. He was smart, good-looking, charming, funny, great with finances, and you could tell he was going to be very successful after he got his master's degree. He was a great catch and had everything you would want in a man. People used to ask us why we never hooked up, and the answer was simple. We knew way too much shit about each other. All the behind-the-scenes stuff that most people would never know about their partners, we knew, and a moment of pleasure was not worth jeopardizing our friendship over, especially when we both had so many other options. So even though I knew it would never work between us, I could see why so many other women fell for him.

Fifteen minutes later, Chris came out with the biggest smile on his face. "You're the best sister ever," he shouted as we got into the car. My brother and I were extremely close and told each other everything, so I knew he was already out there having sex. I wanted Baltimore to make a great impression on him and it did. After he got settled in, he agreed to stay.

Bryan was a general manager at a restaurant and agreed to hook him up with a job. All he needed to do was show up on time and pass orientation, but I soon realized why my mom was having such a difficult time with him. He showed up late and failed orientation. He was so lazy and just wanted to do was lie around the house and drink beer all day. Frustrated, I told him that he would have to go back to Cali if he didn't find a job and get his shit together.

After a month of doing the same shit and running up my cable bill with three hundred dollars' worth of pay-per-view porn, I had to ship his ass back to my mom's. I was extremely disappointed that it didn't work out. But it made me understand my mom a lot more. I got a tiny glimpse on how hard it was to raise teenagers and I was even more grateful that I didn't have any kids.

MY MOTHER AND I WERE ON SUCH great terms–something I thought would never happen. We talked on the phone almost every week. I flew back to Cali regularly every year for either Thanksgiving or Christmas or sometimes both. While I was on the phone with her, I asked her whatever happened to my G-mom. She said after they had a falling out, she moved to Vegas, and she hadn't spoken to her since but wished she could find her.

My G-mom was such a huge part of my life growing up, and I always felt like something was missing when she left. The more and more I thought about her, the more I wanted to find her. I decided to look her up on Myspace and found a guy who looked like he could be my godbrother, so I sent him a message saying that I was looking for my godmom.

I didn't know at the time, but my godbrother was such a whore. He had twelve kids by six different baby mamas. Even though he was married, he was with his side chick when my message popped up. She thought I was just another ho trying to get at him and started cursing him out. Especially when my G-mom didn't recognize me but once they started scrolling through my pictures and saw a baby photo of me, she started screaming.

A couple of minutes later, I got a message to call this number. When I called, my G-mom was screaming so loud, you would have thought she was on speaker phone and said, "Ooooooh, my God, Angie! I can't believe it's you. I have been trying to find you all for years!" I was shocked. I couldn't believe I was hearing her voice after all this time. It sounded exactly like I remembered it as a kid.

We talked for hours and hours on the phone, catching up on everything. Even though I hadn't seen her since I was like nine or ten, it was like she had never left. She told me everyone nicknamed her Madea and after speaking with her, I could tell why. She was hilarious, blunt and crazy just like Madea was. It was so funny listening to her talk. She had me cracking up the whole time. I told her everything that had happened between my mom and I after Curtis moved out. She cried and said she wished she had never lost contact with us because none of that would have happened had she been around, and I knew hands down that was true.

One of the things I loved about her was how brutally honest she was. Even if it hurt, you could ask her anything, and she would always keep it real with you, which was the complete opposite of my secretive mother. So I decided to ask her about my father, since she was there before I was born.

The first thing she said was, "Ooooh Angie. Your father loved you sooo much. He ..."

"Wait for what? What do you mean he loved me? My mom told me he left because he didn't want me," I said, still in shock to hear those words that my father loved me.

"Oh no, that is so far from the truth. He loved you so much. The last time I saw him, you were around one years old. He had just gotten back in town and came over to give you a letter that said he went back to Honduras to learn how to speak English so he could be able to speak to his beautiful baby. He also wrote that he loved you very much. When I called to tell your mom that he had dropped off this letter, she told me to throw it away but never told me why. As you know, your mom is a private person and only tells you what she wants you to know, so I didn't think much of it when I threw it away. Had I known that would be the last time we heard from him, I would have kept it for you. I'm so sorry I did that. I really wish I never threw it away," she started to cry.

I could tell how bad she felt, but just her telling me what my father said meant the world to me. After hearing all this, I was so hurt to know my mom had lied to me my whole life about my father. When I began to voice my frustrations, my G-mom said, "Your mom was only seventeen when she had you and was going through a really difficult time in her life. Shit, I was her best friend, and she never even told me how she ended up in the group home. I didn't know much about your grandmother either, but I could tell she was a very cold woman to be around. Every time she visited your mom, you could cut the tension in the room with a knife. I know your mom is not the best at expressing her emotions, but I do know all she ever wanted in life was to be a mom. And she loved you kids, with everything she had. That I know for sure."

When I started to think about it, I realized she was right. Maybe the same way she treated me was how my grandmother had treated her, and that's the only way she knew how to be. I was fortunate enough to go through years of counseling to figure how to break the cycle, but what if I didn't? We all handle life differently. I made a lot of mistakes growing up but all I needed was some time to learn from them to grow into the person I am today, and so did my mom. She was far from perfect, but I know she loved us. It wasn't easy, but she really did do the best she could to raise three bad kids on her own, and I knew that now.

I loved the relationship my mother and I had and didn't want to ruin it, so I never brought this up to her, but I knew I needed to find my father now more than ever. That following week, I grabbed the white pages and saw thirty names in California with my father's last name. Out of the thirty numbers, I decided to call seven of them that lived in the Los Angeles area, which was the last known place for him to be. Out of those seven, half of them told me I had the wrong number, and the other half I left voice messages for.

Later on that night, I received a call from a young girl who said, "Hi, I'm Alicia. I got your message about you looking for Jerson." I didn't think much of it and thought she was going to tell me that I had the wrong number or something.

"Yeah, I'm just trying to see if he's my father," I replied.

"Yes, he's your father, and you're my sister, and we've been looking for you!" I sat there frozen in disbelief, and there was a long pause. At first, I thought it was a prank call, but when I heard her start to cry, I knew shit got real.

"Are you serious?" I asked.

"Yes, the whole family has been looking for you ever since I can remember. You have ten brothers and sisters who also have been looking for you. We're all Honduran, and you were the only one mixed with Black, so it made us even more curious about you," she said with a little laugh.

I was still in shock and could barely speak. "Oh my God, I can't believe this. This is sooo crazy. Wow, I have ten siblings, that's so crazy! So is my father there? Can I talk to him?" I asked. There was another long pause. I was too afraid to hear the answer, so I waited for her to pull it together and say, "I'm so sorry, but he died back in '98, but he loved you so much. He only married my mom, and they both would go door to door looking for you. So she is just as excited as we are to have found you. She knew how much you meant to our father. Just a week before he died, he told my oldest sister to make sure she found you. I know he's looking down on us and is so happy right now." She struggled to get those last words out.

"Oh, wow, so how did he die?" I asked.

"I'd rather tell you in person. Right now, I want to hear all about your life and where you have been this whole time."

We talked for about three hours, and then I asked, "Do you have a picture of him? I would love to see his face and how much of me looks like him."

"Yeah, I'll text it to you now and a picture of me," she said.

The crazy thing about all of this was, I had never dreamt about my father before until a week prior to this call. I was at a train station, and as I was getting off the train, I saw a bright light from above that was almost blinding. When I gained my focus, there was a man was standing above me on a bridge, smiling down at me. Without saying any words, I felt him tell me that he loved me and was always watching over me. When my sister texted me a picture of him, it was the same man I saw in my dreams, and it gave me chills all down my body. There was no DNA test needed. I had his nose, and my sister and I looked like twins.

Alicia then said, "Our dad used to always say if his kids didn't have his nose, then they weren't his kid." We both laughed, and it blew my mind to hear those words "our dad." I never thought I would ever hear that in my lifetime.

I couldn't believe it. After twenty-seven years, I was finally looking at my father for the first time. After we hung up, tears filled my eyes as I stared at his picture but was quickly interrupted when my phone started ringing off the hook. First, it was my sister who lived in Watts, then my other sister in Long Beach. Next, it was my sister in Miami who was only one year younger than me. She was in a nightclub when she heard the news and ran outside to call me. I could hear the music blasting in the background when she said, "The last time our family had seen or heard from you was when you were around one years old, and your mother came by our dad's house to drop off some baby pictures. My mom answered the door and said our dad was in Honduras and that she was pregnant by him. After that, your mom moved, and he couldn't find her."

Now everything was starting to make so much more sense. My mom probably got piss when she found out my dad had gotten someone else pregnant and decided to cut him off by moving away. I was so disappointed I would never be able to meet him in person, but I felt blessed that I got to see his face and find out how much he loved me. Everything seemed so surreal, and I still couldn't wrap my head around the fact that out of the seven calls I made, I left four voice messages, and out of those four, three of them were my sisters. Sisters! Wow, I couldn't believe I now had sisters. I was so anxious to call everyone, especially my G-mom and tell them how I found my father, but it was almost 3 a.m., and I still had to be at work in less than five hours.

After I got off work, I immediately called my mom while I was driving home. "Hey, are you sitting down?" I asked. She laughed and said, "No, why?"

"I think you should. I have something to tell you."

"What, are you pregnant?" she anxiously said.

"Umm noooo, even better. You ready … I found my father!"

"Whaaat?!" she asked.

"Yeah, I found my father." I explained to her how I'd located him and that I had ten siblings who knew all about me and had been looking for me since I was a baby. She actually seemed genuinely happy for me and said she was glad that I found them. My G-mom was so excited when I told her that she screamed even louder than the day I first found her. Bryan was also very happy for me too. We had shared countless stories about our lives growing up, so he knew how much it meant to me to find him.

OUR RELATIONSHIP HAD BEEN DOING SO well we decided to move in together, and he said while I was in Cali visiting my family, he would take care of all of the moving, so I didn't have to worry about anything except spending time with them. Even though everything was going so great between us, there was always something about him I didn't trust. He was the type that would lie about the littlest things, and whenever he told a story, it would keep changing the more he told it, so it was hard for me to know when he was telling the truth. As much as I loved him and always had fun with him, I couldn't fully trust him, and it held me back from me letting my guard down and giving him my heart completely.

The time came for me to fly to Cali. I was so anxious I barely got any sleep the night before. As soon as I landed in LAX, I rented a car and headed over to Alicia's house, who lived about thirty minutes from the airport. I was so nervous as I walked up to the front door and knocked. A dog started barking as our brother and their mom Danielle answered the door. They both greeted me with a big hug and kiss. Alicia was still working at Victoria's Secret, so I decided to drive up there and surprise her.

When we walked in Victoria's Secret, I saw her hanging up some clothes on the wall. As soon as she turned around, she immediately spotted me and burst out into tears. We hugged for what seemed like minutes. I always wanted a younger sister, and since she was the first one I'd spoken to when I found them, we had this instant bond like we had known each other our whole lives. After she got off, we went back to her house so she could change her clothes, and so we could head over to Long Beach to meet our other two sisters and all my nieces and nephews.

While she was changing, she handed me a photo album with so many pictures of our father. Toward the end, I saw pictures of him lying in a casket. She noticed me staring at it, and she said, "Our father was a wonderful dad and loved all his kids very much, but he wasn't the best man to be with. He had a lot of women, and at times, could be very abusive. The night he died, he had gotten into a huge fight with my mom. I heard her scream out for me, so I ran out into the living room, where I saw him on top of her with his hands around her throat, but he told me they were just playing around and to go back to bed and that he loved me."

When she said that, it sounded eerily familiar and gave me goosebumps. She continued and said, "When I woke up the next morning, the house was filled with police officers, and one of the officers then asked me what I would do if my dad died. Still, to this day, I don't understand why she would ask a seven-year-old that, but it scared the shit out of me, so I ran out looking for him and saw a pile of blood on the floor." Her mom jumped in and said after they had gotten into that fight, she told him it was over and threatened to call the cops on him if he didn't leave. He became so enraged that he pulled out his gun and started threatening to kill her with it. They argued back and forth until he eventually put the gun to his head and shot himself in front of her. "This was not the first time he threatened to kill himself," she said tearing up.

I sat there in disbelief. That was not the story I was expecting at all. I was thinking more like a motorcycle accident since he loved to ride or a heart attack or something, but I never would have guessed that the reason why I would never get the opportunity to see my father was because he took his own life. I started to get angry about how selfish and cowardly it was for him to do that. *How could someone take their own life and leave their family behind like this?*

Then I remembered I had almost done the same thing. And had I been successful, I would not be here to meet my siblings. I then started to feel great sadness for him. How much pain and depression he must have felt to grab a gun, pull the trigger, and end it all in front of his wife and with his kids in the next room. I wished he would have known how much I needed him, but maybe I needed him more as a guardian angel in heaven, than I did a father on earth, who knows.

I tried to just focus on the positive and how blessed I was to get this chance to know who he was. I know there's millions of people out there who would never get to know who their parents are. Not only did I get to know who he was, but I now knew he'd loved and wanted me, and to top it off, I had a whole new family to get to know. I honestly couldn't ask for anything more.

When we got to our other sister's house, they all welcomed me with open arms. They cooked amazing Honduran food, bought me gifts, and of course, had a bottle of tequila on deck. We talked, laughed, and partied all night. It was like I had known them my whole life. They showed me a lot of pictures of our father and shared so many stories that I felt like I knew everything about him. I could tell I had his temper and stubbornness, but I also had his adventurous side, big heart and the need for always wanting to help others. He was constantly flying back to Honduras, where the rest of our family was, to bring them food, clothing, and money. He was smart and worked several different jobs to provide for his family. I knew if he had still been alive, I would have so been a daddy's girl. I had the best time getting to know him and everyone else in my family. It was the best Thanksgiving I'd ever had, and to top it off Alicia and I decided to get matching tattoos of the word love in Chinese.

When I arrived back home, everything was moved into our new apartment as promised. Everything was unboxed and even all my clothes were hung up. I was so grateful to Bryan that I rewarded him with some of that super head he loved. Our apartment was so dope. We had a large two-bedroom, with two bathrooms, a game room with a pool table in it, and we turned the second bedroom into a guest/sex room. The sex room had all kinds of sex toys we would use when we had our drunk and high sex nights. He bought me a stripper pole for my birthday, and even put mirrors up and built a small stage for it right next to the game room.

I hadn't been on a pole in almost ten years, so I bought this pole dancing lesson by Flirty Girl Fitness on DVD and practiced while he was working late nights. Once I felt like I learned my old moves I thought I'd surprise him when he got home from work. As soon as he walked in, he was shocked when he saw me dressed up like a sexy waitress. I walked over and handed him a towel, washcloth, and told him go freshen up, and that when he got out, I'd show him to his VIP table. At first he was confused, but soon realized what was going on, and got super excited as he rushed to take a shower. When he got out, I took him to a small table I had set up for him in front of the pole and sat him down where I handed him his tray to roll up his blunt.

I then came out of the kitchen with his favorite drink, Henny and Coke, and told him to relax, and that his personal dancer would be right in. I went into the room and changed into a sexy red lace panty set and put on my six-inch-red high heels. Even though it was just Bryan, I was still super nervous like I was about to perform in front of a real crowd, so I took shots of Henny until my alter ego Mercedes came out.

She walked out with so much swag and confidence. Bryan's eyes lit up like he was seeing me for the first time. Trey Songz album "Ready" was on, and the song "Jupiter Love" started playing. I walked around him slowly, grabbing him around his chest and kissing him softly behind his ears before stepping on stage. I danced around the pole so seductively, you would have thought I was auditioning for Diamond in Playas Club. I then did an upside-down flip and slid down the pole with my legs spread open.

Bryan yelled out, "Oooooh shit," with a big ass smile on his face. He sat there like a little boy who was looking at first nudie magazine. He then pulled out his wallet, threw all his cash on the stage as I slowly took my bra off. "You Belong to Me" started playing, as I swung around the pole one more time, before I slid my panties off. Then I crawled over to him, unbuckled his pants, and proceeded to suck him off. Just as he was about to cum, I sat on his dick and rode him until I felt every drop inside, and he deflated like a balloon.

"Damn, that shit felt good," he said, pulling his boxers back up. I kissed him on his cheek and said, "Hope you enjoyed yourself and will cum back real soon." I smiled as I walked into our bedroom to change.

When I came out back out, I yelled, "So where the fuck have you been all night?" He looked baffled and responded, "Wha-what do you mean? I was with you!"

"No, the fuck you weren't. It's almost two o'clock in the morning, and you just now getting home, plus you smell like weed and pussy. So where the fuck you been all night?"

It took him a second, but he finally understood I was still role-playing. "Ooooooh, shit. I was at my brother's house." We both laughed about how scared he was when he thought I was serious.

For his birthday, I decided to take him to Aruba. A few weeks before we were scheduled to go, we went out for drinks with Rick, Darryl, and their girls plus my girl Melissa and her husband. I met Melissa at the Subway next to my job, where I would always go for lunch. She was this cute Columbian chick who had the cutest accent. Every time I would go in there, she would make me laugh, so one day I told her we should hang out sometime, and we did. We were all having a good time, when all of sudden Melissa leaned over and kissed me out of nowhere. I was shocked because I had no idea she was into girls like that. I looked at Bryan to make sure he was okay with it, and when he gave me the okay nod, I kissed her back. Had that been Kevin, he would have flipped out, and Kovas would have smacked the shit out of me, but Bryan was such a freak and I loved it. It turned me on, and I couldn't wait to go home and fuck him again.

We decided to leave at the same time Melissa and her husband were leaving. Bryan told me to stay on the corner with Melissa while he and her husband went to go get the cars. About fifteen minutes later, I called him, but it kept going straight to voicemail. Another ten minutes went by, and he finally stumbled in from around the corner. He claimed they'd gotten lost, but he always lied about everything, so I didn't know what to believe, and became furious at him for having us wait on the corner for so long.

By this time, Rick, Darryl, and their girls all came out of the bar and said the cars were parked in the opposite direction. While we were all walking, Bryan kept wanting to talk about why I was so mad, but I didn't feel like talking to him about it in front of everyone, so I kept trying to walk ahead of him. He grabbed my arm, but I snatched it back and threw down the rose he'd bought me inside the bar on the floor. He grabbed me by the back of my neck to bend me down to pick it up. Out of reflex, I snapped and turned to pop him in his eye, not realizing I had my high heels in my hand since my feet were hurting. When I looked, blood started gushing out his eye. It was so bad Darryl had to take off his shirt and place it on his face to stop the bleeding.

Even though I didn't mean to hit him that hard, I was still angry that he grabbed my neck like that and told Darryl to drive me home. When we got to the house, Darryl, his girl, and I were sitting on the couch, talking about what had just happened when Bryan walked in. By now, the liquor had worn off, and when I saw how swollen his face and eye was, I immediately began to feel bad.

As soon as Darryl and his girl left, Bryan broke down. "AyeYoo, I'm so sorry. I swear I didn't mean to grab you like that. You know I grew up watching my dad hit my mom, so I would never put my hands on a woman. I don't know what the fuck I was thinking. You have every right to be mad, especially after everything you told me about your past, but just know that I'm truly sorry."

I could tell he meant every word of that, and it was just a drunken accident on both parts. That was the first serious argument we ever had since we had gotten together. I apologized to him too, and we had the best make-up sex ever. The next morning, his eye was swollen shut, and his face was so puffed-up he started to look like Martin after he lost the fight to the Hitman Hearns, so we went to the emergency room.

The first doctor told us it was possible he could lose sight in that eye. When I heard that, I started freaking out and broke down in tears. "Oh my God, I'm soooo sorry. I swear I didn't mean to hit you like that." He grabbed my hand and told me it wasn't my fault and not to worry but I could tell he was scared too. The doctor came back and said they needed to run more test and sent us to a specialist. Luckily that doctor had better news. He said he wasn't going to lose his vision but would need five stitches on his eyelid.

I held his hand as they put them in one by one and felt his pain with every stitch. The stitches were out by time we left for Aruba, but he still had a visible scar. However, it didn't stop us from having the best time ever out there. We had so much fun relaxing by the beach, feeding all of the iguanas and having sex in places we shouldn't like in an alleyway and on the balcony of a hotel we weren't checked-in to.

AFTER I FOUND MY FATHER'S SIDE, something inside me began to change. The desire for me to move back to Cali kept growing stronger every year. I used to be okay with just visiting my family a couple of times a year, but now I was starting to feel homesick and get depressed more than usual, especially during the winter.

I had done volunteer work over the years from homeless shelters to mentoring kids in group homes to joining the Big

Brother and Sister program. At first, I started out volunteering to make up for all the bad shit I had done but it ended up becoming very therapeutic for me when I realized by sharing the "PG version" of my story it was helping kids to open up more.

One boy named Justice stood out to me the most while I was working at a group home for boys in Hyattsville, MD, back when I was married to Kevin. Everyone said he was this troublemaker and to keep an eye out for him. But it reminded me of when people use to call me a troublemaker when I wasn't—I was just troubled. I knew there was something deeper going on, and I wanted to help him. When I first arrived, he would blow me off every time I tried to talk to him but one day, he overheard me talking to another boy about what he wanted to be when he graduated and surprisingly Justice said he had an interest in becoming a marine biologist.

I was so surprised he was finally starting to open up. I wanted to take advantage of this moment, so I decided to buy a bunch of tickets with my own money to the Baltimore Aquarium and take the boys out on a field trip. It took some convincing to get approved. But I had been volunteering there for a while, and they saw the amazing work I was doing like teaching the boys about finances, credit scores, and balancing a checkbook, so they trusted my judgment and let me take them.

However, I quickly found out why they said to keep an eye out for him. Not even ten minutes after we got there, he asked to use the bathroom and disappeared. I was so scared something had happened to him. We ended up calling the police and filing a missing person's report. After hours of searching, we had no choice but to make the long drive back without him.

A couple days later the group home received a call about his whereabouts and picked him up. Apparently, he was from Baltimore and caught a bus back to his old hood. I felt so stupid like I had just gotten played and expressed my disappointment in him. He seemed not to care at first, but when he saw I wasn't paying him any more attention, he started lashing out toward some of the other boys. After breaking up a fight, I took him outside to find out what was going on.

"What do you care? You're just like the rest of them. Soon you'll leave just like they all do," he said.

"I do care. I care because I've been in your shoes before and understand what you're going through," I replied.

"Just because you read my file, don't mean you know the shit that I've gone through. You never been in my shoes. You probably grew up in some rich neighborhood like Bowie or Rockville."

"Actually, I grew up in Cali and ..."

"Wow, really? I always wanted to go to Cali." His interest sparked.

"Yeah, and I bounced from home to home just like you. Sometimes I was homeless and while I was living on the streets, I had to do some things I wasn't proud of just so I could eat and have a place to stay. I was even caught up in a drive-by once, when I was hanging with this gang. They got into a fight and shot up the place while I was in the car. I was so scared."

"Wow, I never would have guessed that about you. You don't even look like the type that would hang with a gang or have been through any of that," he answered.

"Looks can be deceiving. Everyone here has gone through something. Yes, some worse than others, but there's nothing that you or anyone here has done or been through, that we can't overcome," I said, patting him on his back.

"I don't know about that. There's a lot you don't know."

"Like what? Tell me," I replied.

He was very reluctant but eventually began to share that his mom had been on drugs his whole life, and she would leave him home alone for days or weeks at a time. She constantly had men in and out of the house, and one of her boyfriends ended up beating him up real bad after he stole some money from him, which led to him being placed in this group home.

He said what we didn't know was that when his mom would leave, his boys from the hood would look out for him, and to prove his loyalty, he had to do some things that he was too ashamed to say. When I asked him if he ever killed someone, the look in his eyes said everything I needed to know. He broke down and cried in my arms. One of the other volunteers came out to check on us but I signaled for him to leave. I didn't want to lose this moment. I spent the next half hour reassuring him that we all make mistakes, and no matter what he did as long as he learned from it, and became a better person because of it, it was never too late to turn his life around.

It took some time, but after a while he started to make a positive change. I even taught him how to fill out a job application which got him a job at Checkers. Unfortunately, he was right about one thing. Eventually I did leave. This was during that time I was separating from Kevin and moved to Baltimore. I tried to volunteer as much as I could, but I was going through so much during that time. A couple times a week turned into a couple times a month until it eventually I stopped going altogether.

As much as I wanted to move back to Cali to be near my family, I was so scared that all of my old demons would come back to haunt me. So I decided not to make the move yet and focus more on volunteering. At the group home, I saw how the system just didn't give a fuck about these kids, and the ones that did give a fuck were just too overworked make a real difference. Some of these kids had been through some traumatic situations it made my childhood look like the Cosbys. I wished I could save them all and could have done more for Justice.

When I talked to my mom about it, she told me how she had become a court appointed special advocate and joined the CASA program. She said they trained her to provide support for abused or neglected children, and she had to make sure they were living in a safe and healthy environment. If not, she had to report it to the courts. When I heard this, I thought this would be the perfect way for me to do something more, so I immediately joined and was so proud when I got sworn in by a judge. This was the third proudest moment of my life.

Usually, volunteers were assigned one child, but since they didn't have enough volunteers, I was given two sisters who had been taken from their home due to their stepfather sexually abusing one of them. During the first few visits, they were shy and timid, but through time, they started opening up to me, especially when I shared some of the things that I had gone through. At first, I was visiting them only a couple of times a month, but it soon turned into every other weekend, and they become like my little sisters. I would take them everywhere, from bowling to roller skating to just hanging out at the mall. It made me feel like the impact I was having on their lives gave my life purpose, but as much as I enjoyed giving back, I still felt like something was missing in my life.

My youngest sister Alicia had just graduated high school and said she wanted to come to live with me, so I flew her out, and we turned our sex room into her new bedroom. I thought maybe if I had family here, it would fill that missing void. I could tell she had been very sheltered growing up. She was just as naïve as I used to be. She even thought she was pregnant the same day she lost her virginity. I knew she needed to be around me so I could school her on life. Plus, she had never been around Black people growing up, and I wanted her to learn and understand our culture just as much as I wanted to know about hers.

For her eighteenth birthday, I took her to the Two O'clock Club, which was a male strip club, that got fully nude. She and I were both shocked to see how large some of these men were. I usually went to female strip clubs with my boys like Norma Jean's so this was the first time I'd seen dicks this big in person too. Alicia was so freaked out, she said she was never fucking a Black man because it would tear her to shreds. I laughed and said, "Trust me. Not all Black men are that big and not all White men are small."

When she moved in, things started to change dramatically between Bryan and me. He was becoming more and more jealous of our relationship. He didn't like how much time we were spending together and felt like he was being pushed to the side. After I caught him in another lie, things took a turn for the worse. Since he was the general manager at a restaurant, he worked long hours and wouldn't come home until two or three in the morning. On rare occasions when he would have to open up that same morning, he would just get a hotel, so he didn't have to make that long drive back and forth. For some reason this night when he told me he was getting a room I didn't believe him. I had this gut feeling something wasn't right. I was never the type to go through my man's phone or check up on him when he told me he was going out, but that night something told me to check, and I'd learned a long time ago to never to ignore my instincts.

When he checked in his hotel, he called me, told me he loved me, and would see me tomorrow when he got off. After we hung up, I called the hotel and asked for his room, but the man said there was no one there by that name that checked in.

I then called Bryan back and said, "Hey babe, what hotel did you say you were in again?"

"Ahhh, the Boston Inn, why?" he stuttered.

"Oh, because I just got off the phone with Darryl, and he said his cousin was staying in some hotel out that way too, but I don't think it was the Boston Inn though. What room number are you in?" I asked.

"Umm, 211."

I could tell he was nervous as shit, which made me even more suspicious. "Oh, okay. Yeah, I don't think he's at the same hotel. Well, get some rest. I love you, goodnight!" Once again, we hung up, and I called the hotel and asked for room 211, but this time he said they didn't even have a room 211.

"Are you sure?" I asked.

"Yes, I'm sure. We only have a hundred and twenty rooms."

"How about room 111?" I replied.

"Nope, no one has checked into that room yet."

"Oh, okay, thank you," I said, hanging up. I immediately called Bryan back. "Why the fuck is you lying to me about staying at a hotel?" I yelled.

"What are you talking about?" he asked.

"I just called the hotel, and they said there's no one there who checked in with your name, and there's not even a fuckin' room 211. So why the fuck is you lying to me?!"

He was so lost for words he didn't know what to say except that the man was lying, and he really was at the hotel. As soon as he said that I become even more angry and told him we were over and hung up the phone. Even though we had such a fun relationship, I just couldn't tolerate the lies anymore. *How could I be with someone I didn't trust?*

A few minutes later, my phone rang, and it was the same man from the hotel. "Hi ma'am, you called earlier asking for Bryan Miller in room 211. I'm so sorry, but I made a mistake. He is checked into that room. I'm new here and didn't realize we had a 211, but I can buzz you through if you like."

Out of curiosity, I said okay, and a couple of seconds later, Bryan answered the phone.

"See, I told you I was here," he said.

What Bryan didn't know, was that I had already looked up the hotel online and saw they really did only have a hundred and twenty rooms. So not only was he lying to me, but now he had this poor guy wrapped up in his web of lies.

"Okay, so you won't mind me coming up there, right?" I asked. There was a long pause. "Heeeeello," I said.

He finally broke down and confessed that he was going to a party and lied to me about it because his ex was going to be there, and that he went to the hotel to pay the guy to lie for him.

"I can't believe you went to that extreme to lie to me. What else have you been lying about? You know what, it doesn't even matter because we're done." I hung up the phone and was so pissed. I knew if he would lie over this, there was probably so much other shit he had lied to me about but just never got caught, and I would never be able to trust him again.

He knew this time he had really fucked up and tried his hardest to win me back, but nothing worked this time. It really started to hit him when he saw I was entertaining other men. Out of all my past relationships, this one had hurt the most because we had only argued four times during the five years we were together, including this last one. Other than that, our whole relationship was nothing but great and fun times. We'd traveled to Aruba, the Bahamas, Puerto Rico, and he had even taken me on a cruise to all the Virgin Islands for my 30th birthday. He was also the best sex I ever had. I hated to lose him, but I knew a relationship could never survive without trust. If I couldn't trust him after five years, then I knew I would never be able to. Plus, he wanted to get married and have kids, but I didn't want that with him. I knew it was time for me to set him free.

When I broke the news to him, it was like ripping out his heart, stomping on it, and handing it back to him. He cried, pleaded, and begged for me to stay, and I almost gave in, but I knew it would just be prolonging the inevitable. He finally realized my mind was made up and agreed to move out. He was never good at managing his money. He was the type of guy that if he had the money, he would spend it and would never save. So when we first moved in together, he would give me his whole paycheck except for his spending money, and I would pay all the bills that we split then put the rest of his money into his savings account. When I gave him the passcode to his savings, and he saw that he had over ten thousand saved up, he was so thankful. In return, he decided to pay his half of the rent for the remainder of the lease, and he even let me keep the security deposit.

AFTER BRYAN MOVED OUT, ALICIA AND I began dating guys and partying a lot more together. I was really starting to enjoy being single for the first time in over ten years. Although it wasn't off to a great start. I was at a Redbox picking out a movie in front of a McDonalds when an older man driving in a black Mercedes drove into the drive thru. As he waited in line, he stared at me through his car window. He smiled and nodded his head at me, but he wasn't my type, so I didn't pay him much attention and kept scrolling through all the movie titles. He ordered his food then disappeared around the corner. I selected *The Blind Side* and waited for the movie to come out.

The Baltimore Ravens was my favorite football team, ever since they sponsored this holiday party at the stadium for the Big Brother and Sister program that I had been volunteering for. So I couldn't wait to watch this movie again with my sister who had never seen it, over a bottle of Stella Rose. I grabbed my movie and turned around to see the black Mercedes stopping in front of me. He got out of the car and introduced himself as Dewon and then asked if he could take me out sometime.

At first, I told him I wasn't interested, but the more he talked the more I found myself intrigued by him. The way he spoke was hypnotizing like a poet and I was drawn to him like the words to a pen. The way he spoke was kind of like Kovas, but he was way more sophisticated, nothing like I had ever dated before. I could tell I would probably learn a lot from him, so I took him up on his offer when he asked me out again.

I agreed to meet him at one of my favorite restaurants, "Sushi Ya" in Ownings Mills. The conversation flowed naturally, and we talked about everything from politics to our beliefs to how we grew up. He seemed so interested in hearing everything about my life. I had never done this much talking on a first date before, except with Kovas. A couple times when I would say something, he would just stare at me and smile like he was mesmerized by what I was saying.

"Look, I'm just going to cut to the chase. I really like you and want this to go somewhere. Let's just lay everything out on the table. What exactly is it that you're looking for in a man and what are some deal breakers?" he asked leaning back in his chair.

"Honestly, I just got out of a long-term relationship, so I'm not looking for anything serious. I just want someone who's like my best friend. Someone I can tell any and everything to and he does the same in return. My last ex used to lie about everything, which is part of the reason why we broke up. I'm the type you can tell anything to, and as long as you always keep it a hundred with me, we'll be good," I responded. I could tell he was very happy when I said that by the big-ass grin on his face.

He leaned in closer and said, "I'm glad you said that. I want to be upfront and honest with you about everything, so I do have some things I want to share with you."

"Okay," I responded.

"I have two kids."

"Ookay, that's cool," I said.

"And I'm the pastor of a Baptist church."

"What the hell!" I shouted. "Oh shit, I'm so sorry I didn't mean to curse like that." I covered my mouth to prevent even more ungodly words coming out.

"It's okay, you don't have to apologize. You can be yourself around me," he said, laughing.

"Wow, that's so crazy. One of my homegirls is pregnant by some pastor. You know the one that was on the news for cheating on his wife?" I shook my head.

"Oh yeah, that's my boy, we go way back. Who's your friend?" he asked.

"Ooooh, shit. I'd rather not say. I've already said too much. I didn't know you knew him like that, and she told me not to tell anyone."

"It's okay, I'm sure I'll find out later anyway, but there's one more thing I do need to tell you. I'm also married."

Now, it's one thing to date a man who had kids or was a pastor but being a pastor's side chick, was just something not even I could do. "Check please," I said waving the waitress down. I wanted to end the date immediately, especially after we got into it when I called him a hypocrite and a holy pimp for using the church's money to take women out.

He got very defensive and said, "I'm human. I'm not God, and I'm not perfect. I make mistakes just like everyone else. People need to stop holding their pastors up on these unrealistic pedestals."

When he said that, I felt like a kid who had just found out Santa wasn't real. I started to doubt everything I had been raised to believe. He was right. Pastors are human, and humans make mistakes all the time, so how did I know if the bible was even real when it was written by man? I used to get in trouble at Sunday school all the time because I would question everything when things didn't make sense. I had always felt like religion was just a way to scare and control people, but after hearing this, I lost the little bit of faith I had left. Now don't get me wrong, I have always believed in God and always will, but I no longer believed in religion.

Normally men would always pay for the first date, but I didn't want his church money paying for my sushi. I threw sixty dollars down on the table to cover my half and bounced, never seeing him again. My sister's dating life, on the other hand, was nothing like mine. Even though she said she was never going to fuck a Black guy after seeing that big-ass stripper dick, she ended up fucking one and had been hooked ever since. Especially after she started dating this EMT that made her squirt.

Darryl, Rick, and I loved to spend our weekends riding dirt bikes on the streets and watching the 12 o'clock boys' wheelie up and down Northern Parkway and Druid Hill Park. One time, I even got to ride on the back of their dirt bike, praying I didn't fall off like some girls had as they wheelied for what seemed like miles. Now that we were older, we all decided to upgrade and get motorcycles. I was so excited when I got my first Suzuki 600 that I had a photoshoot to show it off.

As a sexy female rider, I would get so much attention when I wasn't surrounded by my boys. My dating life was the shit during this time. Once we got our bikes, we rode everywhere, from TGI Fridays in Greenbelt to Fells Point in Baltimore. One weekend we were headed down to Canton Park to link up with some fellow riders. As we were riding down the interstate 83, a chick with long hair flew past us. We were going pretty fast, so she had to be doing over a hundred.

When we pulled up to the parking lot, we saw her standing next to a bunch of other guys. My boys kept talking about how bad she was when she hit that turn so sharp her knee damn near touched the pavement. I was just as curious as they were to see what she looked like. She still had her helmet on, but I could tell she was cute by her thin frame with long curly hair that touched the tip of her nice firm ass. We all walked over when she took her helmet off, and realized she was a he. I busted out laughing. All my boys tried so hard to play it off like he wasn't the one they were all talking about, but he was, and I never let them hear the end of it.

Sadly that same day, another rider was killed. After we left the park, we were about to get back on 83 but had to make a detour when we saw police blocked it off. Every rider knew how dangerous 83 could be with its sharp winding turns and prayed it wasn't a fellow rider. Unfortunately, we found out later it was. While making that sharp turn, a rider lost control and hit the wall so hard his head came off while still being in his helmet.

I always used to hear, "There are two types of riders. Those who have crashed and those who will," so I knew it was just a matter of time before I fell. Fortunately, that day never came. Mostly because my boys always protecting me. Whenever I rode with them, I would ride in the middle, which allowed my boys to prevent cars and even a truck from hitting me. When I rode alone, it was my guardian angel who watched over me. I had so many close calls, like the time I had come to a complete stop, and the car behind me didn't hit the breaks in time and came stretching by, inches away from hitting me.

Even with all the danger, those were some of the best times of my life. Everything was going so great, except with Alicia. She started to get more and more out of control with her dating. She was doing disrespectful stuff around the house like leaving a used condom out on the kitchen floor or inviting random guys to the house who she'd just met. I tried to explain to her since we were two females living alone, it wasn't safe to bring randoms to the house like that, but she was young and didn't want to listen just like I didn't at her age. I remembered how bad I used to be and tried to be understanding but since I was ten years older than her, I didn't want her to make the same mistakes I did. I started to become more like her mom than her sister, and she hated that, which started to cause a rift between us.

With me and Alicia starting to bump heads more and more, and Rick engaged to his high school sweetheart and getting ready to be deployed, and Darryl getting ready to enter the police academy, I started to feel like we were all growing apart and headed down different paths. My one-year lease was about to be up for renewal and thought if I wanted to move back to Cali, now would be the perfect time to do it, so I finally gave my job my letter of resignation. Since I had been there for almost eleven years, I wanted to give them more than just two weeks' notice so I told them I would stay until they found the perfect person, which ended up taking over three months.

During that time, I just wanted to have as much fun with my friends as possible before we all went our separate ways. When I wasn't riding with my boys, I was out partying with my girl Ashley, who I had met years prior at a company function. She was one of the onsite managers and had a kid by an NBA player.

Ashley had gorgeous dark brown skin that looked like melted chocolate with luscious curves and a phat ass. Guys would break their necks to look at her ass every time we went out. She got so much attention that a lot of females were constantly jealous of her, so she didn't have many friends. Since I wasn't the jealous type and always had hot friends, we instantly clicked. I hated the spotlight. I was like Janet, very shy and timid, and it took liquid courage for me to become Ms. Jackson. So it never bothered me when my friends got all of the attention.

Our favorite place to party was in DC. One night we were at Stonefish Lounge, and she made a comment to one of my boys, "I never been attracted to light-skinned people, but I would fuck the shit out of Angie." When he came back and told me this, I was shocked, but assumed it was just the liquor talking. Later that night, we went back to her house, and I lay on her couch like I usually did when I stayed the night, but this time, she didn't stay upstairs. She came back down wearing this tight sexy black silk nightie that hugged her curves like a motorcyclist coming down 83.

She cuddled up behind me on the couch and I started to think about what my boy had told me earlier and became nervous as fuck. My palms were sweating, and my heart started racing like I was a virgin being touched for the very first time. Besides the kiss with Melissa and Jasmine going down on me at the strip club, I had never fully been with another woman before. She started rubbing on my body and grabbed my breasts. Then she turned my head toward her and started kissing me. When she heard me moan, she got on top and kissed me again. She felt so soft, I started to relax and kiss her back. She began sucking on my nipples and worked her way down to my pussy.

However, when she went down on me, I was very disappointed. I thought women would be better at it than men, but Bryan was way better, so I flipped her over and licked and sucked on her the way he used to do me. To my surprise it didn't take her that long to cum. After she came the first time, I continued, and after the second time, she moaned even louder than the first one. By the time I went down on her for the third time, the sun was starting to come up, but she tasted so good that I didn't want to stop. Finally, after her third nut, she couldn't take me anymore and pulled me up, and we fell asleep for a few more hours.

When we woke up, it was a little awkward, so I decided to head home, and it never came up until a couple weeks later when we hung out again. After leaving the Park at 14th nightclub, she wanted a threesome with this guy she had been fucking. But I wasn't really feeling him when he came over and decided to go upstairs instead. I heard her tell him that I was the best head she'd ever had, and even did it better than him. He laughed about it, then they started fucking. After he left, she came upstairs and tried to kiss on me, but something about that whole situation rubbed me the wrong way. Maybe I was a little jealous that she didn't want it to be just me and her and brought this guy over without asking me first. After that, we never hooked up again but still remained cool.

I WAS IN WALMART WITH MY SISTER, standing in line, when this Asian guy cut in front of us. I politely said, "Excuse me, I'm in line." He apologized then cut in front of the guy standing in front of us with his two kids. He told him the same thing I did and pointed to the end of the line, where he eventually realized he was supposed to go. We all started laughing about it, and the guy introduced himself to me as Travis. He was an older man in his mid-forties, but I could tell he worked out a lot by the muscles coming out of his shirt. He asked me for my number, and at first, I hesitate because he had two kids, but figured since I was leaving anyway there shouldn't be in harm in just exchanging number.

We talked over the next couple of weeks, before I agreed to meet up with him at Corinthian Lounge & Restaurant for our first date. As we were waiting for our waitress to bring out our food, I got a text message from Darryl about meeting up to ride later on that day. As I started to reply, Travis snatched the phone out of my hand and told me how rude it was to text on a date.

"What the fuck, don't be snatching the phone out my hand like that. Are you crazy? You don't know who I'm texting. It could be important," I said, snatching my phone back.

"I'm sorry. I didn't mean to snatch the phone out your hand like that, but I think it's rude when people be more on their phones than being in the moment, especially on a first date."

I was still a little mad, but he did have a point, so I let that one slide and put my phone away and focused on him for the rest of the date, which turned out to be great. I told him how my best friend was now a cop, and he told me that he also had a close friend that was a Baltimore County detective. He also shared with me how he was a single dad and raising two kids by himself. I had never dated a single dad before and was a little nervous about it.

Over the next couple of weeks, we went on a few more dates, then he invited me to his house for dinner. I was surprised to see his kids there. Usually, they would be gone when I came over, but this time they were waiting at the dinner table when I walked in. They recognized me from Walmart, and we joked around about it, which broke the ice. I had a really good time and it made me less nervous about dating men with kids.

On our next date, I decided to invite him to my place and take things to the next level. I was pleasantly surprised to see how big his dick was, but it threw me off on how loud he was. He even cried during us having sex and said that he loved me. I was not expecting that at all and didn't feel the same way in return. He knew I was planning on moving back to Cali soon and wasn't looking for anything serious, but I think he thought he could change my mind. I was dating other guys too, but the one I was really feeling the most at this time lived in New Orleans.

He was this sexy fitness model that I'd met on Facebook through a mutual friend. Since I had a brother who also lived in New Orleans on my dad's side, I decided to fly out and kill two birds with one stone. As soon as he picked me up from the airport, we had to rush to the hospital. His best friend, who worked as a security guard, was shot in a nightclub while trying to break up a fight. Once he found out his friend would be okay, we got to enjoy the rest of our time together. We walked the French Quarter, got some drinks, ate some gumbo, got some dessert at Café du Monde, and took a romantic dinner cruise across the Mississippi River. I then meet my brother for the first time inside a mall. It was hard at first because he didn't speak much English, but we made the best of it and had a great time.

When I got back home, I decided to have a few friends over for some drinks, including Travis. While we were all chilling in my living room, New Orleans called me. We talked for a few minutes. Then when I went to end the call, he told me to tell him that I loved him. He wanted to see if I would say it in front of all my friends, which I did. After we hung up, I could tell Travis was bothered, especially after he made a comment to one of my homegirls about me always being on the phone. As soon as they left, he went off and got all in my face about me talking to other men in front of him.

I yelled back, "WE ARE NOT TOGETHER! I can talk on the phone to whoever the fuck I want to talk to."

The way he looked at me was like he wanted to hit me, but my sister came out of her room to see what all the yelling was about. When she moved in, she had brought her dog with her. But when my apartment complex found out, they gave us a notice to get rid of the dog or we would be evicted. Since Travis lived up the street in a single-family house with a yard, he agreed to let her dog stay at his home, but after this, he told me we had to come to get the dog, which we did. After that, I blocked him from ever calling me again.

A week later, there was a knock on the door, and it was the police. When I answered, they asked where I was last night. I told them I had been at my house all night. Then they asked if I had been by Travis's house at all. I told them no since we'd stopped talking last week, and I'd picked up my sister's dog from his home. They then told me all four of his tires had been slashed, and he said I had something to do with it. In my mind, I was thinking, *Good, that's what his ass gets*, but I didn't have anything to do with it, and was pissed he was blaming me for it. Luckily, I lived in a gated community with cameras and a security guard at the gate, so anytime we left in and out, it was documented, and I told the police if they checked they would see that I was home all night.

Since my lease was over, I decided to move in with Havana until I finished training the new guy that had just been hired to take over my position. Alicia wasn't ready to move back to Cali since she loved Baltimore, so she moved in with this guy she had been dating. I told her she shouldn't do it, but she was very stubborn like I used to be and did what she wanted.

As we were packing, she got a call from an unknown number. At first, she didn't answer it, but after the fourth time, she finally did. It was Travis, telling her to tell me if he didn't get the money for slashing his tires, I was going to be sorry. I snatched the phone from her and told his bitch ass I didn't have anything to do with his tires and to stop calling me. I hung up and had her block his number. A few hours later, we heard another knock at the door, so I answered it, and it was the police again. This time they said he claimed I had broken into his house and stole some items. I started laughing and told the police how he had just called me that morning telling me I was going to be sorry if I didn't pay him and now suddenly, someone had broken into his house–how convenient.

"This is not a laughing matter. These are serious charges," one of the officers said.

"It's a laughing matter to me because I know I had anything to do with it. It's obvious he's pissed about me breaking up with him and just trying to get me back," I explained.

I then started to remember when we first started dating, Travis told me that someone had broken into his house months before we even met, then again after we started dating and they stole five thousand dollars from his basement. He even asked to borrow some money from me, which I refused. After putting two and two together, things were starting to look suspicious.

"You might want to look into his record before you start excusing me of anything. This has been happening to him since before we even met. So if you guys don't have anything else, I need to finish packing," I said.

They asked if they could take a look around to see if I had any of the items he claimed was stolen. I knew I didn't, so I agreed, and they looked all around and in all the packed boxes. I chuckled as they said everything was clear and left, but inside I was heated at the fact that he was trying to set me up like this. Luckily, I only had a few more weeks to go. Then I'd be in Cali and would never have to deal with his ass again.

The following day I moved in with Havana, and it was starting to hit me that I was leaving Maryland after twelve years. I was excited about starting this new chapter in my life but also sad I'd be closing another simultaneously. One of the hardest parts was breaking the news to my two little girls from the CASA program. They had become just a big part of my life, so when I told them I was leaving they cried. They said everyone they love always ends up leaving them, which broke my heart even more. I felt so guilty I was leaving like this again. I promised them that even though I was moving three thousand miles away, I would always be there for them no matter what.

Alicia moved in with her boyfriend, and I decided to spend the rest of my time with Anthony, who I had known for years. I met him at a nightclub called Dream in DC back when I first started dating Bryan. But he lived in Virginia with his girl, so we just became Facebook friends. That was until I had caught Bryan lying to me about the hotel. So while Bryan was away on a business trip. I invited Anthony over to stay the night. He was shocked but jumped at the chance. He had been trying to hook up with me for years, but we never had the opportunity until now. The rain was pouring down so hard I thought he was going to change his mind about coming but he finally made it. When he came in, I showed him into the sex room where I had the windows open so we could see the thunderstorm. Candles lit up around the room as I started to give him the kind of massage Keith gave Stoney in *Set It Off*. Anthony had the sexist lips. The kind that LL Cool J would lick, and I wanted to kiss them all night long. After we made Keith and Stoney love, we talked until it was time for him to go home. That was when I knew things were truly over between me and Bryan.

After Bryan moved out, I hooked up with Anthony every chance we got. He was definitely someone I would have been in a relationship with had we lived closer. He was my sexy Aquarius twin and resembled Trey Songz so much that when we took a trip to Atlantic City with his boys, we got into the nightclub for free and had free table and bottle service all night. Women kept wanting to take pictures with him, especially since a couple of his boys were big enough to look like his security guards. When I decided to move to Cali, we made it a point to spend as much time as we could with each other and even came up with a "Fuck-it list," which is a list of all the places we wanted to fuck before I left.

We had already checked off the Ferris wheel at Kings Dominion in broad daylight, which wasn't easy. I had to wear an easily accessible sundress, and we had to ride it a few times to make sure it stopped at the perfect angle where not too many people could see. Once it stopped, I sat on his lap from the back and bounced on it until he busted, which was just in time before it started moving again.

We fucked on my boss's desk one late at night after work, which felt like a scene out of a movie. I was his naughty secretary who got called into his office to be reprimanded for wearing inappropriate work attire. But instead of writing me up, he stuck his dick inside me after I purposely dropped my pen and bent over, exposing my wet pussy. I loved to role play and would come up with the craziest scenarios. I always wanted to try the burglary scene where he would crawl in through the window and take me while I was sleep, but I could never make it all the way through without laughing.

We also fucked at the Potomac River near the Eisenhower memorial where we could see the Monument and new Martin Luther King, Jr. Memorial that had just been built. Now we had to tackle the biggest challenge yet–his job. He was the head of security at the World Bank in DC and gave me the code to get in the front door. Once I got in, he told me to go to the elevator and wait for him on the 10th floor.

On the way there, I decided to role play again. This time I was going to be Stoney, and I had stolen the code from Keith while he was sleeping in his bed. But he woke up as I was sneaking out of his house and followed me to the bank where I had planned to rob it. He caught me just as I was getting into the elevator and was about to turn me in, but I seduced him, and after we made love, I sliced his throat and robbed the bank as planned. Then I flew to Cuba, where I met up with Tupac, and we lived happily after.

Okay, okay, I know that sounds crazy, but that's what I was fantasizing about on that long drive from Baltimore to DC. When I finally got there, I was wearing nothing, but a red bra and panty set underneath my trench coat. I was so nervous but excited at the same time. I went to the front door and punched in the code, but it beeped loud and wouldn't open. Then I noticed one of the security guards stand up and start walking toward me. I hurried up and entered the code again, and this time it made a clicking noise, and the door opened. I tried not to make eye contact with the security guard as I rushed over to the elevators. My heart was pounding like an African drum.

When I made it in, I squatted down and let out a big sigh of relief. I was so scared that I was shaking as I texted Anthony that I was here. Shortly after I got to the 10th floor, he came up, and we went back into one of the elevators where he locked it with his key so it wouldn't move. He then picked me up and passionately kissed me against the wall. He opened my coat and smiled when he noticed what I was wearing. I got down and slowly took my jacket off, letting him get a good look at my body. He then grabbed my face and kissed me again. I ripped off his clothes and started sucking his dick. Then I got up, took off my panties, and he picked me back up, placing my legs over his shoulders, while eating my pussy until it was dripping down his chin. Then he slid me down and fucked me with my legs still over his arms. After a few minutes, he put me down, and I bent over to hit it from the back until he came.

"Damn, I'm going to miss this shit," he said, buckling up his pants.

"Come on, let's go in one of the conference rooms," he said.

I put my coat on and placed my panties in my pocket and followed him out to one of the conference rooms, where he picked me up, laid me across one of the tables, and ate my pussy again until he got hard. I hopped off the table and rode him on one of the chairs until he busted a second time.

After that, he said he wanted to take me to the rooftop where it overlooked all of DC. It was so beautiful. We could see the Monument, the Capitol, the White House, and the Thomas Jefferson Memorial. He held me tightly from behind, and we both took a deep breath, realizing that our crazy sex affair was coming to an end. We reminisced about all the good times we'd shared throughout the years, and right before we were getting ready to go back in, I said, "We have to fuck out here!"

He laughed and said, "Again? … aight, fuck it!"

I pulled his pants down and sucked him off until I could feel every vein on his dick begin to throb inside my mouth. I then sat on one of the air conditioning units, and he fucked me again as we kissed the entire time until he busted his third and final nut. Then he walked me down to my car, where we kissed goodbye.

The following week, while I was at work, an officer showed up at my job. I thought, *Not again*, but she said she was just there to get my new address to close the case for Travis, so I gave her Havana's address. Later that night, I was on my way to meet up with Anthony again so we could fuck at this Japanese restaurant in Columbia where you could get your own private room.

I stopped at McDonald's on the way to grab a coffee and noticed a car following closely behind. Then when I went through the drive thru, I saw the same car waiting for me in the parking lot, and then it started to follow me again when I drove out onto the street. I knew something was up, so I pulled over to confront whoever it was, but before I could get out of the car, I was surrounded by two other vehicles with their sirens on. They told me to step out of my car and to put my hands in the air.

Then I was handcuffed and taken back to Havana's house, where they told me they had a warrant to search my car and her home. However, no one showed me the warrant or said what it was for. When I tried to call Darryl, they snatched the phone out of my hand and said they were taking it into evidence. After they searched her home and my car, they took me down to the Baltimore County police station where I was interrogated like a serial killer.

There were two officers. One was playing the good cop, the other the bad one. The bad one pushed me down on the chair real hard and started yelling at me about where I was on these specific days. I was so scared I couldn't even remember what I had done the day before. Then they finally told me why I was there. They said Travis's home was burglarized again, and this time arson was involved. Not only did the perpetrator steal money from his house again, but they also tried to burn his house down and killed his turtle. Travis said that he had broken up with me, and I had become violent with him and started threatening him.

Now I know what y'all must be thinking–if I tried to burn down my mama's house then I probably did do that shit. But anyone who knows me, knows as crazy as I am there's no way, I would ever hurt a child or an animal, so I would never kill his turtle or risk setting fire to his house that his kids could be in. No matter how much I hated Travis, I wouldn't wish that on him or anyone else.

I tried to explain to the officer's that I was the one who cut him off for tripping about me talking to other guys, and that I even had the texts and Facebook messages to prove it. If they were smart, they would have already done this research, and seen that he was the one that kept calling, texting, and harassing me. But no matter how much I pleaded, it seemed like they weren't believing shit I was saying. Then I started to remember that he said he had a police friend who worked in this station and thought maybe it was probably one of them, so I shut down and asked for a lawyer, but they said they were not charging me with anything, and I was free to go anytime I wanted. I knew after that something shady was going down.

The next day I called Darryl and had him do some investigating of his own. I was finally able to get a copy of the warrant and saw that the judge had only issued it because Travis said I was getting ready to move to California and flee the area. I was also able to look online and see he had a long history of domestic violence with his ex-wife, armed robbery charges, possession of an illegal weapon, and drug charges. He'd even filed countless police reports for burglary on his home way before we even met. Later I found out through a mutual friend that he was running an insurance scam. He would burglarize his own house and file false reports to get the money and use his police friend to do it.

I was so pissed. I began to make calls to internal affairs, who seemed genuinely interested in what was going on. However, without having the name of his police friend, they said there was not much they could do but would look into it. After that, everything was dropped, and I was able to get my phone back. As much as I wanted to sue him and the police department for what they'd put me through, I let it go because I just wanted to enjoy my final weeks in Maryland without any drama.

Rick was about to get married and made me one of his grooms-women. Darryl was the best man. We decided to take Rick to Atlantic City for his bachelor party with the other groomsmen. Even though Rick was one of my best friends, I had never met any of his groomsmen before who were his friends from college. I immediately had my eye on his friend Daniel, who was 6'7. I had never been with a guy that tall before and was pleasantly surprised when he told me he was an engineer and didn't play basketball. An intelligent man always impressed me more than an athletic one. After flirting all night with him in the strip club, we ended up fucking in the hotel bathroom.

Then a couple days later I watched my best friend get married. It was such a bittersweet moment. On one hand I was extremely happy for him and glad I got to be a part of their journey. I even witness him proposing to her. I was so proud of the man he had become. But on the other hand, I knew this was the end of our journey and we would no longer be the three musketeers anymore. Sure, we would always stay in touch, but I knew things would never be the same between us, which was evident when I threw my going-away party and Rick couldn't be there because he had been deployed.

"I'M GOING GOING, BACK BACK, TO CALI Cali" by Biggy was playing as I packed up my SUV with as much as I could fit and had it shipped it off with my Gixxer to my mom's house. Then I flew back to Cali with my two cats and moved back into with Mom, where my brother Chris and his girlfriend Stacy were also staying. I couldn't help but to get this eerie feeling when I started to move my things back into my old bedroom. I had so many bad memories there but was trying to be optimistic and focus on creating good ones.

I had enough money saved up that I could take my time to find the right job and location where I wanted to live in. After I got settled in, I started to go on job interviews every week. I was excited to be back home, but I kept having this feeling that something bad was going to happen, and it didn't take long before something did.

Every morning I would wake up to Coco sleeping at the edge of my bed. However, this morning he wasn't there, so I got up to look for him and noticed the back door was cracked open, which Chris would sometimes do after going outside to smoke a cigarette. I slammed it shut and started to freak out. I woke my mom up, who helped me search everywhere for him.

We even put up five-hundred-dollar reward signs all throughout the neighborhood. I know some people might say *Oh, it was just a cat*, but he wasn't just a cat to me. I'd had Coco for over ten years ever since I was twenty-one, and since I didn't want kids, he was my fur baby, and when he went missing, it was like losing a child to me. I was so devasted I cried almost every night.

I searched for him every day, when in the pouring rain, which ended up giving me tonsillitis and was admitted to the hospital for severe dehydration. I got several calls from people who thought they had found him, but it was never him, and I began to lose hope that I would ever see him again. I was so mad at my brother Chris that I cursed him out and told him that never to talk to me again. It began to be too painful for me to be in that house. So I decided to give my luck a try in Vegas.

I drove down and stayed with Tisha and her four kids and started applying for all kind of accounting jobs. While I was there, I got a Facebook message from one of my old military buddies I was stationed with at Fort Belvoir, who also lived in Vegas. He said he had always had a crush on me and would love to take me out to dinner. I was thrilled to catch up with an old military friend, so I agreed. I picked him up from his house and noticed that he was acting strange the moment he got in my car. I kept asking him if he was okay, but he just said he was nervous to see me after all this time.

We pulled up to a casino and sat inside at one of the restaurants. He then got up, handed me his credit card and said to order whatever I wanted, and he'd be right back. I was so confused about why he would give me his card if he was going to be right back. I waited for a while to see if he was going to return, but when he didn't, I ordered the most expensive things on the menu: lobster, shrimp, and steak as well a couple of drinks. I figured if I was going to eat alone, I was going to eat good. After I ate all my food and he still hadn't come back, I started to be nervous about using his card, thinking it probably would get declined or something, but she came out with the receipt and told me to sign for it.

I didn't want to wait for him anymore, so I was grabbing my purse to head out when I saw security holding his arm and bringing him over to me. "Is he with you?" the security guy asked.

"Umm yeah, why?" I responded.

"He was getting ready to get kick out of the casino, but he said you were sitting here waiting on him, so I'm letting you know he has to leave right now."

I was so lost and had no clue on what the fuck was going on or why this kind of shit always happens to me. "What did he do?" I asked.

"You need to ask him that, but he needs to leave like right now. I only came over as a courtesy to you."

We both left the casino, and when we got into my car, I asked, "What the hell was that all about?" He kept saying was security was tripping off him for going to the bathroom but wouldn't give me a straight answer. So I told him, I was dropping him back off at his house. Once I said that, he started flipping out and broke down crying. I was scared he was going to do something crazy, especially being a war vet, but he finally calmed down enough to talk and said, "My life is fucked up, ever since I got out the military. I saw some real fucked-up things oversees that he just couldn't get out of my head no matter what I try to do. I'm not going to lie. I did some coke in the bathroom. That's why security was throwing me out, but I didn't mean for all that shit to happen. I wanted to impress you today, but I just keep fucking up. Nothing I ever do is right. I shouldn't even be alive anymore," he cried. He went on about how he had started doing porn to make ends meet and how much he wanted to kill himself over it. When he said all that, I felt so bad for him and tried to console him as best as I could.

At first, I was planning to drop him off and never speak to him again, but after hearing this, I could tell he just needed a friend. Not to mention I had been in his shoes before and since I had lost my father to suicide, I knew I couldn't leave him like that. I told him, I would be here for him and we could hang out again, later on that week. A few days later, he told me he had gotten two tickets from his friend to see the Mayweather fight and asked me if I wanted to go. I loved boxing and was thrilled to say yes.

Then out the blue he sent a text message asking if he could eat my pussy before for the fight. I was so pissed that he would send me something like after I had spent hours trying to convince him how much his life was worth saving. Once he sent that, I didn't want to have anything else to do with him. I told him to lose my number and never call me again then I blocked his number and unfriended him from Facebook.

A couple days later, I saw RIP and pictures of him all on my FB timeline. I called one of our mutual friends and he told me he had died from a drug overdose. I felt like shit and realized the words you say to someone could be your last. I called Chris to work things out and forgive him for what happened to Coco. I also decided Vegas was not for me either, especially after going on several failed interviews. I wanted to put all of my energy into finding a job anywhere in Cali, so I went back to my moms and started applying to jobs no matter how far it was.

Weeks went by, and I still couldn't find a job that paid anywhere near what I used to make. I was willing to take a pay cut, but not if it paid what I was making ten years ago. The jobs that did pay well always asked for a college degree, which I didn't have. It was now my third month, and the longest time I went without having a job since my teenage years. I fell into a deep depression and it felt like I had made the biggest mistake of my life by moving back out here. I thought with my eleven years of accounting experience, it would be easy to find a job, but it wasn't. Everything I had worked so hard for had fallen apart in a matter of months.

One lady even told me without having a degree, no one is going to hire me at the rate I want and that I should lower my standards. I was down to my last dime and thought maybe she was right. I mean I guess it's better to have a low paying job than having no job. So I applied at jobs that paid over half of what I made but couldn't even get those because they felt like I was overqualified. I didn't know what to do anymore. I was starting to lose all hope, but then I began to remember everything I had been through in my life, and no matter how bad it got, God always came through for me when I needed him. I got down on my knees and prayed, "God, I have faith in everything you do. I know I didn't come this far for nothing. I know the reason why I didn't get those jobs I wanted was because you have something more amazing in store for me. I just pray that it happens soon. Please God, bless me with the job that I'm meant to have. Please, please, please. Amen."

After I finished praying, I remembered what my old boss at the HOA company once told me. He'd pulled me in his office and asked me where I saw myself in five to ten years from now. I told him hopefully still working here. He laughed and told me to think beyond that. He said there was always something special about me and I had the potential do anything I set my mind to. I never heard anyone tell me that before, and it made such a deep impact on me. I decided to do the opposite of what the lady suggested. Instead of lowering my standards, I raised them even higher and applied to jobs I thought I was way underqualified for.

Two days later, I got a call for a CFO position at a music company in Los Angeles, which was over two hours away. But I didn't care and agreed to come in that Friday. I spent that whole night researching everything I could about the company. I had been on so many job interviews I was a pro at it and knew I'd nailed it when I had the owner in tears as he described how he started his company from scratch out of his one-bedroom apartment. He said he and his wife had lived off beans and hot dogs for years before turning it into the multi-million-dollar company it is today. I told him I admired people like him who could turn nothing into something and help people the way his company did. I shook his hand, and he thanked me for coming in and said he would be making a decision soon and would be in touch.

The next day, he called and offered me the position. I couldn't believe it. He said the reason he chose me was I had really done my research about his company and the fact that I gave my job three months' notice to find someone instead of two weeks really impressed him. He needed someone who wasn't just smart but also trustworthy and I demonstrated all of the qualifications he was looking for. He then asked me if I could start on Monday, which of course I agreed to do. As soon we hung up, I jumped up and down, screaming at the top of my lungs. Not only was I making way more money than I had in Maryland, but I also getting my own office, which was double the size of my old boss's. That day was the fourth proudest moment in my life.

I MOVED IN WITH MY UNCLE IN WEST Covina, who was the only person I knew that lived close enough to my job. However, it was still a three hour a day commute, but I didn't care at all. I was just so happy to have the job I wanted and did the commute for four months until I'd saved up enough money to get my own apartment and furnish it with brand-new furniture.

By this time, Alicia was fed up with her cheating boyfriend when his baby mama confronted her and said they were still messing around. After almost fighting her over him, she decided to move back to Cali and move back in with our brother. I had missed her so much and was glad to hear she was coming back. We started hanging out just like old times, except this time we weren't living together, and all of the tension was gone. Without having all that tension, we got to party like sisters again. I decided to take her to Supperclub for her 22nd birthday. That was a crazy night that felt like the movie Hangover. Weird things just kept happening. Like someone flashing us their dick, taking pictures in a Playboy bunny's party bus, breaking bottles on the streets with homeless people, skinny dipping in Santa Monica beach, sticking a piece of paper down someone's dick hole. Yeah, as I said, that was a crazy but fun night.

About a year later, once I got settled in, I traded my SUV in for a BMW convertible which I had always wanted since Kevin crashed my first convertible. I also sold my bike to Rick. Riding just wasn't the same without my boys. I never felt safe enough when I rode in Cali without them, so my gut feeling told me it was time to get rid of it. Rick ended up crashing it not too long after he got it. Thank God, he wasn't hurt but the bike was totaled.

Tatiana was in the military and stationed up north, but her sister and her friends were still living in the Inland Empire, so I started hanging out with them a lot, especially with Emera and Stephanie. It felt like the good ol' days, except now we were all grown, and I didn't have to worry about sneaking out of my mama's house to party with them. We partied everywhere together from LA to Palm Springs to Ensenada to ATL to Miami.

One night we were on our way to a Rick Ross album release party in LA. We thought since we knew one of the promoters, we could show up anytime, but by the time we got there, security told us they were no longer allowing anyone else in. So we decided to hit up another club. As we were walking down the street to catch an Uber, I saw a heavy-set man walking out the club's back door with an entourage. Mind you, I was drunk, and I rarely watched music videos. I had no idea what Rick Ross really looked like except that he was a big Black man with a beard, and when I saw the same type of man coming the club with an entourage following behind him, I assumed it was him, and I said, "Oh, shit, there goes Rick Ross."

The next thing I heard was, "Bitch, you better watch who the fuck you are talking to. Do you know who the fuck I am?"

I honestly had no idea, so I responded, "Yeah, Rick Ross, right?" All my girls were on the floor laughing, and I couldn't understand why until Emera ran up to me and said, "Nooooo, that's Suge Knight!" and started laughing again.

Everyone thought it was funny except him and he responded, "You need to watch who the fuck you talking to before you get fucked up."

I was still in disbelief and too drunk to realize it was Suge Knight, so I responded, "This is not Suge Knight. Suge is way bigger than this," which made my friends laugh even harder.

Emera was like, "Ang, this is Suge, look!" She then showed me a picture of him on her phone, and it finally hit me it wasn't Rick Ross, and they looked nothing alike.

"Ooooh shit, my bad," I said.

"You lucky I don't fuck you up," he said.

"Why you so aggressive? Were you not loved as a child or something? Do you need a hug? No, you know what you need? You need a finger in your ass!" I stumbled over toward him with my finger in the air.

I don't know why but every time I drank, I always had this fetish for sticking fingers in assholes, so that was all I could think about saying at the time.

"What the fuck did you just say?" he said, walking up on me like he was about to punch the shit out of me. "Man, get the fuck out of here with that shit. How would you like it if I shove my dick in your mom's mouth?" he continued.

"I don't know. If you shaved your balls, she might like it," I said as Emera covered up my mouth and pulled me back away from Suge before I could say anything else. He must have realized I was either just as crazy as him or drunk as fuck because he had no response and just walked away. We ended up getting in our Uber and laughing about it the whole way.

The next day, Emera posted some pictures of all of us from that night and one of her close friends from high school named Quan hit her up and asked about me. After she responded to him about what a crazy but great friend I was, he sent me a message that he wanted to know me. He was attractive, but when I saw that he lived in Sacramento I quickly dismissed him since long distance relationships had never worked out for me. Later in life, I realized that was a huge mistake because he ended up being my soul mate, but that's be continued in a whole other chapter of my life.

Alicia had been talking to a guy who was mixed with Jamaican and African. She wanted to invite him over to my house so they could hook up. As I was getting into bed, I realized I'd forgotten my phone charger and yelled out to them that I needed to get it out the living room. I heard him yelled, "Okay," so I opened my bedroom door and witnessed them fucking, doggy style, on my couch. "Really, what the fuck?" I said, covering my eyes.

"Oh, we thought you said can we bring you your charger," he said laughing.

I ran over, grabbed my charger then ran back into my room, where I tried burning that imagine out of my mind. Come to find out it was the day my nephew was conceived. At first, I was extremely disappointed she had gotten pregnant because she could barely take care of herself. But after I saw the first ultrasound, my heart melted, and I instantly fell in love. I couldn't wait to be another auntie-godmom, but I knew from day one that there was something more special about this one, so I called him my nephew-son.

Before she got pregnant, we had planned to go to Honduras together on our dad's birthday in May to visit his grave and to meet the rest of my family for the first time. But since her due date was at the end of April, she could no longer make the trip. Most of my family only spoke Spanish except my stepmom and I really needed someone else to be there with me, so I didn't feel so out of place. I hit up my girls, and Emera volunteered to go.

During the end of April, I started to get nervous that she would have the baby while I was in Honduras, but luckily her water broke at my house and we headed straight to the hospital. When I was living in Maryland, Havana had gotten pregnant for the fourth time by some guy she was dating, and

I got to witness the birth of her youngest daughter who also became my godniece. However, Havana had a C-section which seemed a lot easier than what Alicia was going through. I had never heard someone scream that much in pain before and it scared the shit out of me. I kept thinking something was wrong.

By time we got the hospital it was too late for her to get an epidural and she had to give birth the natural way. It was so hard to watch. I cringed with every push. She said it felt like all of her bones where breaking one by one. Finally, after an excruciating hour, my nephew-son was brought into this world. I even got to help pick out his name.

When the doctors came in, they asked my sister if she wanted him circumcised, but she couldn't afford it, so I offered to pay for it. I couldn't have my nephew-son walking around with a turtle dick, which he took like a champ and didn't even cry when they did it.

A FEW WEEKS LATER, EMERA AND I WERE getting ready for our flight to Honduras. I knew it would be a very emotional trip, so I decided to play a practical joke on her to lighten up the mood by placing a huge dildo in her carry-on bag so TSA would see it when she went through the check point. However, my joke didn't go as planned. She was so late, by the time she got to the airport, we damn near missed our flight. I was so worried that I had forgotten all about the dildo and the joke was on me because it ended up staying in my bag the whole time.

When we arrived in Tegucigalpa, Honduras, I was overwhelmed with the amount of family that showed up at the airport. It was my stepmom, uncle, aunt, brother, and so many cousins I couldn't even count. I felt so loved seeing them all standing there waiting for me as I came down the escalator. They all gave hugs and took some pictures before headed out to a nice Honduran restaurant, where I was greeted with even more family. We cheered to my arrival with tequila shots. I knew at that moment they were my blood. I couldn't stop staring at my uncle, who closely resembled my father. He kept telling me how happy my father would have been to see me.

After dinner, we went back to my stepmom's house to unpack. Just as I pulled dildo from my bag, my stepmom walked in the room. It was brand new and still in the package, so she thought I had brought it for her. We all laughed so hard as she took it and put it in her room.

The next day she took us to my grandmother's house, who had passed away after my father. She had so many pictures of him on the wall, and even had a photo album with some of my baby pictures in it. My stepmom said he use to always show me off and was so proud to have me as a daughter. My uncle gave me a sheet from his photo album with some pictures and a card that Mom had given my dad.

Staying in Honduras was a very humbling experience. They only had running water that would come on for a couple hours, once a week. Most of the time we had to bathe out of buckets of water. After we came back from my grandmother's, we got excited when we realized the water had come back on. Emera and I rushed to take showers while my stepmom filled up the buckets. Emera went in first and came out feeling brand-new. As I grabbed my stuff for the shower, my stepmom turned the water off, thinking we were done. But I hadn't showered yet, and when I went to turn the water back on, only one little drip came out. I was so disappointed I had to take another birdbath.

We also couldn't put toilet paper in the toilets because their sewage systems couldn't handle solid waste. I learned this the hard way when I took a shit at my uncle's house and clogged up his toilet. The bathroom was right next to the dining room where everyone was sitting at the table. I was so embarrassed when I had to stick my head out and whisper for help.

The next day we drove three hours down to a small ranch in San Marcos de Colon, where my father and stepmom grew up. On the way, I realized how Left Eye died on these streets. Hondurans drive crazy as fuck. There are so many one-way streets, and they play chicken to move around slower vehicles. Cars were coming straight at us, and a couple of times, my stepmom had to swerve off the road to avoid getting hit. I was okay with it, but Emera was having a difficult time since she had been in a severe car accident when she was younger that almost killed her. A few times, she would scream out when other cars got too close. I tried not to laugh, but it was kind of funny. We ended up getting pulled over at a checkpoint where they asked us to show them our IDs and passports.

"Oh shit!" I said realizing that I had left my passport in my other bag.

They were speaking in Spanish, so I didn't understand what was being said when my stepmom tried to explain this and show them my California driver's license instead. I knew something bad was about to happen when they told me to step out the car. They took my ID and walked into a brown building. I asked my stepmom what was going on.

"They say you get deported if you don't show valid passport. I think they just want some money, mija. You have some?" she asked in her Spanglish accent.

I handed her a twenty and waited for them to come back out. When they did, they started speaking more aggressively in Spanish. My stepmom pulled one of them over to the side and begin speaking to him in a softer tone. I saw her hand him the twenty and he signaled for us to leave.

"Come on, mija," she said placing her hand on my back and escorting me back in the car. She said they told her next time I would be deported. *Of course, this shit would only happen to me*, I thought.

When we got to the ranch, I could tell it was in a very poor part of Honduras and was infested by mosquitos. The moment we stepped out of the car, Emera and I were being sucked dry. Apparently, they only had a taste for American blood. It got so bad that we had to drive back into the nearest small town and go on the hunt for repellent. Three stores later, we finally found some and sprayed it all over ourselves like it was it was liquid gold.

When we got back to the ranch, I was amazed to watch how they made all of their food from scratch and cooked everything outdoors. I even got to milk a cow for the first time, which felt so disgusting–like an eighty-year-old penis. They had no electricity, so after the sun went down, we sat by the fire and tried to communicate the best we could. The hardest part was trying to use the outhouse in the dark. After my first piss, I decided just to hold it until the next morning.

The showers were outdoors too but it felt so amazing to take one outside. It had been so long since I had a real shower, I didn't even care that the water wasn't that warm. I was extremely grateful that I got to experience where my father grew up, but I was ready to get the hell out of there and head back to Tegucigalpa.

Once we got back, we wanted to do some sightseeing, so we went to see the Comayagua Cathedral, which had the oldest clock in America. It was built by some Arabs during their time in Spain around the year 1100. It was crazy to see something that old. Speaking of old, while I was sitting outside waiting on my stepmom to come out the store, I got cursed out by some old Spanish lady. I had no idea what she was saying until my stepmom came out and started cursing back at her.

"What was that all about?" I asked.

"Oh, she thought you were part of some gang because of your back tattoo. Out here most people that have visible tattoos are gang affiliated," she explained.

I wished I had known that before I packed all these crop tops, I thought.

The next day we drove another three hours to San Pedro so I could meet the rest of my siblings. My sister from Miami had flown out to meet us so she could be there when I met our oldest brother, another sister, and my nephew who was also mixed with Black. He was twelve at the time and was so excited to meet me. He said it was nice to finally see someone like him since he was the only one mixed with Black where he lived. Sadly, while I was writing this book, he was shot and killed in front of his home. He was only eighteen. I was so grateful that I got to spend that precious moment with him before he died.

I had now met nine out of my ten siblings, but there was still one more left–our transgender brother Hancel, who had been infected with AIDS. Because of this, I knew he didn't have long to live and how important it was for me to see him. But I never got that chance. He had gotten jumped days before I arrived, and his cell phone was stolen, so we couldn't get ahold of him while I was out there. Then a couple of years later, he passed away due to health complications.

I was crushed that I never got to meet him. Luckily, I did have an opportunity to talk to him on the phone and hear his voice tell me how much he loved me, and I told him the same in return. He was so sweet. I know we would have been close had we grown up together but now he was with our father watching over us.

When we got back to Tegucigalpa, and my uncle surprised me by taking all of us to see the *Christ* at "El Picacho," which is a monument that stands at the height of 4,353 feet above sea level. It was such an amazing view. As we were overlooking all of Tegucigalpa, he pulled out a bottle of tequila. We all took shots to celebrate family, our amazing time together, and my father, whose grave I was about to visit.

IT WAS NOW THE MOMENT I HAD BEEN waiting my whole life for–being reunited with my father. As I walked toward his grave, I was overwhelmed with so many different emotions. I always believed that there was something above putting in double time to watch over me, and now it felt like I was meeting that guardian angel for the first time. I approached his grave and fell to my knees, closed my eyes, and imagined that he was right there next to me.

I could feel him putting his arms around me as I squeezed him tight around his big ol' belly. I felt his beard tickling the side of my face as he gently kissed me on my forehead and whispered in my ear, "Fly, Black Butterfly, fly," and just like that, all of the anger, hate, resentment, and pain that had once consumed me was finally set free. I felt like this massive weight had been lifted off my shoulders, and I was instantly filled with love, happiness, self-worth, and forgiveness. That's when I looked up, noticed my wings, and began to fly …

"She was never meant to be in a cage. Her spirit was born to fly and when she was finally set free, she showed the world she was never a caterpillar, she was just a butterfly who had lost her wings."
– Black Butterfly

Epilogue
Monarch Reign

LOOKING AT ME NOW, YOU WOULD never have known that I went through even half of what I did. My scars are no longer visible, but the pain still runs deep. I spent most of my life being chased by my past and haunted by the bad decisions I've made. It took a long time for me to realize that everything I ever wanted was on the other side of fear.

Writing this book was one of the hardest things I ever had to do. Having to go back to that dark place and relive all of those horrible memories I tried so hard to forget became so painful that at times it felt like I was writing with my own blood. I wanted to quit so many times and sometimes I did. But I kept thinking about how hard it must have been for so many others who shared their stories. Had they stopped or given up, they wouldn't be who they are today, and I probably wouldn't be here either.

So I kept pushing through. And by the end, it was like looking into a mirror for the first time. I got to see how much I had actually accomplished in my life. I had no idea, the amount of shit I went through until I wrote it all down. The fact that I'm still alive and have a smile on face is a miracle, and I'm so proud that I never gave up on myself. My past no longer haunts me. Instead, I embrace it. Like colors to a painting, I saw how my mistakes helped to create my masterpiece.

I have no regrets in life. Well except for shaving my eyebrows like we all did in the 90's, I really regret that shit. Other than that, I have no regrets. Everything I went through shaped me into who I am, and I love the person I've become. I'm still crazy and fuck up from time to time. But that's what life is all about—making mistakes and learning from them. The wisest person doesn't just learn from their own, they learn from others.

My editor asked me, now that my book is complete, what would make it a success. As much as I would love for my story to help and inspire others, just me being able to complete this chapter of my life has been a major achievement for me. This was the fifth proudest moment of my life. You don't have to be rich to be successful or be famous to feel accomplished. You just have to defy the odds and do something that you never thought you would be able to do. I never thought I would be able to fly without wings until now.

Acknowledgments

I WANT TO ACKNOWLEDGE ALL OF THE women that helped mold me into the person I am today, starting with my mother. As a kid, I never appreciated you, and I took you for granted. You did the best that you could, and I know that now. I'm so blessed that you're still alive so I can tell you that your tough love made me a strong, independent woman, and I love and appreciate you for that.

To my godmom, who taught me to always speak and live in my truth. When the world told me I was too outspoken, you said, "Fuck them, who gives a fuck what they think? Always be yourself." And I always have been, thanks to you. My mom may have given me her blood, but you gave me your backbone, and my strength.

To the "Fords," thank you making me a part of your lives. I don't know where I would be if you had never taken me in. You are proof that you don't have to be blood to be family.

My second mom, Kem. You were there for me regardless of what I did and taught me the true definition of unconditional love. I will never forget that.

To the unknown lady that took me in and gave me another chance at life. You will forever be known as the one guardian angel that I got to meet in person.

Reading Group
Questions & Topics for Discussions

1. What is the significance of the title? Did you find it meaningful, why or why not?
2. What did you like most about the book?
3. What did you like the least?
4. What are some passages that you underlined, or that particularly affected you?
5. How did the book make you feel? What emotions did it evoke?
6. Do you think the author succeeded in what they set out to do?
7. What is the most important point the author makes in this book?
8. Did you find the author's story compelling?
9. What was the most shocking part of the book?
10. What aspects of the story could you most relate to?
11. Why do you think the author chose to write her memoir?
12. Is it ever right to withhold information from a child about their parent?
13. What did you learn from hearing this author's story?

14. Are there any areas you wish the author had elaborated upon further?
15. Are there any people in the book whose perspective you would want to hear?
16. Do you think the author was honest about everything that happened?
17. How did the book compare to other memoirs you've read?
18. How did the memoir make you reflect on your own life?
19. Has this book changed your perspective on anything? If so, in what way?
20. Would you want to see this memoir turned into a movie?
21. If you could talk to the author, what burning question would you want to ask?

____

____

____

____

____

____

____

____

Made in the USA
Monee, IL
06 December 2022

19876180R00154